AUTHORS IN CONTEXT examines the work of major writers in relation to their own time and to the present day. The series provides detailed coverage of the values and debates that colour the writing of particular authors and considers their novels, plays, and poetry against this background. Set in their social, cultural, and political contexts, classic books take on a new meaning for modern readers. And since readers, like writers, have their own contexts, the series considers how critical interpretations have altered over time, and how films, sequels, and other popular adaptations relate to the new age in which they are produced.

MICHAEL H. WHITWORTH is a senior lecturer in the English Department, University of Wales, Bangor. The author of *Einstein's Wake: Relativity, Metaphor, and Modernist Literature* (2001), he has also written articles and chapters on Joseph Conrad, T. S. Eliot, and Virginia Woolf, and on the relations of science and literature.

OXFORD WORLD'S CLASSICS

*For over 100 years Oxford World's Classics have brought
readers closer to the world's great literature. Now with over 700
titles—from the 4,000-year-old myths of Mesopotamia to the
twentieth century's greatest novels—the series makes available
lesser-known as well as celebrated writing.*

*The pocket-sized hardbacks of the early years contained
introductions by Virginia Woolf, T. S. Eliot, Graham Greene,
and other literary figures which enriched the experience of reading.
Today the series is recognized for its fine scholarship and
reliability in texts that span world literature, drama and poetry,
religion, philosophy and politics. Each edition includes perceptive
commentary and essential background information to meet the
changing needs of readers.*

OXFORD WORLD'S CLASSICS

═══

MICHAEL H. WHITWORTH

Virginia Woolf

═══

OXFORD
UNIVERSITY PRESS

OXFORD
UNIVERSITY PRESS

Great Clarendon Street, Oxford OX2 6DP

Oxford University Press is a department of the University of Oxford.
It furthers the University's objective of excellence in research, scholarship,
and education by publishing worldwide in

Oxford New York

Auckland Bangkok Buenos Aires Cape Town Chennai
Dar es Salaam Delhi Hong Kong Istanbul Karachi Kolkata
Kuala Lumpur Madrid Melbourne Mexico City Mumbai Nairobi
São Paulo Shanghai Taipei Tokyo Toronto

Oxford is a registered trade mark of Oxford University Press
in the UK and in certain other countries

Published in the United States
by Oxford University Press Inc., New York

British Library Cataloguing in Publication Data

Data available

Library of Congress Cataloging in Publication Data

Data available
ISBN 0–19–280234–8

1

Typeset in Ehrhardt
by RefineCatch Limited, Bungay, Suffolk
Printed in Great Britain by
Clays Ltd., St Ives plc

For Jessica Maynard

ACKNOWLEDGEMENTS

For permission to quote from the works of Virginia Woolf, I am grateful to The Society of Authors, as the literary representative of the Estate of Virginia Woolf.

I would like to thank the English Department, University of Wales, Bangor, for granting me the study leave in the second semester of 2001–2 which enabled me to begin writing this book. I am grateful to Patricia Ingham, Judith Luna, and Boyd Hilton for their advice and suggestions at all stages in its composition, and to the copy-editor, Rowena Anketell. I have been fortunate in the students who have chosen to study Woolf with me at Bangor at undergraduate and postgraduate level: their enthusiasm has been stimulating and their insights illuminating. Likewise I owe much to the organizers of, and participants in, the Annual Conferences on Virginia Woolf at St Louis, Delaware, UMBC, Bangor, and Smith College.

Finally, for encouraging and distracting me at appropriate moments, wholehearted thanks are due to Liz Barry, Lindsey Gillson, Mark Stanton, Alex and Alison Hewitt, and Sharon Ruston.

CONTENTS

LIST OF ILLUSTRATIONS

A CHRONOLOGY OF VIRGINIA WOOLF

	Life	*Historical and Cultural Background*
1882	(25 Jan.) Adeline Virginia Stephen (VW) born at 22 Hyde Park Gate, London.	Deaths of Darwin, Trollope, D. G. Rossetti; Joyce born; Stravinsky born; Married Women's Property Act; Society for Psychical Research founded.
1895	(5 May) Death of mother, Julia Stephen; VW's first breakdown occurs soon afterwards.	Death of T. H. Huxley; X-rays discovered; invention of the cinematograph; wireless telegraphy invented; arrest, trials, and conviction of Oscar Wilde. Wilde, *The Importance of Being Earnest* and *An Ideal Husband* Wells, *The Time Machine*
1896	(Nov.) Travels in France with sister Vanessa.	Death of William Morris; *Daily Mail* started. Hardy, *Jude the Obscure* Housman, *A Shropshire Lad*
1897	(10 April) Marriage of half-sister Stella. (19 July) Death of Stella. (Nov.) VW learning Greek and History in the Ladies Department of King's College, London.	Queen Victoria's Diamond Jubilee; Tate Gallery opens. Stoker, *Dracula* James, *What Maisie Knew*
1898		Deaths of Gladstone and Lewis Carroll; radium and plutonium discovered. Wells, *The War of the Worlds*
1899	(30 Oct.) VW's brother Thoby goes up to Trinity College, Cambridge, where he forms friendships with Lytton Strachey, Leonard Woolf, Clive Bell, and others of the future Bloomsbury Group (VW's younger brother Adrian follows him to Trinity in 1902).	Boer War begins. Births of Bowen and Coward. Symons, *The Symbolist Movement in Literature* James, *The Awkward Age* Freud, *The Interpretation of Dreams*
1900		Deaths of Nietzsche, Wilde, and Ruskin; *Daily Express* started; Planck announces quantum theory; Boxer Rising. Conrad, *Lord Jim*

	Life	*Historical and Cultural Background*
1901		Death of Queen Victoria; accession of Edward VII; first wireless communication between Europe and USA; 'World's Classics' series begun. Kipling, *Kim*
1902	VW starts private lessons in Greek with Janet Case.	End of Boer War; British Academy founded; *Encyclopaedia Britannica* (10th edn.); *TLS* started. Bennett, *Anna of the Five Towns* James, *The Wings of the Dove*
1903		Deaths of Gissing and Spencer; *Daily Mirror* started; Wright brothers make their first aeroplane flight; Emmeline Pankhurst founds Women's Social and Political Union. Butler, *The Way of All Flesh* James, *The Ambassadors* Moore, *Principia Ethica*
1904	(22 Feb.) Death of father, Sir Leslie Stephen. In spring, VW travels to Italy with Vanessa and friend Violet Dickinson. (10 May) VW has second nervous breakdown and is ill for three months. Moves to 46 Gordon Square. (14 Dec.) VW's first publication appears.	Deaths of Christina Rossetti and Chekhov; Russo–Japanese War; *Entente Cordiale* between Britain and France. Chesterton, *The Napoleon of Notting Hill* Conrad, *Nostromo* James, *The Golden Bowl*
1905	(March, April) Travels in France, Portugal, and Spain. Writes reviews and teaches once a week at Morley College, London.	Einstein, Special Theory of Relativity; Sartre born. Shaw, *Major Barbara* and *Man and Superman* Wells, *Kipps* Forster, *Where Angels Fear to Tread*
1906	(Sept. and Oct.) Travels in Greece. (20 Nov.) Death of Thoby Stephen.	Death of Ibsen; Beckett born; Liberal Government elected; Campbell–Bannerman Prime Minister; launch of HMS *Dreadnought*.
1907	(7 Feb.) Marriage of Vanessa to Clive Bell. VW moves with Adrian to 29 Fitzroy Square. At work on her first novel, 'Melymbrosia' (working title for *The Voyage Out*).	Auden born; Anglo-Russian Entente. Synge, *The Playboy of the Western World* Conrad, *The Secret Agent* Forster, *The Longest Journey*

	Life	Historical and Cultural Background
1908	(Sept.) Visits Italy with the Bells.	Asquith Prime Minister; Old Age Pensions Act; Elgar's First Symphony. Bennett, *The Old Wives' Tale* Forster, *A Room with a View*
1909	(17 Feb.) Lytton Strachey proposes marriage. (30 March) First meets Lady Ottoline Morrell. (April) Visits Florence. (Aug.) Visits Bayreuth and Dresden.	Death of Meredith; 'People's Budget'; English Channel flown by Blériot. Wells, *Tono-Bungay* Masterman, *The Condition of England* Marinetti, *Futurist Manifesto*
1910	(Jan.) Works for women's suffrage. (June–Aug.) Spends time in a nursing home at Twickenham.	Deaths of Edward VII, Tolstoy, and Florence Nightingale; accession of George V; *Encyclopaedia Britannica* (11th edn.); Roger Fry's post-Impressionist Exhibition. Bennett, *Clayhanger* Forster, *Howards End* Yeats, *The Green Helmet* Wells, *The History of Mr Polly*
1911	(April) Travels to Turkey, where Vanessa is ill. (Oct.) VW and Vanessa take lease on Asheham House in Sussex—VW to spend increasing periods there in 1913. (Nov.) Moves to 38 Brunswick Square, sharing house with Adrian, John Maynard Keynes, Duncan Grant, and Leonard Woolf.	National Insurance Act; Suffragette riots. Conrad, *Under Western Eyes* Wells, *The New Machiavelli* Lawrence, *The White Peacock*
1912	Rents Asheham House. (Feb.) Spends some days in Twickenham nursing home. (10 Aug.) Marriage to Leonard Woolf. Honeymoon in Provence, Spain, and Italy. (Oct.) Moves to 13 Clifford's Inn, London.	Second Post-Impressionist Exhibition; Suffragettes active; strikes by dockers, coal-miners, and transport workers; Irish Home Rule Bill rejected by Lords; sinking of SS *Titanic*; death of Scott in the Antarctic; *Daily Herald* started. English translations of Chekhov and Dostoevsky begin to appear.
1913	(March) MS of *The Voyage Out* delivered to publisher. Unwell most of summer. (9 Sept.) Suicide attempt. Remains under care of nurses and husband for rest of year.	*New Statesman* started; Suffragettes active. Lawrence, *Sons and Lovers*

	Life	*Historical and Cultural Background*
1914	(16 Feb.) Last nurse leaves. (Oct.) Moves to Richmond, Surrey.	Irish Home Rule Bill passed by Parliament; First World War begins (4 Aug.); Dylan Thomas born. Lewis, *Blast* Joyce, *Dubliners* Yeats, *Responsibilities* Hardy, *Satires of Circumstance* Bell, *Art*
1915	Purchase of lease on Hogarth House, Richmond. (26 March) *The Voyage Out* published. (April, May) Bout of violent madness; under care of nurses until November.	Death of Rupert Brooke; Einstein, *General Theory of Relativity*; Second Battle of Ypres; Dardanelles Campaign; sinking of *SS Lusitania*; air attacks on London. Ford, *The Good Soldier* Lawrence, *The Rainbow* Brooke, *1914 and Other Poems* Richardson, *Pointed Roofs*
1916	(17 Oct.) Lectures to Richmond branch of the Women's Co-operative Guild. Regular work for *TLS*. VW begins work on *Night and Day*.	Death of James; Lloyd George Prime Minister; First Battle of the Somme; Battle of Verdun; Gallipoli Campaign; Easter Rising in Dublin. Joyce, *Portrait of the Artist as a Young Man*
1917	(July) Hogarth Press commences publication with 'The Mark on the Wall' and a story by Leonard Woolf.	Death of Edward Thomas. Third Battle of Ypres (Passchendaele); T. E. Lawrence's campaigns in Arabia; USA enters the War; Revolution in Russia (Feb., Oct.); Balfour Declaration. Eliot, *Prufrock and Other Observations*
1918	Writes reviews and *Night and Day*; also sets type for the Hogarth Press. (15 Nov.) First meets T. S. Eliot.	Death of Owen; Second Battle of the Somme; final German offensive collapses; Armistice with Germany (11 Nov.); Franchise Act grants vote to women over 30; influenza pandemic kills millions. Lewis, *Tarr* Hopkins, *Poems* Strachey, *Eminent Victorians*
1919	(1 July) Purchase of Monk's House, Rodmell, Sussex. (20 Oct.) *Night and Day* published.	Treaty of Versailles; Alcock and Brown fly the Atlantic; National Socialists founded in Germany. Sinclair, *Mary Olivier* Shaw, *Heartbreak House*

Life	*Historical and Cultural Background*
1920	Works on journalism and *Jacob's Room*.	League of Nations established. Pound, *Hugh Selwyn Mauberley* Lawrence, *Women in Love* Eliot, *The Sacred Wood* Fry, *Vision and Design*
1921	(7 or 8 April) *Monday or Tuesday* published. Ill for summer months. (4 Nov.) Finishes *Jacob's Room*.	Irish Free State founded. Huxley, *Crome Yellow*
1922	(Jan. to May) Ill. (24 Oct.) *Jacob's Room* published. (14 Dec.) First meets Vita Sackville-West.	Bonar Law Prime Minister; Mussolini forms Fascist Government in Italy; death of Proust; *Encyclopaedia Britannica* (12th edn.); *Criterion* founded; BBC founded; Irish Free State proclaimed. Eliot, *The Waste Land* Galsworthy, *The Forsyte Saga* Joyce, *Ulysses* Mansfield, *The Garden Party* Wittgenstein, *Tractatus Logico-Philosophicus*
1923	(March, April) Visits Spain. Works on 'The Hours', the first version of *Mrs Dalloway*.	Baldwin Prime Minister; BBC radio begins broadcasting (Nov.); death of K. Mansfield.
1924	(9 Jan.) Purchase of lease on 52 Tavistock Square, Bloomsbury. Gives lecture that becomes 'Mr Bennett and Mrs Brown'. (8 Oct.) Finishes *Mrs Dalloway*.	First (minority) Labour Government; Ramsay MacDonald Prime Minister; deaths of Lenin, Kafka, and Conrad. Forster, *A Passage to India* O'Casey, *Juno and the Paycock* Coward, *The Vortex*
1925	(23 April) *The Common Reader* published. (14 May) *Mrs Dalloway* published. Ill during summer.	Gerhardie, *The Polyglots* Ford, *No More Parades* Huxley, *Those Barren Leaves* Whitehead, *Science and the Modern World*
1926	(Jan) Unwell with German measles. Writes *To the Lighthouse*.	General Strike (3–12 May); *Encyclopaedia Britannica* (13th edn.); first television demonstration. Ford, *A Man Could Stand Up* Tawney, *Religion and the Rise of Capitalism*
1927	(March, April) Travels in France and Italy. (5 May) *To the Lighthouse* published. (5 Oct.) Begins *Orlando*.	Lindburgh flies solo across the Atlantic; first 'talkie' films.

Life	Historical and Cultural Background
1928	(11 Oct.) *Orlando* published. Delivers lectures at Cambridge on which she bases *A Room of One's Own*.	Death of Hardy; votes for women over 21. Yeats, *The Tower* Lawrence, *Lady Chatterley's Lover* Waugh, *Decline and Fall* Sherriff, *Journey's End* Ford, *Last Post* Huxley, *Point Counter Point* Bell, *Civilization*
1929	(Jan.) Travels to Berlin. (24 Oct.) *A Room of One's Own* published.	2nd Labour Government, MacDonald Prime Minister; collapse of New York Stock Exchange; start of world economic depression. Graves, *Goodbye to All That* Aldington, *Death of a Hero* Green, *Living*
1930	(20 Feb.) First meets Ethel Smyth; (29 May) Finishes first version of *The Waves*.	Mass unemployment; television starts in USA; deaths of Lawrence and Conan Doyle. Auden, *Poems* Eliot, *Ash Wednesday* Waugh, *Vile Bodies* Coward, *Private Lives* Lewis, *Apes of God*
1931	(April) Car tour through France. (8 Oct.) *The Waves* published. Writes *Flush*.	Formation of National Government; abandonment of Gold Standard; death of Bennett; Japan invades China.
1932	(21 Jan.) Death of Lytton Strachey. (Apr. and May) Tour of Greece. (13 Oct.) *The Common Reader*, 2nd series, published. Begins *The Years*, at this point called 'The Pargiters'.	Roosevelt becomes President of USA; hunger marches start in Britain; *Scrutiny* starts. Huxley, *Brave New World*
1933	(May) Car tour of France and Italy. (5 Oct.) *Flush* published.	Deaths of Galsworthy and George Moore; Hitler becomes Chancellor of Germany. Orwell, *Down and Out in Paris and London* Wells, *The Shape of Things to Come*
1934	Works on *The Years*. (Apr.) Tour of Ireland. (9 Sept.) Death of Roger Fry.	Waugh, *A Handful of Dust* Graves, *I, Claudius* Beckett, *More Pricks than Kicks* Toynbee, *A Study of History*

	Life	*Historical and Cultural Background*
1935	Rewrites *The Years*. (May) Car tour of Holland, Germany, and Italy.	George V's Silver Jubilee; Baldwin Prime Minister of National Government; Germany re-arms; Italian invasion of Abyssinia. Isherwood, *Mr Norris Changes Trains* T. S. Eliot, *Murder in the Cathedral*
1936	(May–Oct.) Ill. Finishes *The Years*. Begins *Three Guineas*.	Death of George V; accession of Edward VIII; abdication crisis; accession of George VI; Civil War breaks out in Spain; first of the Moscow show trials; Germany reoccupies the Rhineland; BBC television begins (2 Nov.); deaths of Chesterton, Kipling, and Housman. Orwell, *Keep the Aspidistra Flying*
1937	(15 March) *The Years* published. Begins *Roger Fry: A Biography*. (18 July) Death in Spanish Civil War of Julian Bell, son of Vanessa.	Chamberlain Prime Minister; destruction of Guernica; death of Barrie. Orwell, *The Road to Wigan Pier*
1938	(2 June) *Three Guineas* published. Works on *Roger Fry*, and begins to envisage *Between the Acts*.	German *Anschluss* with Austria; Munich agreement; dismemberment of Czechoslovakia; first jet engine. Beckett, *Murphy* Bowen, *The Death of the Heart* Greene, *Brighton Rock*
1939	VW moves to 37 Mecklenburgh Square, but lives mostly at Monk's House. Works on *Between the Acts*. Meets Freud in London.	End of Civil War in Spain; Russo–German pact; Germany invades Poland (Sept.); Britain and France declare war on Germany (3 Sept.); deaths of Freud, Yeats, and Ford. Joyce, *Finnegans Wake* Isherwood, *Goodbye to Berlin*
1940	(25 July) *Roger Fry* published. (10 Sept.) Mecklenburgh Square house bombed. (18 Oct.) Witnesses the ruins of 52 Tavistock Square, destroyed by bombs. (23 Nov.) Finishes *Between the Acts*.	Germany invades north–west Europe; fall of France; evacuation of British troops from Dunkirk; Battle of Britain; beginning of 'the Blitz'; National Government under Churchill.
1941	(26 Feb.) Revises *Between the Acts*. Becomes ill. (28 March) Drowns herself in River Ouse, near Monk's House. (July) *Between the Acts* published.	Germany invades USSR; Japanese destroy US Fleet at Pearl Harbor; USA enters war; death of Joyce.

ABBREVIATIONS

All the editions listed are published by Oxford University Press, except where noted otherwise.

BTA	*Between the Acts*, ed. F. Kermode (1992)
CE	*Collected Essays*, ed. L. Woolf (London: Hogarth, 1966–7)
CSF	*The Complete Shorter Fiction*, ed. S. Dick, rev. edn. (London: Hogarth, 1989)
Diary	*The Diary of Virginia Woolf*, ed. A. O. Bell, 5 vols. (London: Hogarth, 1977–84)
EVW	*Essays of Virginia Woolf*, ed. A. McNeillie, 4 vols. to date (London: Hogarth, 1996 onwards)
JR	*Jacob's Room*, ed. K. Flint (1992)
Letters	*The Letters of Virginia Woolf*, ed. N. Nicolson, 6 vols. (London: Hogarth, 1975–80)
MB	*Moments of Being*, ed. J. Schulkind, introduced and revised by H. Lee (London: Pimlico, 2002)
MD	*Mrs Dalloway*, ed. D. Bradshaw (2000)
MW	*The Mark on the Wall and Other Short Fiction*, ed. D. Bradshaw (2001)
ND	*Night and Day*, ed. S. Raitt (1992)
O	*Orlando*, ed. R. Bowlby (1992)
PA	*A Passionate Apprentice*, ed. M. A. Leaska (London: Hogarth, 1990)
ROO	*A Room of One's Own*, in *A Room of One's Own and Three Guineas*, ed. M. Shiach (1992)
TG	*Three Guineas*, in *A Room of One's Own and Three Guineas*, ed. M. Shiach (1992)
TL	*To the Lighthouse*, ed. M. Drabble (1992)
VO	*The Voyage Out*, ed. L. Sage (1992)
W	*The Waves*, ed. G. Beer (1992)
Y	*The Years*, ed. H. Lee (1992)

Note on Coinage. There were 12 pence ('*d.*' from Latin 'denarius') in the shilling, and 20 shillings in the pound. The price of four pounds, ten shillings, and sixpence, for example, is represented as £4. 10*s*. 6*d*. The 'guinea', originally a gold coin, was worth 21*s*.

CHAPTER I

THE LIFE OF VIRGINIA WOOLF

THE first-time visitor to Monk's House, Virginia Woolf's home in Sussex from 1919 until her death, might be surprised not only by its modest scale and asymmetrical structure, but also by the rooms most closely associated with Virginia. Her writing 'lodge', a small wooden structure, is positioned across the lawn against the churchyard wall, with views of the river meadows above the river Ouse and of the hills beyond. Her ground-floor bedroom, separate from that of her husband, Leonard, is attached to the main house, but accessible only through an outside door. 'I used to think how inconvenient it must be to have to go out in the rain to go to bed,' recalled their cook Louie Mayer.[1] An uninformed visitor might conjecture that there had been an 'estrangement' between husband and wife, but that term is quite inadequate to the close and supportive relationship they formed: they were very rarely apart. Nevertheless, the structure of the house suggests Virginia's need for privacy and independence. Moreover, it suggests that the story of her life is not simply the story of the composition of her books, nor of her friendships and family relations, but also of the places she lived in and how she shaped them to herself. Virginia Woolf was fond of metaphors of snails, of vulnerable souls secreting protective shells.

She was born Adeline Virginia Stephen on 25 January 1882, at 22 Hyde Park Gate, Kensington, London, her home for the next twenty-two years.[2] The house, which survives, was remembered by her as tall and dark; and if its remembered darkness reflects in part her sense of oppression there, its height reflects practical considerations faced by her parents. When they married in 1878, Leslie Stephen and Julia Duckworth were both widowed, and both had children from their previous marriages; they were to have four more, Vanessa, Thoby, Virginia, and Adrian. They added two additional storeys to the already tall house, using them for a study and nursery rooms.[3]

Julia Duckworth, née Julia Prinsep Jackson in 1846, was born into a family that traced its ancestors back to pre-revolutionary France and the court of Versailles, which remained well connected in English and in Anglo-Indian society, and in which the female off-spring were noted for their beauty; Julia herself was the model for the Pre-Raphaelite painter Edward Burne-Jones. She had married the young lawyer Herbert Duckworth in 1867, and bore three children by him, George (1868–1934), Stella (1869–97), and Gerald (1870–1937), born two months after his father's sudden death.

Leslie Stephen was born in 1832 into an equally well-connected and financially secure middle-class family. His grandfather, James Stephen (1758–1832), had been involved in the campaign against slavery, and had thus become connected with the 'Clapham Sect', a group of middle-class evangelical Christians centred on Clapham, south London. Their evangelicalism, it should be noted, gave them an orientation towards conscientious and pragmatic public duty, rather than dogmatic scriptural literalism. What the Stephen family culture passed to Leslie was not Christianity—he was agnostic—but a sense of intense self-discipline, of individual responsibility, and of social duty. Leslie was educated at Eton and at Cambridge; on graduating, he entered literary journalism, not from 'an overpowering love of letters', he later recalled, but because religious doubts prevented him from becoming a tutor.[4] He wrote for journals with respectable middle-class readerships, such as the *Saturday Review and Pall Mall Gazette* (it is telling that he describes the 'middle' articles as 'lay sermon[s]'), though always with a sense that the trade of literary journalism was not quite respectable; he believed more strongly in his philosophical studies. He went on to edit the *Cornhill Magazine*, a literary journal in which he was proud to have serialized Henry James's *Daisy Miller* and Thomas Hardy's *Far from the Madding Crowd*.[5]

He had married Harriet Thackeray (known as 'Minny'), daughter of William Thackeray, in June 1867. Their daughter Laura was born prematurely in December 1870; Minny died following the premature birth of their second child in November 1875; the child did not survive.[6] It was Minny's death, and the problem of caring for Laura, which brought Leslie Stephen and Julia Duckworth together. Laura had been slow to develop, and after her mother's death her mental deficiencies became all the more apparent. She learned to read, but only slowly, and never learned to write; she spoke incoherently, rapidly, and spasmodically.[7] She lived with Leslie and Julia

Stephen and their other offspring until some point in the early 1890s, when she was committed to an asylum; she remained institutionalized until her death in 1945. As Hermione Lee has argued, she must have been a disturbing presence for Virginia.[8] Mental illness and mental handicap were not so clearly distinguished by the Victorians, and the influence of heredity rather than that of environment was the most commonly cited cause. Virginia's own mental illnesses must have led her to reflect on the history and treatment of her half-sister.

In the year of Virginia's birth, Leslie Stephen resigned the editorship of the *Cornhill*, having been invited to become the editor of the *Dictionary of National Biography* (*DNB*), which aimed to provide brief, authoritative, and accessible biographies of the great figures of British history. Leslie Stephen wrote 378 of the entries himself, edited the articles in the first twenty-six volumes, while managing contributors 'who were not accustomed to being managed'.[9] At the same time he undertook other work reviewing and lecturing. The workload told on his health, and he frequently regretted the 'drudgery' of the work and the 'insane verbosity' of some contributors.[10] His children noticed: Thoby, aged 5, presented him with a box that he called his 'contradictionary box'; asked why, he said that it was 'full . . . of rubbish'.[11] The 'gleams of epigrammatic satire' that had entered Thoby's head had also entered Virginia's: her father's absorption in the project anticipates Mr Ramsay's absorption in his philosophical work in *To the Lighthouse*. Mr Ramsay's conception of himself as a mountaineer (*TL*, pp. 49–50) draws upon Leslie Stephen's love of mountaineering, a pursuit that he fell back on when doctors enforced temporary retirement from the *DNB*, and upon his friend Frederic Maitland's depiction of the dictionary as a heroic physical feat, a 'snowfield' to be crossed in spite of the threat of a muttering storm and a lightning flash.[12] The project also began Virginia's doubt over whether a life can be easily summarized by reference to facts alone; whether, indeed, a life can be known at all without distortion. Eventually, in May 1891, Leslie Stephen passed the editorship over to his assistant. When it was completed in 1900, the sixty-three volumes of the *DNB* contained over 29,000 articles by over 650 contributors.[13]

Virginia Woolf's earliest memories are connected not with Hyde Park Gate, however, but with Talland House, a holiday retreat in

St Ives, Cornwall. Leslie Stephen had bought the leasehold in 1881, and though it was certainly second-best to the Alps, he recognized its charms. He writes lyrically of the sea breezes, 'as soft as silk', with 'a fresh sweet taste like new milk'; and of its 'little garden'

which is not much to boast of; and yet it is a dozen little gardens each full of romance for the children—lawns surrounded by flowering hedges, and intricate thickets of gooseberries and currants, and remote nooks of potatoes and peas, and high banks, down which you can slide in a sitting posture, and corners in which you come upon unexpected puppies— altogether a pocket-paradise with a sheltered cove of sand in easy reach (for 'Ginia even) just below.[14]

Though the editor of the *DNB* could be a forbidding figure to his children, this passage shows his ability to view the world from a child's perspective; in a memoir of him, Virginia recalled her impression that her father 'was not very much older than we were'; his involvement in their games so complete that there was 'a perfectly equal companionship'.[15]

Woolf's recollections of Talland House, written towards the end of her life in 'Sketch of the Past', also dwelt on its fecundity: not only of fruit and flowers, but more abstractly, of colours, 'pale yellow, silver, and green' and sounds, falling as if through 'an elastic, gummy air' (*MB*, pp. 79–80). But Woolf also remembered, with a quite contrasting clarity, an incident from when she was aged 6:[16]

There was a slab outside the dining room door for standing dishes upon. Once when I was very small Gerald Duckworth lifted me on to this, and as I sat there he began to explore my body. I can remember the feel of his hand going under my clothes; going firmly and steadily lower and lower. I remember how I hoped that he would stop; how I stiffened and wriggled as his hand approached my private parts. But it did not stop. His hand explored my private parts too. I remember resenting, disliking it—what is the word for so dumb and mixed a feeling? It must have been strong, since I still recall it. (*MB*, p. 82)

The incident—there is no evidence that Gerald repeatedly abused Virginia—and its psychological consequences have been interpreted in many ways.[17] Woolf herself interprets it, using it to explain her shame on seeing her reflection, as there had been a mirror in the same hallway. However, the arguments and speculations with which she frames the recollection do not seem adequately to contain it. The memoir leaves the impression that even in her late fifties, she had not come to terms with it.

Though Gerald Duckworth's abusive explorations in or about 1888 might figure as the serpent in the paradisaical garden, it was another event, the death of Julia Stephen in 1895, which was to cast the Stephen family out of the garden, and which was to prove the more immediately and massively damaging to Virginia's health. Julia Stephen was only 48, but had spent a great deal of her energy on running the household, often carrying out tasks which would normally, in her social class, be carried out by servants. She had also found time for much charitable work: Mrs Ramsay's philanthropical excursions in *To the Lighthouse* echo Julia Stephen's in the 'small, dingy, and crowded quarters of St Ives'.[18] 'She sank', Woolf later wrote, 'like an exhausted swimmer, deeper and deeper in the water, and could only at moments descry some restful shore on the horizon to be gained in old age when all this toil was over' (*MB*, p. 11). If this makes her death sound a long and gradual process, the death of Mrs Ramsay suggests that it was entirely unexpected. The truth lies somewhere between the two: in late February 1895, Julia Stephen fell ill with influenza; though she had apparently recovered by early April, the illness can only have weakened her, and she died of rheumatic fever on 5 May 1895.[19]

In the period following her mother's death, Virginia had some sort of nervous or physical breakdown: records are sketchy, but she recalled it as a state of 'physical distress' characterized by a 'racing pulse'; doctors prescribed 'No lessons, no excitement: open air, simple life'.[20] The simple life of St Ives was, however, closed to Virginia; even before Julia's death the family had decided to give up the lease of Talland House, a new hotel having obstructed their sea view; her death made the decision seem inevitable.

The loss of her mother was in no way made easier for Virginia by her father's inconsolable grief, an emotion which was often self-pitying, often self-dramatizing, and always demanding. Leslie Stephen's 1903 recollection of Thomas Carlyle embarking on 'his long pilgrimage . . . through regions of gloom and sorrow' after the death of his own wife in 1866, sounds suspiciously like a self-portrait. Vanessa's sketch of her father gives a flavour of the lasting resentment created by his metaphorical pilgrimage: the family were left in charge of 'a melancholy, deaf, rather helpless man of over

Virginia Woolf with her father, Sir Leslie Stephen, *c.*1902

Stephen/Duckworth family photo

sixty, who had never had to face domestic problems and was fearful of the workhouse if his balance at the bank dropped, as it sometimes did, to less than £3,000'.[21]

The situation was eased at first by Stella Duckworth, who took over the day-to-day management of the household. But Stella had for some time been courted by a young solicitor named Jack Hills. She had rejected his proposal of marriage in March 1896, but in August of that year, reassured that she could reconcile her sense of duty towards the family with her feelings for Jack, she accepted. Leslie Stephen had at first insisted that they live in 22 Hyde Park Gate, but the practical inconvenience and emotional delicacy of such an arrangement soon became obvious and they settled instead on the plan of living nearby at number 24. Jack and Stella were married in April 1897. On their return from honeymoon, Stella was suffering from 'a chill'; her condition rapidly grew worse with a condition which at the time was spoken of as appendicitis or peritonitis, but which may have been a retroverted uterus, or an ectopic pregnancy.[22] The uncertainty and the association with pregnancy made it all the more disturbing: as with Prue Ramsay's death in *To the Lighthouse*, the vagueness of 'some illness connected with childbirth' (*TL*, p. 180) is as troubling as the death is shocking. Virginia was particularly attentive towards Stella, but was herself growing ill, having difficulty sleeping. On 14 July Stella was soothing away Virginia's 'fidgets' (*PA*, p. 114); on 18 July she was undergoing an operation, and by the early hours of 19 July she was dead.[23]

In 1897 Julia Stephen's sons were gradually establishing independent lives. The Duckworth brothers still lived at 22 Hyde Park Gate: since 1892 George had been working as an unpaid secretary to the pioneering social reformer and sociologist Charles Booth, while Gerald was in the process of founding the publishing firm Duckworth and Co. (*PA*, p. 133). Thoby was at boarding school, Clifton College in Bristol; in 1899 he entered Trinity College, Cambridge. Adrian, who had always been more delicate in health, was not a boarder, but a 'day boy' at Westminster School in London; he too would go to Cambridge, in 1902. Vanessa was studying at a school of art in nearby Queen's Gate, but it was on her, when the family returned from their long summer vacation in September 1897, that the domestic responsibilities fell. Not only was she the older of the two sisters, but she was the more pragmatic and confident. Virginia recalled her being 'strong of brain, agile and determined' (*MB*, p. 26); Vanessa recalled descending into the basement kitchen every morning to confirm arrangements for meals with Sophie Farrell, the family cook.[24] Though the practicalities of ordering and preparing food were entirely Sophie's duty, this gave Vanessa all the anxiety of managing the budget with little of the necessary control: 'The utmost one could do by way of economy was to suggest that perhaps strawberries were still rather dear or salmon more expensive than whiting'.[25] It is clear that the 18-year-old Vanessa did not feel comfortable being in a position of authority over Sophie, who was in her mid- to late thirties. Neither sister was ever to achieve completely harmonious relations with their servants. Vanessa was not particularly strong at arithmetic—neither sister had been properly educated in it—and checking the weekly account books with her father exposed her to his now characteristic 'groans', 'sighs', and 'explosions of rage'.[26]

The 'darkness' of 22 Hyde Park Gate was literal in the basement, but metaphorically it spread through all quarters of the house, and as Leslie Stephen's health declined, the house grew darker. He had suffered occasional 'fits' for some years: in 1889, he had been struck down at the Athenaeum club while explaining to a friend how strong he was.[27] The fit he suffered at the start of 1900 was not only in itself disturbing to his family ('I thought he was on fire', recalled Virginia), but may have been a first symptom of the bowel cancer that was diagnosed in the spring of 1902. By October 1902 he was writing letters of a valedictory kind to his friends, but the end was still some way off.[28] An operation in December brought temporary relief, though by Easter 1903 his strength had begun to wane. He made further preparations for death, writing reminiscences of his early life in June, but he continued to read; he even wrote a lecture on the eighteenth century for Oxford, though it had to be delivered by his nephew. His doctors predicted that the end would come at Christmas time, but Leslie Stephen proved them wrong, and survived until 22 February 1904.

In this period, the emotionally unstable George Duckworth effectively became the head of the family, and he interpreted this role in a distinctive and damaging way. There was increasingly a clash of cultures within 22 Hyde Park Gate: Vanessa and Virginia were by nature '[e]xplorers and revolutionists', living ten years ahead of their times, while George and Gerald were Victorians, forty years behind (*MB*, pp. 149–50). The more benign aspect of George's new-found patriarchal power was his insistence on introducing Vanessa and Virginia to 'society': by convention, a young woman would 'come out' at the age of 18, attending dances and evening parties during the London 'season' (February to July), with the object of finding a suitable husband; a 'rich old Etonian' was the ideal George had in mind.[29] Vanessa had come out in 1897, but had 'gone in again' following Stella's death.[30] When George renewed his efforts, Vanessa found it difficult 'to turn from the horrors of illness, death, and long conversations about the dead' to the 'cheerful society' she was being offered; when Virginia's turn came, she felt equally out of place.[31] Vanessa was more comfortable with her art school friends; and Virginia with her reading; when she returned from one party, Virginia's mind turned immediately to the more exciting prospect of learning classical Greek the following day (*MB*, p. 42).

However, while in public George was insensitively adhering to social norms, in private he was diverging in a disturbing way. Woolf recalled one night in June 1903, when: 'It was long past midnight that I got into bed and sat reading. . . . There would be a tap at the door; the light would be turned out and George would fling himself on my bed, cuddling and kissing and otherwise embracing me' (*MB*, p. 44). This was, he later told Virginia's doctor, to comfort her for the fatal illness of her father. Although Woolf begins this account on a particular occasion, the 'would' makes it clear that George repeatedly intruded on Virginia in this way. Whatever George's own motivations and feelings during these incidents, and regardless of whether there was a more aggressively sexual aspect to them than Woolf could record, they were at the very least deeply intrusive at a time when she was emotionally vulnerable. The dances and parties were humiliating, but George's attentions were psychologically damaging. Had their mother been alive, George would most probably not have troubled her; had Stella not died and her father not been slowly dying, she might have psychologically survived them, but as it was, in the summer of 1904 she suffered a nervous breakdown.

In the immediate aftermath of Leslie Stephen's death Virginia had travelled with her sister, brothers, and George, to Manorbier in Pembrokeshire, to recuperate. With George came emotional claustrophobia: 'He never lets one alone a moment. Very well meant, but wearisome' (*Letters*, i. 132). In April the Stephens and Gerald travelled to Venice, and on their return to London in May, Virginia suffered her breakdown. She was placed in the care of the eminent psychiatric doctor Sir George Savage, and then of Violet Dickinson (1865–1948), a friend and mentor whom Virginia had met through Stella Duckworth, and who remained a close friend for the rest of the decade. During her time with Violet she hallucinated, as she later recalled, the sounds of birds 'singing Greek choruses', and of King Edward in the azaleas 'using the foulest possible language' (*MB*, p. 45). Both hallucinations allow a wide range of psychoanalytical explanations.[32] The first of them Woolf later gave to Septimus Warren-Smith in *Mrs Dalloway* (*MD*, p. 21), in spite of the improbability of his knowing Greek. She also suffered intense headaches, something she was to take in later life as a warning symptom of a recurrence of her illness; and she attempted suicide, though the window she chose to leap from was too low for the purpose.

By August she was well enough to join her family in Nottinghamshire on their summer vacation; she then went on to Cambridge to continue her recovery with her aunt Caroline Emelia Stephen, a spinster and Quaker known in the family as 'the Nun'. She made occasional brief trips to London, where Vanessa was organizing the move from Hyde Park Gate to 46 Gordon Square, Bloomsbury. George had married in September, and Gerald was persuaded to move to a separate flat. Virginia left Aunt Emelia in December 1904, and a new phase of her life began.

Virginia's recollections and those of Vanessa both figure 46 Gordon Square as a place of light, space, and freedom after the darkness and claustrophobia of 22 Hyde Park Gate; as a place of rational if slightly chilly beauty after the ugliness of their old home.[33] In place of the dark colours and intricate William Morris wallpapers of Hyde Park Gate, they decorated their walls with washes of plain distemper. This break with the surroundings of the Victorian period was paralleled in their social lives. Both Vanessa and Virginia had their own sitting rooms in which to read or see friends, in addition to which there was a large double drawing room. Thoby had graduated and was studying law in London; missing his former circle of Cambridge friends, he instituted an 'at home' on Thursday evenings; it was through these events that Virginia was to meet (among others)

Lytton Strachey, exotic, tall, thin, and possessed of a distinctive high-pitched voice; Clive Bell, a man both aesthetic and robustly masculine, described by Thoby as 'a sort of mixture between Shelley and a sporting country squire'; and Desmond MacCarthy, who was to spend a lifetime in literary journalism without ever writing the great novel everyone expected of him. Leonard Woolf was part of this circle of friends, but he had departed for a post as a colonial administrator in Ceylon. Thoby's Thursday group was the core of the 'Bloomsbury Group'. At first these educated young men, who had acquired almost mythical proportions in Thoby's accounts, were disappointingly silent in the presence of the Stephen sisters; accustomed to exclusively male society, they were no doubt ill at ease. But as they grew more comfortable, they included the sisters as equal partners in 'astonishingly abstract' conversations that ran on into the night, criticizing the sisters' arguments as severely as their own, and dispensing with the etiquette that had characterized the parties of the Hyde Park Gate period (*MB*, p. 51). Vanessa was soon to institute a 'Friday Club' for the exhibition and discussion of new paintings.[34] The group acquired new members, and others drifted away in the following years. Importantly, Clive Bell was to introduce the art critic Roger Fry, and the abstract discussions of beauty were to be applied to particular paintings. The economist John Maynard Keynes became part of it in 1911. Although Vanessa became a less significant member after 1918, choosing to spend more of her time in Sussex and France, and though regular events such as the 'Thursdays' ceased, the group continued to function as a recognizable and mutually supportive social network.[35]

Virginia inherited her father's sense of anxiety about income. Late in 1904 she began to review books for a Church of England newspaper, the *Guardian*, recording her 'great pleasure' when her 'first instalment of wages', £2. 7s. 6d., arrived (*PA*, p. 219). In March 1905 she began to review for the *Times Literary Supplement* (*TLS*), recently established, but far more prestigious. She continued to review for the rest of her life, though as she became more financially secure in the late 1920s, the quantity of reviewing diminished.

She also, in January 1905, began unpaid teaching work, giving evening classes at Morley College, an institute for working men and women. It is surprising that she took this on, not only considering her breakdown, but also the unsystematic and informal nature of her own education. Her mother had taught her and Vanessa Latin, French, and History (she had also taught Thoby, until he was old enough to go to preparatory school); she was not a great success, and when they were temporarily taught by a 'harmless, ordinary, little governess', Vanessa found it a great relief.[36] Her father's lessons in arithmetic had been even more difficult to bear. There were also classes in more conventionally feminine accomplishments such as music and dancing. As Virginia grew older, her father increasingly had given her freedom to choose from his library and so to broaden her self-education: she read voraciously in literature, history, and biography. In 1897, she had taken classes in Greek and Latin in the Ladies Department of King's College in Kensington; from 1899 she took private lessons in these subjects. Fortunately, Morley College did not impose any syllabus or examination teaching on Virginia: she began by teaching 'composition'; after some weeks her students requested 'history', so she improvised a series of lectures.[37] Her struggles with problems of representation begin here: on the one hand, giving her students 'hard dates to take home', 'something solid to cling to'; on the other, trying 'to make them feel the flesh & blood in these shadows'.[38]

The family also continued to take holidays together: Adrian and Virginia in France, Portugal, and Spain in April 1905; all four in Cornwall in August 1905; Vanessa and Virginia in Norfolk in August 1906. Their most ambitious holiday was the tour of Greece in September and October 1906 which was to lead to further tragedy for the family. Thoby and Adrian departed in August, and were met in Olympia on 13 September by Virginia, Vanessa, and Violet Dickinson. Vanessa soon fell ill with appendicitis and had to be nursed by Virginia and Violet; she continued ill for the rest of the holiday, though they travelled on to Constantinople. Thoby returned to London early, and the rest of the group followed, returning on 1 November. They were greeted with the news that Thoby was in bed with a fever and diarrhoea. It was typhoid, but it was initially misdiagnosed as malaria; Violet, who had become ill on the journey home, had also contracted it. Thoby's typhoid led to a perforation of the bowels, and an operation on 17 November did not save him; he died three days later.

Though Virginia's mental fragility tends to dominate accounts of her life, it is a sign of her mental toughness that she survived this appalling and unexpected loss. In the weeks after Thoby's death, Virginia wrote an extraordinary sequence of letters to Violet Dickinson which maintained the pretence of Thoby being alive, giving accounts of his being 'cross with his nurses' because they wouldn't give him mutton chops and beer, eating chicken broth, and slowly recovering. The pretence ended when Violet saw a reference to his death in a literary journal. Though the letters might seem to indicate some kind of mental and emotional imbalance—at worst psychotic, at best an unwillingness to come to terms with Thoby's death—they more probably indicate that, in a very level-headed way, Virginia was seeking to protect Violet from the shock of the news. To say that is not to deny that Virginia did find it difficult to come to terms with Thoby's death, an absence made more complex by the aloofness that he had shown to Virginia in life.[39] The figure of the promising but reserved young man was to appear as Jacob in *Jacob's Room* and to recur as Percival in *The Waves*. The experience of nursing both him and Vanessa was to filter into *The Voyage Out*, the first versions of which (as 'Melymbrosia') Virginia began to write in 1907 or 1908.

Virginia faced another loss and another change of address. Two days after Thoby's death, Vanessa agreed to marry Clive Bell. Though Bell was to be a valuable and encouraging critic of 'Melymbrosia', Virginia was at first a little suspicious of the country squire aspect of his persona, and found this difficult to reconcile with his 'capable brains and great artistic sensibility' (*Letters*, i. 276). Vanessa and Clive were married on 7 February 1907, and it was agreed that on their return they would take 46 Gordon Square as their home; Virginia and Adrian found a new house at 29 Fitzroy Square. As the two squares were only a few streets away from each other, the Bloomsbury Group was able to continue its meetings: there were Thursday evening gatherings at Fitzroy Square, and a short-lived play-reading society was instituted at Gordon Square; members of the group often holidayed together. This was essential to Virginia, as her relationship with Adrian was not an easy or happy one. These social circles were further extended when, late in 1908, Virginia was to meet Lady Ottoline Morrell, wife of a Liberal MP, and a society hostess with as much interest in the arts as in politics. The people who attended Ottoline's gatherings at 44 Bedford Square, and who stayed at Garsington Manor near Oxford (acquired by the Morrells in 1915), were a mixture of artists, writers, and politicians; Virginia Woolf was to characterize the atmosphere and diversity of these events in much the same terms she used to describe Mrs Dalloway's party.[40]

One occasional entertainment during these years was the costume party—Virginia attended one as Cleopatra in the summer of 1909—and in February 1910, Adrian and his friend Horace Cole carried dressing up to more dangerous and subversive extremes, in what became known as the *Dreadnought* Hoax.[41] At a time when the strength of the British Navy was a matter of heated political debate, a group of Adrian's friends, including Virginia, dressed themselves as the Emperor of Abyssinia and his entourage, and gained access to HMS *Dreadnought* in Weymouth. They obtained costumes from a company of theatrical costumiers in London; the false beards and black make-up were not robust enough to allow them to eat on board ship, but they excused themselves by reference to religious dietary restrictions. They were greeted at Weymouth by a naval officer in full uniform, and the ship's band played a national anthem. (Not, as it turned out, the Abyssinian national anthem, for which they didn't have the music, but the anthem of Zanzibar, which the bandmaster considered 'the next best thing'.[42]) Knowing no Abyssinian, Adrian (who took the role of the party's interpreter) tried to learn Swahili on the train from London to Weymouth; on board, having exhausted his one phrase of Swahili, he made the best of his classical education, and used phrases from Virgil's *Aeneid*, breaking them up in the hope that no officer would recognize their source. Extraordinarily, Commander William Fisher, Adrian's cousin, failed to recognize him, even though Adrian, 6 foot 5 inches tall, was very distinctive. The group returned to London undetected, though a few days later the story reached the newspapers, and questions were asked in the House of Commons. The Navy exacted retribution on several of the conspirators in the largely symbolic and strangely ritualistic form of caning on 'the hindquarters'; Virginia escaped punishment.[43] The episode shows the satirical and anti-authoritarian side of Bloomsbury, something that would develop into an important part of Virginia's work. It must too have given Virginia some insight into the theatricality of social identity. As Adrian recalled it, by the time they had reached Weymouth 'It was hardly a question any longer of a hoax. We were almost acting the truth. Everyone was expecting us to act as the Emperor and his suite, and it would have been extremely difficult not to'.[44]

During the Fitzroy Square period, Virginia continued to review books, primarily for the *TLS*, and to work on 'Melymbrosia'. At the beginning of 1910 she assisted in the campaign for women's suffrage, in the quite menial role of an addresser of envelopes. She was unwell from March of that year, and in June was recommended to take a rest cure; she returned to Fitzroy Square in September. In November 1910 the first exhibition of 'post-Impressionist' art in London opened; organized by Roger Fry, it featured more than 250 works, including paintings by Cézanne, Gauguin, Van Gogh, Manet, Matisse, and Picasso. Though these painters are now accepted masters of modern painting, they were greeted with a 'wild hurricane' of abuse in the newspapers, being seen as 'degenerate' and as a rejection of civilized values.[45] The ensuing arguments strengthened the Bloomsbury Group's sense of artistic identity.

In November 1911 Virginia and Adrian moved across Bloomsbury once again, from Fitzroy Square to 38 Brunswick Square. The move represented a further experiment in styles of living: they planned to share the house with their friends Duncan Grant and John Maynard Keynes; all the 'inmates' would contribute to household expenses; meals were to be provided individually by Sophie, the cook who had been with the family since Hyde Park Gate. It was highly unusual for an unmarried woman to be living in such circumstances, and the scheme led to a cooling of relations with Violet Dickinson, who considered it improper.[46]

Adrian and Virginia soon found a tenant for the top floor, Leonard Woolf, who in June of that year had returned on leave from his post as colonial administrator in Ceylon. Leonard had met Virginia briefly in 1904 before his departure, and on returning soon found himself falling in love. Virginia had not been without suitors in the previous years: in February 1909, Lytton Strachey had proposed to her, possibly in an attempt to 'renounce' his homosexuality; on the following day they both agreed it had been a terrible mistake. Virginia was later to describe him as being 'perfect as a friend, only he's a female friend' (*Letters*, i. 492). In May 1909, the aspiring politician Edward Hilton Young had proposed to her.[47] In July 1911 Walter Lamb, a Cambridge friend of Clive Bell, made his feelings clear to her, and in November 1911 Sydney Waterlow, a diplomat

The *Dreadnought* Hoaxers

Virginia and
Leonard Woolf
in 1912

with philosophical leanings, had also proposed and been gently rejected.[48] Leonard Woolf was to propose on 11 January 1912, but Virginia took some time to decide; the situation affected her mental health, and she spent several weeks in a nursing home in Twickenham. Underlying Virginia's delay was her realization that Leonard felt very genuinely and intensely for her, and a feeling that she could not accept him unless her own feelings had at least something of the same quality. In a letter of 1 May 1912, she set out her predicament: she did not want to be merely 'quite happy', or to look on marriage 'as a profession' (*Letters*, i. 496–7). She also admitted that his being Jewish, and seeming 'so foreign', was an obstacle to her; in announcing her acceptance, she wrote of him as 'a penniless Jew' (*Letters*, i. 500, 501). She continued to find his mother, Marie Woolf, an extraordinary figure, and large Woolf family gatherings slightly overwhelming; however, she recognized the snobbery in her own attitude, and came to see that what she first rejected as vulgarity could also be valued as vitality (*Letters*, iv. 195).

They were married on 10 August 1912, and honeymooned in Provence, Spain, and Italy for six weeks. Soon after returning they left 38 Brunswick Square, and took rooms at 13 Clifford's Inn, one of the Inns of Court. They settled down to work as professional writers: though Virginia had a substantial regular income from inherited capital, it was not quite sufficient. Though Leonard concentrated on political journalism, he also completed a novel, *The Village in the Jungle*, in 1912, and was to complete another (*The Wise Virgins*, a novel of courtship) in 1914. Virginia completed *The Voyage Out* in March 1913 and delivered it to Gerald Duckworth; he accepted it for publication in April.

However, Virginia, who had been unwell with headaches since December, grew increasingly unwell. The first response was for her to spend more time in the country. She and Vanessa had taken a lease on Asheham House in Sussex in October 1911, and she stayed there for increasingly long periods in the summer of 1913. By July she was seriously ill, neither eating nor sleeping properly and on the advice of Dr G. H. Savage, she first went to the nursing home in Twickenham; and then in August with Leonard to the Plough Inn in Somerset. While they were back in London in September consulting doctors, Virginia took an overdose of veronal, a sleeping drug, which very nearly proved fatal. She was found unconscious by her friend

Katherine Cox; had it not been for Maynard Keynes's brother, a doctor, being nearby and able to obtain a stomach pump, she might not have been saved.[49]

In the period after her suicide attempt, Virginia recuperated first at Dalingridge Place, George Duckworth's home in Sussex, and then from November 1913 to August 1914 largely at Asheham. In her periods of recuperation, writing was often forbidden or allowed for only limited periods, and the documentary evidence can leave the impression that she was isolated and unaware of the world around her; but she was fully aware of the war having broken out on 4 August 1914: Asheham seemed to be 'practically under martial law' (*Letters*, ii. 51). In October 1914 the Woolfs settled in lodgings in Richmond; although Leonard held a prejudice against the suburbs, he decided that they should settle there 'to protect [Virginia] from London' and from 'the devastating disorientation' of 'social life'.[50] They decided to lease Hogarth House, 'the perfect envelope for everyday life', part of an eighteenth-century house which combined 'immense solidity' with 'grace, lightness and beauty'; in the drawing room, 'one felt the security from anything like a hostile world, the peace and quiet, in this tremendous solidity of walls, doors, and windows, and yet nothing could have been more light and graceful, more delicately and beautifully proportioned than the room itself, its fireplace and great windows, its panelling and carved woodwork'.[51] Its attractions clearly related to Virginia's health, and fortunately so: by mid-February she was suffering again from headaches and poor sleep, and by 25 March, the day they took possession, Virginia had again gone to a nursing home. Virginia always experienced great anxiety before the publication of her works, and it may be that the anticipation of the appearance of *The Voyage Out* on 26 March lay behind the breakdown, though her taking a violent dislike to Leonard during this illness might indicate a disagreement within the marriage. Virginia moved to Hogarth House on 1 April, but spent much of the summer at Asheham. By the end of August she was allowed to write cards and short letters to friends; by October she was reading again, and becoming increasingly aware of and concerned about the war and the zeppelin bombing raids (*Letters*, ii. 70, 72). By January 1916 she had resumed reviewing for the *TLS*, and she and Leonard had settled into a fairly regular routine of writing in the morning, taking a walk in the afternoon, and reading in the evening;[52] at some point in 1916 she began work on her second novel, *Night and Day*.

Leonard Woolf was called up for military service in May 1916, but exempted on account of a permanent nervous tremor in his hands, and on account of Virginia's poor health.[53] His brother Cecil was conscripted, and killed by a shell in 1917; the same shell severely injured his brother Philip. Many in Bloomsbury were conscientious objectors; Virginia's own anti-war feelings were reinforced by her impression of it as a peculiarly masculine activity, a 'preposterous masculine fiction' created by people as remote as 'some curious tribe in Central Africa' (*Letters*, ii. 76).

Even before they had moved into Hogarth House, Leonard Woolf had formed the plan of setting up a printing press in the cellar, with the motive of providing Virginia with a manual occupation in the afternoons that would take her mind off her work.[54] In March 1917 they bought a hand-operated press 'small enough to stand on a kitchen table', and in July 1917 they printed their first publication, *Two Stories*, which consisted of Virginia's 'The Mark on the Wall' and Leonard's 'Three Jews'. The establishment of the Hogarth Press gave Virginia a sense of creative freedom: she was now guaranteed an outlet for experimental works like 'The Mark on the Wall' or 'Kew Gardens', which would have been difficult to place with any regular publisher or journal. Though she continued to work on the formally conventional *Night and Day*, and was to publish it in the conventional manner with Gerald Duckworth in October 1919, the Press gave her the opportunity to write longer experimental works. When she began work on *Jacob's Room* in 1920, she saw it as a development of the method of the Hogarth Press short stories; it and all her subsequent novels were published by the Press (*Diary*, ii. 13–14). As soon as they had printed *Two Stories*, the Woolfs entered into a contract for a larger press; as the business grew, they contracted professional printers to print longer works.

The Press also created new friendships and strengthened existing ones within the literary community. In 1916 Leonard had met Katherine Mansfield at Garsington, and the Press's second publication in 1918 was her short story *Prelude*: at sixty-eight pages, not short for the amateur typesetters. The Woolfs approached T. S. Eliot at the suggestion of Roger Fry in October 1918.[55] He had published one volume of poems, *Prufrock and Other Observations*, with the

Egoist Press, and responded positively to Leonard's invitation. The
Press was to publish his *Poems* in May 1919 and *The Waste Land* in
September 1923. In 1924, at the invitation of Lytton Strachey's
brother James, they became the publishers of the authorized English
translation of Sigmund Freud's psychoanalytical writings. Many of
their works came to them through Bloomsbury connections; this
inevitably provoked suspicions of nepotism, but it also gave them a
broad-based list of literary and political works, often innovative, and
sometimes polemical. In the 1930s, Virginia met many younger
writers, both through the Press and through Vanessa's children, and
she appears in many of their memoirs. John Lehmann began as an
assistant at the Press in January 1931, and seven years later was to
buy Virginia's half-share in the business.[56] Under his influence, the
Press developed a strong poetry list in the 1930s. His sister, the
novelist Rosamond Lehmann, indicates what a striking presence
Virginia was to the writers who met her: 'She was extremely beautiful, with an austere intellectual beauty of bone and outline, with
large melancholy eyes under carved lids, and the nose and lips, the
long narrow cheek of a Gothic Madonna. Her voice, light, musical,
with a throaty note in it, was one of her great charms. She was tall
and thin, and her hands were astonishingly exquisite'. Rosamond
recalled her conversation, 'a brilliant mixture of reminiscence, gossip, extravagantly fanciful speculation and serious critical discussion
of books and pictures', her sometimes 'malicious' and 'corrosive
tongue', and her love of jokes.[57]

On 1 March 1919, the Woolfs were given notice to quit Asheham
House. Vanessa had already moved out, and had taken the lease of the
nearby Charleston Farmhouse; on 1 July 1919 Leonard and Virginia
bought Monk's House at auction for £700, and on 1 September 1919
they moved in.[58] It was a small flint and brick cottage, without hot
water or a bath, and with a primitive 'earth closet' for a toilet; the
extensive garden and its fruit trees were the most attractive point
(*Diary*, i. 286; *Letters*, ii. 379). At first the Woolfs shared the main
bedroom, sleeping in separate beds; later Leonard slept in one of the
smaller bedrooms.[59] Later still, Virginia's separate bedroom was
added to the house, one of a number of improvements which made
the house seem all the more rambling. It was remembered by one
visitor as 'untidy', with masses of books on the shelves, on the floor
and up the staircase.[60] Whatever its deficiencies, the house was to

provide an important retreat from London, a place to rest and a place to write, away from the distractions of the Press and social life; it was also a place to which the Woolfs would invite their closer friends. Rest continued to be considered necessary and important, as in the early 1920s Virginia continued to be troubled with the headaches which were taken as early warnings of mental illness. Two months in 1921, for example, were 'rubbed out', spent in 'wearisome headache, jumping pulse, aching back, frets, fidgets, lying awake, sleeping draughts, sedatives, digitalis, going for a little walk, & plunging back into bed again—all the horrors of the dark cupboard of illness once more displayed for my diversion' (*Diary*, ii. 125).

When she was engaged in writing a novel, Virginia Woolf's working routine was almost continuous. She kept pencil and paper by her bed, and would write phrases down; the cook Louie Mayer recalled seeing them by her bed when she brought coffee in the morning.[61] It is clear too that she woke with ideas that could not or had not been written down: she described waking 'filled with a tremulous yet steady rapture', and having to carry her 'pitcher full of lucid and deep water across the garden' to her writing lodge (*Letters*, iv. 218). Sometimes, before going to her writing lodge, she would lie in the bath speaking out loud the sentences she had written in the night, asking herself questions and giving herself the answers.[62] Though this may seem like mere writerly eccentricity, it indicates how important to Virginia were the sound of her writing and the shape of her sentences. When she had formally settled down to work, she very rarely worked at a table, but sat in a low armchair with a plywood board across her knees. In the late morning or afternoon she would type up what she had thus written by hand.[63]

The Woolfs continued to spend a significant amount of time in Richmond, travelling into London for business and pleasure. Virginia felt increasingly 'mute & mitigated' in the suburbs, believing that she was missing the 'life' of the city; she had begun work on *Mrs Dalloway* in August 1922, and the process of vividly imagining London can only have exacerbated her sense of separation. Leonard, though he continued to be concerned for the effects of social pleasures on Virginia's mental health, was persuaded that the fatigue of catching crowded buses and trains was at least as serious, and in November 1923, they began to search for a central London home.[64] On 9 January 1924, Virginia signed the lease for 52 Tavistock

Square, and recorded the moment as soon as she could in her diary, seeing this as her return after a ten-year exile, and as marking the final chapter in the 'series of catastrophes' which had very nearly ended her life (*Diary*, ii. 282–3). The four-storey terraced house was austerely elegant like her previous Bloomsbury houses; it had a basement suitable for the Press; two floors which were sub-let to a firm of solicitors; and two further floors which formed Leonard and Virginia's living quarters. It was to be their London home effectively for the rest of Virginia's life: they decided to move out only in 1939, irritated by the construction of a large new hotel in Tavistock Square, and completed the move into 37 Mecklenburgh Square on 24 August 1939; the outbreak of war and the danger of air raids meant that they spent little time there.

In December 1922, Virginia had met Vita Sackville-West, already the author of two novels, and a woman whose background fascinated Virginia. Vita traced her ancestry back to the Norman Conquest; the family home, Knole in Kent, had been given to the family by Elizabeth I. She was born in 1892; her father was the 3rd Baron Sackville of Knole; her mother, Victoria, was his cousin, the illegitimate daughter of his uncle (the 2nd Baron) and a Spanish dancer, Pepita da Oliva.[65] Though passionate about Knole, she could not inherit it, and had settled nearby at Long Barn; later she and her husband would create a famous garden at Sissinghurst Castle. Though married to the diplomat Harold Nicolson and mother of two children by him, Vita was well known as a lesbian, and, as Harold was homosexual, their marriage was one of companionship rather than sexual passion. Virginia's first account of her was not flattering—'florid, moustached, parakeet coloured'—but a friendship and an attraction soon developed; when Virginia spent three days with Vita at Long Barn at the end of 1925, the relationship became a sexual one. Vita was now seen in altogether more erotic terms, 'pink glowing, grape clustered, pearl hung' (*Diary*, iii. 52). When Vita travelled to Persia in 1926 to join her husband for two months, the physical relationship transmuted into an epistolary one. On her return, Virginia was deep in the writing of *To the Lighthouse*, but they spent further weekends together during 1926. Vita told her husband that she was 'scared' of 'arousing physical feelings' in Virginia, 'because of the madness'; Virginia's reference to being 'bathe[d] . . . in serenity' late in 1926 suggests a great sense of physical ease in Vita's company, if not a sexual relationship.[66] They remained close for the next few years, though the relationship chilled in 1929 as Vita became close to Hilda Matheson (*Diary*, iii. 239). And, as Hermione Lee has noted, there was an intermediate stage in its transformation when in January 1927 Virginia saw Vita at Knole: her existing sense of the centuries of history behind Vita's passions was deepened, and the transformation of Vita into a fiction began.[67]

In March of that year, Virginia devised the plot of *Orlando*, a comic fantasy that embodied her attraction to Vita's ancestry. She intended it from the outset to be a self-satirizing, mocking book, an 'escapade' after the intensity of *To the Lighthouse* and before the 'mystical poetical work' she had been contemplating, which was eventually to become *The Waves* (*Diary*, iii. 131). It was a 'writer's holiday' (*Diary*, iii. 177; apostrophe inserted). She returned to the idea in September 1927, envisaging Vita Sackville-West as Orlando, and, by the time she began writing in early October, had the outline of the book as it was published: 'a biography beginning in the year 1500 & continuing to the present day, called Orlando: Vita; only with a change about from one sex to another' (*Diary*, iii. 161). Progress was rapid, and Woolf completed the first draft on 22 March 1928; she revised and typed up the manuscript in April and May, and her typescript was sent for typesetting on the first of June; she corrected the proofs later in June, and the book was published on 11 October 1928. *Orlando* sold well, and was at that time Woolf's greatest commercial success (*Diary*, iii. 198, 200).

The publication of *Orlando* marked a turning point in Virginia's life. She was already a novelist of growing reputation, something marked by an increasing number of invitations to deliver lectures, including those which were to form *A Room of One's Own*. But she earned relatively little by her writing: in 1924, she earned £37 from her books, and £128 from her journalism. *Mrs Dalloway* and *To the Lighthouse* had each been more successful than their predecessors, and in 1927 she earned £545 from her books. *Orlando*, though, was a success of an entirely different order, and in 1929 her books brought her £2,306.[68]

This financial success allowed Virginia significantly to reduce the amount of book reviewing she did; it also allowed Leonard to resign as literary editor of the *Nation*. It seems likely that the security provided by the success of *Orlando* emboldened Virginia to begin

Vita Sackville-West in
1934, by Howard Coster

Ethel Smyth *c.* 1938

work on *The Waves* in 1929. She had first had her vision of a fin in a waste of waters in September 1926; in October 1926 she was planning something 'mystic, spiritual' about a solitary woman musing; by March 1927 this idea was connected with the image of a many-petalled flower; the image of the moths, which for a long time provided her working title, came in a letter from Vanessa dated 3 May 1927 (*Diary*, iii. 131; *W*, pp. 104, 191). Yet it was not until August 1929 that she began to work at it seriously. Virginia's financial success also allowed her and Leonard to extend their garden, to buy a car, and to take more frequent holidays. In April 1931 they travelled in western France; in April and May 1932, in Greece with Roger Fry and his sister; in May 1933, in Italy; in April 1934, Ireland. In May 1935 they travelled through Germany to Italy, alarmed to find themselves driving through a town 'lined with uniformed Nazis', who were awaiting an official visit from the 'Herr Präsident', Goering; children waved Nazi flags, and banners declared that 'The Jew is our Enemy'.[69] The rise of fascism in Europe and the corresponding rise in militarism in Britain were to concern Virginia in her works throughout the 1930s. In the following years, the Woolfs took less nerve-racking holidays in Cornwall, western France, and Scotland.

In February 1930 a 'bluff military woman . . . bounced into the room' and into Virginia's life (*Diary*, iii. 290). Ethel Smyth, wearing her distinctive three-cornered hat and tailor-made suit, was a composer, campaigner, and author who had greatly admired *A Room of One's Own* and wanted to meet its author. Born in 1858, the daughter of an army general, she herself had had to become bellicose, fighting to be given a proper musical training, and struggling to have her works performed. Some of this was due to sexist prejudice, and some because her musical idiom had dated rapidly. During the campaign for women's suffrage she had joined the militant Women's Social and Political Union (WSPU): as Hermione Lee notes, while Virginia Stephen was filling envelopes for the non-violent National Union of Women's Suffrage Societies (NUWSS), Ethel Smyth was breaking windows in Berkeley Square.[70] She had by 1930 published several volumes of memoirs and was to publish several more; in them, she was characteristically outspoken about her passion and affection for other women. She was, in short, 'an emotional, demanding, self-absorbed person with a great investment in her own feelings, a deep fund of loyalty, and a capacity for intense suffering'.[71] She inspired affection and frustration in Virginia in equal measure. Though a great talker, she was by this time severely deaf, and was not a good listener. She would descend on Virginia with little regard for a writer's need for privacy.

Ethel's intrusion might seem a horribly inappropriate reward for writing *A Room of One's Own*, but her presence connected Virginia to a longer history of women's emancipation, and led indirectly to the composition of *The Years*. The beginnings of this novel, and of the polemical book *Three Guineas*, lay in 'Professions for Women', a talk Virginia gave in January 1931 at the National Society for Women's Service. Ethel sat beside her on the platform, though the invitation had come from Pippa Strachey, Lytton's sister. The society worked to 'obtain economic equality for women', and Virginia's talk argued that women, if they were to enter 'the professions', must not only obtain legal equality, but also eliminate the ideological barriers to success; foremost among them, the 'Angel in the House', the Victorian stereotype of subservient womanhood. From this talk, she developed the idea of a 'novel-essay', a form which would combine chapters of fiction with historical commentary. When she abandoned the experiment ('The Pargiters'), the fictional side developed into *The Years*, and the essay side into *Three Guineas*. Summarized thus, the process sounds easy; in fact, the process of composition turned out to be the most gruelling that Virginia had ever undertaken.

The 1930s were punctuated by a series of deaths of close friends, and Virginia's diary took on some of the qualities of the last section of her father's 'Mausoleum Book', in which he had commemorated lost friends and family. In December 1931, Lytton Strachey became seriously ill. It turned out that he had stomach cancer, though doctors initially misdiagnosed him as having an ulcerated colon. He died on 21 January 1932. With concern, the Woolfs visited Dora Carrington, who had lived with Strachey and her husband Ralph Partridge in a complex web of emotional dependency; but she was unreachably depressed, and on the following day shot herself. Lytton's death cast a shadow over the writing of Flush, Virginia's light-hearted biography of Elizabeth Barrett Browning's spaniel; begun at some point around August 1931, it owed something to Strachey's own irreverent biographies in *Eminent Victorians*.

Another close and influential friend, Roger Fry, died of heart failure on 9 September 1934, having injured himself in a fall two days earlier. At his funeral, she thought of 'the fun & the fact that he had lived with such variety & generosity & curiosity'; she was left with a sense of 'the poverty of life' without him, 'the substance gone out of everything' (*Diary*, iv. 243, 242). Figures like Fry not only supported Woolf as personal friends, but as signs that she had an audience. When the novelist Stella Benson had died in December 1933, Virginia felt a sense of loss out of all proportion to their intimacy: they had met briefly in 1932, though Virginia had felt that they could have reached a 'deeper layer' of friendship. What she mourned was the loss of a sense of community, of 'a web' of like-minded thinkers that would fertilize or light up her own works (*Diary*, iv. 193). At the end of October Fry's companion Helen Anrep tentatively asked Virginia to write his biography. The task was in many ways unsuited to her intuitively experimental impulse: in her diaries she toyed with alternative modes of composition, such as a multiply-authored narrative, or beginning at the end of his life with a whole day at his house in the south of France. In the event she took a more conventionally chronological approach, and found the work uninspiring 'drudgery', not completed until May 1940.

In July 1936 civil war broke out in Spain between the fascist forces of General Franco and the Republican side, an alliance of leftist and anarchist elements. Many British writers gave their support to the Republican cause, and several went to Spain either to fight or to undertake pacifist work such as ambulance driving.[72] At the outbreak of war Vanessa Bell's son Julian was working in China as a university professor; in February 1937 he decided to resign to join the International Brigade in Spain. This naturally caused Vanessa and Virginia some anxiety; their feelings were exacerbated by the recent death in Spain of John Cornford, whose parents had been good friends of Virginia around 1911. Julian was persuaded to go as a non-combatant in the Spanish Medical Aid organization. He left London on 7 June 1937, and died on 18 July, killed by a shell fragment which had hit him in his ambulance. Virginia spent the following weeks consoling Vanessa, though her sister never fully recovered from the loss. Virginia also wrote a memoir of Julian, and in writing the second and third sections of *Three Guineas*, she continued her argument with him about how best to fight for liberty.[73] Nevertheless, she found it impossible to assimilate the experience. It seemed as if the future had been 'cut off', 'lopped: deformed' (*Diary*, v. 113).

The outbreak of war in September 1939 not only darkened Virginia's mood, but brought practical difficulties: food rationing was imposed; Virginia found there was 'little fat to cook with' and less variety in her diet; the only way to enjoy food was to 'make up imaginary meals' (*Diary*, v. 343–7). The Woolfs spent most of their time at Monk's House. They experienced not only the common anxiety about the threat from bombing—quite literally brought home by the destruction of 37 Mecklenburgh Square—but also the expectation that, as they were leading left-wing intellectuals, and Leonard was Jewish, they would be particular targets in any Nazi occupation. Like many in their circles, they discussed committing suicide. Leonard stocked up petrol to enable them to asphyxiate themselves with car exhaust fumes.

Virginia completed *Between the Acts* at the end of February 1941. She had often felt despondent on completing a novel, and had often suffered from headaches at those times, but she was more than usually dissatisfied with this one. She described it as 'too slight and sketchy', 'too silly and trivial' (*Letters*, vi. 482, 486). At first she asked Leonard and John Lehmann to decide whether to publish. She continued to feel that writing was impossible: there was 'No audience' and 'No private stimulus', only the 'outer roar' of war and the news of war (*Letters*, vi. 479). She may have attempted to commit suicide on or around 18 March: she came back from a walk soaking wet, and claimed to have fallen in a dyke.[74] In a letter dated 'Sunday' (23 March 1941) she wrote to Vanessa: 'It is just as it was the first time, I am always hearing voices, and I know I shan't get over it now' (*Letters*, vi. 485; apostrophe inserted). She wrote to Lehmann suggesting that the Press withdraw *Between the Acts* from publication; she would rewrite it for publication in the autumn; Leonard, forwarding this letter to Lehmann on the morning of 28 March, wrote that she was 'on the verge of a complete nervous break down . . . The war, food &c have been telling on her and I have seen it coming on for some time'.[75] Later that morning Virginia wrote a suicide note to Leonard, leaving it on her pad in the writing lodge. She returned to the house and put on her coat; she took her walking stick and walked down to the river Ouse. There she must have put a stone or stones in her coat pocket, and thrown herself in. When Leonard found her note at lunchtime, he went down to the river, and found her stick floating there. Extensive searches failed to discover her body, but on

3 April the national press announced that she was presumed dead. Her body was found on 18 April; Leonard attended her cremation alone, and buried her ashes in the garden of Monk's House.

Leonard Woolf lived on at Monk's House until his own death in 1969. Virginia's final letter had told him to 'destroy all my papers', but he did not. He quietly sustained Virginia's literary reputation, overseeing the publication of *Between the Acts* later in 1941, four volumes of her essays, beginning with *The Death of the Moth* in 1942, a volume of short stories in 1944, a selection from her diaries in 1953, her correspondence with Lytton Strachey in 1956, and a collected edition of her essays in 1966.

CHAPTER 2

THE FABRIC OF SOCIETY: NATION AND IDENTITY

THE 'Britain' in which Virginia Woolf died was not the same nation in which Virginia Stephen had been born. The identity of the nation, internally and externally, had changed irrevocably. Though some important turning points occurred outside Woolf's lifetime—for example, the Reform Act of 1867, or the independence of India in 1948—she witnessed many changes that developed from or anticipated these events. Internally, there were great changes in the composition of the electorate and the identities of political parties; in the character of London and its position within the nation; in the role of women; in housing and in the idea of the family; in the relations between social classes; and in education. Above all, the dominant idea of the state changed. Whereas the late nineteenth century had been dominated by the liberal ideal of the maximum of individual liberty and the minimum of state interference, the early twentieth century saw increasing acceptance of the idea that the state should restrict individual liberty for the benefit of the whole nation. Moreover, the state could adopt a positive role in encouraging or managing crucial elements in the fabric of society. The worldwide economic depression of 1929–32 created conditions which for some justified more authoritarian forms of government.

Externally, the relation of Britain to other nations changed. The position of the British Empire as the world's dominant economic power was challenged by the rise of Germany and the United States. The relation of Britain to its imperial possessions was challenged by their development as industrial economies and consequent demands for independence. Politicians argued whether Britain should continue with a policy of free trade, or impose duties ('tariffs') on imported goods; more subtly, they debated whether tariffs should differentiate between the countries of the Empire and those outside it. The Boer War (1899–1902) and the First World War (1914–18) were the most prominent crises in the process of international adjustment. Though the First World War was fought over European territory, it was fought against an imperial rival. The post-war period saw the advent of fascist dictatorships in Italy (in 1922), Germany (in 1933), and Spain (after the Civil War of 1936–7). The Spanish Civil War began a period of instability in Europe which was followed by Germany's annexation of the Sudetenland in 1938 and its invasion of Poland in 1939, the event which precipitated the Second World War (1939–45).

In a change both internal and external, the Irish Easter Rising of 1916 brought to a crisis the question of Home Rule for Ireland; the creation of the Irish Free State in 1922 and the Irish Republic in 1937 changed the composition of the United Kingdom itself. While Woolf's fictions only occasionally depicted these changes directly, the underlying questions of national identity and individual liberty are far more pervasive.

Industry, Empire, and Party Politics

The change in Britain's international fortunes involved both its imperial possessions and its domestic industries. Britain had been involved in many different forms of 'imperial' and 'colonial' relation to other territories, and continued to be through Woolf's lifetime. The crucial distinction is between 'formal' and 'informal' empire, the one involving legal control as well as trading links, the other depending solely on economic dominance.[1] The distinction is relevant to *The Waves*, where Percival can be taken to represent 'formal' empire, and Louis, as a businessman and the son of an Australian banker, to represent 'informal' relations. Britain's relations to India had begun in the guise of trade, under the East India Company, but were formalized following the mutiny of 1857; in 1876 Disraeli declared Queen Victoria the 'Empress'. Relations with Canada and Australia grew gradually less formal during the late nineteenth and early twentieth centuries, Canada being granted 'dominion' status in 1867. Nevertheless, Britons continued to emigrate.

The industrial revolution of the early nineteenth century had given Britain immense economic advantages, but in the late nineteenth century it began to lose ground to Germany and America. Historians have noted the advent of a 'second industrial revolution' during this period. The first revolution had seen the application of steam power to existing industries such the production of textiles and steel; the technologies were relatively simple. The second revolution grew from scientific discoveries in the fields of chemistry and electromagnetics, producing products such as synthetic dyes and telegraphic equipment. It applied new chemical knowledge to existing processes such as steel production. It developed the technologies and procedures of mass production ('Taylorization', after the American F. W. Taylor), such as the analysis of a productive process into separate operations and the creation of assembly lines. Britain, having invested in the older technologies and having developed markets for the older products, was not well placed to join the second revolution. Moreover, as compared to Germany and America, its universities were exclusive and geared towards humanistic rather than scientific education. The development of London as an international financial centre in the 1870s and 1880s had brought a short-term advantage, in that it allowed much of the capital created by the first industrial revolution to be invested overseas; but these investments were at the expense of domestic industry. Once Germany was unified after the Franco-Prussian War (1870–1), it was well placed to develop the new technologies. Likewise America, after the disruption of the Civil War (1861–5), had made up for lost time and had begun to overtake Britain as an industrial nation.[2]

Britain's supremacy as an imperial power was brought into question by the Boer War of 1899–1902. The 1880s had seen increased European involvement in Africa (the 'scramble for Africa'), with Britain's interests focused on the southern area. In the 1890s Britain came into conflict with the Boers of the Transvaal and Orange Free State areas of southern Africa, descendants of Dutch colonists, whose European loyalties were to the Netherlands and Germany. The Boers wished to establish a United States of Southern Africa, and conflict broke out with the British settlers of the Cape region. Britain appeared to have won the war on 25 October 1900, when it formally annexed the Transvaal, but the Boers maintained guerrilla resistance until May 1902. Compared to the First World War, casualty levels were relatively low: 450,000 troops were employed; only 5,774 were killed, though another 16,000 died of disease, and another 22,829 were wounded.[3]

The Boer War focused political attention on the health of the nation and the organization of the state. Social investigators had been documenting the poor health and living conditions of the British working classes for some years, but only when many of the men who volunteered for military service were rejected as being physically unfit did the issue become politically important. Forty per cent of those who joined the army between 1897 and 1902 were rejected as physically or medically unfit; in some cities the percentage was as high as 60.[4] There was a change in political culture, in which the ideal of 'national efficiency' replaced the ideal of individual liberty. Though politicians disagreed on how best to achieve the new ideal, they shared certain key assumptions. The health of the nation was an important concern; it was understood in the terminology of heredity and environment established by the 'eugenics' movement. The business cultures of Germany and America were common points of reference, as was the transformation of Japan into a 'Western'-style nation.[5] 'Centralization' was a significant theme. So too was the more ambiguous term 'organization', which could refer to a separation of functions (as with the organs of the body), or to the fact of their being coordinated by a central purpose. In 1873 Virginia Woolf's uncle James Fitzjames Stephen had argued for the importance of centralized administration in India, and his *Liberty, Equality, Fraternity* anticipated the later debates.[6] While the liberalism of the late nineteenth century had argued that the best form of society was one in which the government interfered as little as possible with individual liberties, and in which free-market competition would 'naturally' create the greatest good for the greatest number, the advocates of national efficiency argued that competition often introduced wasteful duplication of effort, and that in the modern world certain services and industries were best run as state or municipal monopolies.

The Boer War and the growing threat of German naval power encouraged politicians to rethink the relations of Britain to its trading partners, and to propose the abandonment of free trade in favour of various forms of protectionism. In the period 1903 to 1908, two main options emerged: that of a tariff on all imports into Britain, with the exception of those from the Empire; and that of selective tariffs adopted as retaliatory measures. At first these proposals were as important for their symbolism as for their revenue-raising possibilities: they raised the question of whether Britain was to conceive itself in national or imperial terms; whether it was one nation-state trading with others, or part of a continuous economic territory that stretched around the globe.

The period after the First World War saw a continuing decline in Britain's international position and growing calls for independence from imperial nations. In 1917 the British Government had promised 'responsible government' to India, meaning by this that the people of India would be responsible for domestic affairs, while international affairs would continue to be controlled from London; similar 'dominion' status had been granted to Canada in 1867, and was to be granted to the Irish Free State in 1922. Leonard Woolf argued for similar status to be given to Ceylon.[7] In April 1919 a British army general opened fire on an unarmed crowd at Amritsar, killing 379, and alienating the Indian population still further from British rule. However, the Government of India Act of 1919 deferred the granting of responsible government; it was to come, and only in a limited form, with the Act of 1935. The experience of imperial decline led to an amplification of imperial propaganda, encouraged by the Empire League, manifesting itself in events such as imperial exhibitions at Earl's Court and Wembley Stadium, both of which Virginia Woolf witnessed for herself.[8]

In the period before the First World War, the questions of state intervention, tariff reform, and Home Rule for Ireland divided the main political parties, particularly the Liberals. In 1880 the Liberal party contained three overlapping elements: the aristocratic Whigs, the middle-class Moderates, and the Radicals. Home Rule had been a key Liberal policy since Gladstone in 1885, but those Liberals in favour of the 'Union' formed a distinct faction, the Liberal Unionists, who had more in common with the Conservative party. The rise of socialist thinking influenced the emergence of the 'New Liberalism' in the period 1906 to 1914, a political philosophy which saw greater scope for government interference. Though the Conservative party was less fragmented, it was divided on questions of free trade.

The period also saw the rise of the trade unions and of the Labour party. In the 1860s and 1870s trade unions had represented only a limited number of clearly defined trades, usually of a skilled nature. The 'new unionism' that rose in the late 1880s recruited unskilled workers, and sought to create working-class unity. The fundamental power of the unions arose from their power to organize strikes. However, the crushing of particular strikes and legal judgements discouraging strike action forced them to consider parliamentary representation as another lever. As John Davis notes, it is no coincidence that the Independent Labour Party (ILP), founded in 1893, was born in Bradford: two years previously a textile workers' strike had been defeated there by the local Liberal establishment.[9] The ILP fielded its first candidates, twenty-eight of them, in the 1895 election. The Trades Union Congress formed the Labour Representation Committee (LRC) in February 1900 with the aim of electing working men to Parliament; however, many unions were unwilling to support the LRC. Then in 1901 came the 'Taff Vale judgement': the House of Lords awarded damages to the Taff Vale Railway Company against the union which had organized a strike in the previous year; the case cost the union at least £23,000.[10] The case set a legal precedent which discouraged strike action; it was not until 1906 that the Trade Disputes Act removed liabilities for civil damages. Many of the unions which had been sceptical about the LRC were persuaded to back it: the number affiliated rose from 41 to 165. This was certainly an important factor in the election of the first Labour MPs in 1906. The introduction of salaries for MPs in 1911 removed a further obstacle to working-class representation: the first generation of Labour MPs had been largely dependent on the unions for their income. The Trade Union Amendment Act of 1913, intended to frustrate the political activities of trade unions by separating their political from their general funds, actually assisted the Labour cause. Because unions could find little else to do with their political funds, they were less reluctant to give them to the Labour party. The party's income increased tenfold.[11]

The First World War sharpened the sense of class conflict. Rapid retail price inflation in the first year of the war caused hardship and engendered suspicion. Businessmen were suspected of profiteering, and of using the war as an excuse to overrule agreements about working hours and practices.[12] In the post-war period the unions organized several coordinated general strikes, the most significant of which was the General Strike of 1926. The General Strike began with a dispute over the reorganization of the coal industry, including the removal of government subsidies instituted immediately after the war. The dispute broadened when print workers refused to print an inflammatory leading article in the *Daily Mail*, and became a general strike, involving railway, tram, and dock workers from 3 May to 12 May 1926. It persuaded some centrist Liberals (such as Sir John Simon) to move rightwards. In its aftermath reactionary politicians and commentators became more strident in their patriotism.

Legislation for a New Nation

The election of a Liberal government in January 1906 inaugurated six years of revolutionary legislation which changed the nature of the British state for most of the century. Virginia, along with her brother and sister, went to Trafalgar Square to celebrate the victory.[13] With Jack Hills, who had become a Conservative MP in 1906, she discussed protectionism and the recruitment of underpaid Chinese labourers to the mines of South Africa; the latter policy had weakened the credibility of the Conservative party with working-class voters, and had contributed to their defeat.[14] Though Woolf was engaged with political questions for the rest of her life, when characters in her novels refer to specific legislation, it often dates from this period. In *The Voyage Out*, Rachel's father is said to be 'a strong Protectionist' (*VO*, p. 177); Evelyn Murgatroyd declares that the questions 'that really matter to people's lives' are 'White Slave Traffic', 'Women's Suffrage', and 'the Insurance Bill' (*VO*, p. 289). In *Night and Day* the mechanisms of suffrage campaigning are depicted directly, but other issues are mentioned: Mary's friendship with Ralph is based on their common interest in questions such as 'the housing of the poor' or the 'taxation of land values' (*ND*, p. 82). The former was the subject of a series of ineffective Acts (see the section 'Houses, Households and Families', below), the latter the most contentious element of David Lloyd George's 'People's Budget' of 1909. In *Jacob's Room*, Jacob ponders the question of Home Rule (*JR*, p. 133), as does Miss Marchmont (p. 144). In the drafts of *Mrs Dalloway*, land values interest Peter Walsh, though the decline of the Liberal party in the post-war years had marginalized the issue.[15]

Lloyd George's budget of 1909 is the crucial event; though proposals for Home Rule and women's suffrage dated back to the nineteenth century, the budget and the events that surrounded it brought fundamental changes to the nature of Parliament. In April

1909 Lloyd George was faced with an 'enormous' increase in government expenditure.[16] This was primarily due to the cost of the Old Age Pension scheme, which had come into effect on 1 January 1909, and to additional naval expenditure on dreadnoughts, though Lloyd George also noted that the increase in motor traffic was causing additional costs in road maintenance. His was an explicitly anti-militarist budget. Like other Liberals; he dismissed fears about German naval strength, saying that it would be 'an act of criminal insanity' to spend £8,000,000 building 'gigantic flotillas to encounter mythical Armadas'; he would prefer to spend money easing the hardships of the poor than creating 'huge machines for the destruction of human life'.[17] However, his limitations on naval expenditure did not balance the budget. To raise additional revenue he proposed several measures, including a 'super-tax' on the very rich, and, most controversially of all, the taxation of land values.

Lloyd George argued that the value of land had increased immensely in the previous twenty or thirty years, primarily in cities and in areas with large mineral wealth. In the case of urban land values, the increase was due not to the efforts of the landowners, but 'to the energy and enterprise of the community'.[18] The tax was to be levied whenever ownership changed through inheritance or sale. It is a sign of the change in political culture that a Liberal Chancellor of the Exchequer was employing an essentially socialist argument. The argument had been advanced by several writers in the 1890s. J. A. Hobson had noted that the state not only increasingly intervened to restrict the freedom of workers and employers, for the sake of wider community interests, but that it also increasingly undertook 'productive works' such as conveying letters and telegrams, producing and distributing gas, or building drainage systems and sewage works.[19] Such works benefited all, but they rewarded landowners with an 'unearned increment'.[20] The Lancashire town of Bury provided a pointed example: the municipal authorities had wanted to raise £60,000 from the rates to provide sewage-works; the greatest single beneficiary of the scheme would have been the dominant local landowner, Lord Derby, as the 'ground value' of his land would have greatly increased.[21] Socialist thinkers went one step further than Liberals, generalizing the argument about land value to apply to all forms of capital. The growth of an individual's capital was due not to 'his solitary efforts', but to 'the assistance lent by the community'.[22]

What unites Lloyd George and the socialists is that they adopt a new model of the state: not as a collection of individuals, but as an interconnected web, in which each individual depends on the efforts and investments of others. Woolf alludes to the unearned increment in *Night and Day*, where Katharine Hilbery benefits from a metaphorical increment in the value of the poetic works of her grandfather (*ND*, p. 37). More generally, throughout her career Woolf tried to find ways of describing in fiction the hidden connections between individuals.

Unsurprisingly, Lloyd George's proposal for a land tax was unpopular with the landowners in the House of Lords. Though by convention, the Lords did not use their power of veto on taxation legislation, since the Liberal landslide of 1906 they had been asserting their undemocratic authority. In November 1909 they rejected the budget, provoking a constitutional crisis which, after the general elections of January and December 1910, led to the Parliament Act of 1911.[23] The Act limited the powers of the House of Lords: the Lords could not reject financial legislation; they could reject other legislation twice only; a Bill which was passed by the Commons in three successive sessions would become law.[24] The Act altered the balance of power in the country. The Lords, with their in-built conservative majority, were permanently weakened; the democratic electorate—albeit an all-male electorate—was strengthened. However, as John Davis notes, the Liberal party paid dearly for allowing the House of Lords to retain a right of veto: the Lords used their powers to the full, and after the radical transformations of 1909 to 1911, parliamentary activity slowed down considerably.[25]

The 'Insurance Bill' which Evelyn Murgatroyd considers so important in *The Voyage Out* was the National Insurance Bill of 1911. Introduced in the Chancellor of the Exchequer's statement in May 1911, it aimed to provide insurance against sickness for the whole working class, and insurance against unemployment for certain trades. Unlike the Old Age Pension, the health insurance was a contributory scheme: for every 4*d.* that the employee was required to pay, the employer would pay 3*d.*, and the state would make a contribution equivalent to 2*d.* Contributory health insurance had hitherto been organized by the Friendly Societies, and the Act recruited them, along with the trade unions, to administer the benefits. In its rationalization of previously ad hoc schemes, the National Insurance

Act is typical of the 'national efficiency' movement in the wider sense of the phrase; in its concern with the health of the nation, it typifies the narrower concerns of the movement. It also laid the foundations for later, larger schemes. The existing ad hoc arrangements had been described by Winston Churchill in 1908 as the 'social security apparatus', provisions that were to be combined with 'state safeguards' to create an ideal system.[26] Churchill's phrasing implies a contrast between 'society' and the 'state', but the 1911 Act and its successors effectively made 'social' security a state responsibility. While the 1911 Act did not create a national health service, it greatly increased the role of the state in providing health care. While it provided unemployment insurance to only a limited number of trades, it paved the way for the Unemployment Insurance Act of 1920, which insured all workers.

The campaign for Irish Home Rule gained momentum as soon as reform of the Lords became a possibility. Unionists opposed the Parliament Bill on the grounds that it would inevitably lead to a measure of Home Rule, and so the issue was debated long before the formal introduction of the Government of Ireland Bill on 11 April 1912.[27] The Bill proposed to establish a separate Parliament for the whole of Ireland with power over domestic affairs; the Westminster Parliament was to remain the imperial Parliament. In two successive sessions the Bill was passed by the House of Commons and rejected by the Lords. As time drew on, it became clearer that the status of Ulster was the sticking point for Unionists, the 'Ulster' in question sometimes consisting of as few as four counties in the north of Ireland, sometimes as many as eight.

This clarification of the problem was accompanied by growing militarization in the north. The Ulster Volunteer Force had been founded, quite legally, in January 1912, and two days before the introduction of the Home Rule Bill, a review of its 80,000 volunteers had been held. Not only did its founder, Sir Edward Carson, take the salute, but so too did the leader of the Unionists in the Commons, Bonar Law.[28] The officers of the British army in Ireland were largely drawn from the Anglo-Irish gentry, and by November 1913, Bonar Law was openly appealing to them to disobey orders. In March 1914, in what became known as the 'Curragh Mutiny', a large group of officers made it clear that they would not enforce the Home Rule Bill on Ulster.[29] The breakdown of government control in Ireland greatly facilitated gun-running to the Ulster Volunteers. Although the Home Rule Bill completed its third reading in the House of Commons on 26 May, it was clearly a measure that was impossible to implement. Further negotiations began in July 1914, but the deterioration in continental politics and the entry of Britain into the war on 4 August 1914 meant that the Bill was never implemented.

During the Easter Rising of 1916, the nationalists declared an Irish Republic; after the elections of 1918, the Sinn Fein party established an independent Irish Parliament, the Dáil. The situation was politically confused, but initially pacific. Then in 1919 the Irish Republican Army (IRA) began a guerrilla war against British Government in Ireland; the brutal response of British units (first the Black and Tans and then the Auxiliary Division) deepened resistance. Lloyd George attempted to implement the Government of Ireland Act (1920), which legislated for the creation of an Irish Free State of twenty-six counties in the south, and an Ulster of six in the North, with separate parliaments in Dublin and Belfast. This was not accepted by the Unionists in the North or the Sinn Fein Nationalist party in the South. A further treaty in December 1921 caused a split in the nationalists, and a civil war broke out in Ireland, lasting from June 1922 to April 1923. Eventually Ireland was divided along the borders proposed by Lloyd George in 1920.

The passage of women's suffrage legislation was equally complex. The pressures which led to the demand for equal voting rights were many. A politically forceful women's movement had arisen in the 1870s and 1880s, campaigning to repeal the Contagious Diseases Acts. It was reinforced by the increasing educational opportunities for women from 1870 onwards. Female ratepayers were permitted to vote in local elections from 1869, and to serve on School Boards and as Poor Law guardians. This gave women some experience in public life, and increased awareness of the power of central government. The reorganization of local government removed women from London local authorities in 1899 and from School Boards, which were abolished in 1902; such loss of influence almost certainly stimulated women such as Emmeline Pankhurst to renew the campaign for women's suffrage.[30]

The opposition to women's suffrage often appealed to mute prejudice rather than to rational argument. Those arguments that were advanced usually claimed that something in the essential physiological or psychological nature of women made them unsuited for politics. The 'argument from force' maintained that because women were physically 'unsuited' to military service, they should not be allowed to take political decisions which might lead to war.[31] Woolf was aware of the idea: in 1910, reviewing a pro-suffrage adaptation of Aristophanes' *Lysistrata*, she drew attention to its having put the 'physical force argument' into 'the mouths of the old men'.[32] The argument that the proper sphere of 'woman' was the home (or, by association, child-rearing and education) had more varied affiliations. The idea that women had a distinct sphere of activity could be employed by anti-suffrage campaigners, and suffragists attempted to refute them; however, it could be employed by pro-suffragists, on the grounds that these spheres of activity needed to be represented in the electorate by those who understood them best.[33]

The campaigners for and against suffrage did not have clear affiliations to political parties. There were two main suffrage organizations, the National Union of Women's Suffrage Societies (NUWSS), founded in 1897, and the Women's Social and Political Union (WSPU), founded in 1903. Though the terms 'suffragist' and 'suffragette' are now often used interchangeably, at the time the former was the label of the NUWSS, while the latter, originally intended as a derogatory term, was adopted and reclaimed by the WSPU. The WSPU became the more militant body, supporting window-smashing campaigns and other violent actions. Its leader, Emmeline Pankhurst, notoriously autocratic, was recalled by one very detached supporter as a forerunner of Lenin, Hitler, and Mussolini.[34] Politically it became the more closely associated with the Conservative party; on the outbreak of war it suspended its campaign and became strongly patriotic and militaristic. The NUWSS was non-militant, and more closely associated with the Liberal and Labour parties. However, although the suffrage cause was natural liberal territory, the Liberal leader Asquith was personally strongly opposed to it. Rather than openly declaring and justifying his opposition to the idea, he repeatedly made ambivalent promises, and allowed Bills to be introduced in Parliament, but then refused to allow parliamentary time for them to proceed: hence, in *Night and Day*, Mary Datchet's belief that Asquith 'deserves to be hanged', and the reference to the Government's 'latest evasion' (*ND*, p. 133).[35] The best opportunity for achieving suffrage came when the election of January 1910 was

Suffragette march,
London 1911

'The Right
Dishonourable
Double-Face Asquith',
suffragette poster, 1909

called; although this election was conceived as a vote on the 'People's Budget' of 1909, the suffrage campaigners worked hard to make votes for women an electoral issue. The election of December 1910 seemed to be another such opportunity. In the end, it was the war which brought about women's suffrage. From March 1916 onwards the Government was considering post-war conditions (Asquith formed a 'Reconstruction Committee' in that month), and in late 1916 a parliamentary committee was formed to consider electoral reform. Its primary purpose was to enfranchise army conscripts, but it also recommended that the vote be given to women. The Representation of the People Act of 1918 gave the vote to women at the age of 30 if they were local government electors or married to one. It was not until April 1928 that an Act lowered the voting age for women to 21, giving women complete suffrage equality with men. The winning of the vote was not the only success: the Sex Disqualification (Removal) Act of 1919 removed many of the legal barriers that prevented women from entering the professions; however, many informal cultural barriers remained in place. By 1938, in *Three Guineas*, many of Woolf's references to the 1919 Act are bitterly ironic.[36]

The legislative and political ferment of the years 1906 to 1912 conjured a whole range of images of a future Britain. It could be a peaceful and democratic nation, in which all adults participated equally; or a militaristic, patriarchal, and aristocratic one, in which the Lords and army officers overruled the wishes of the people. It could be an agglomeration of local communities, each taking responsibility for education and social welfare, or it could be a centralized state, with a central government overseeing social policy and, when necessary, conscripting its citizens into the armed forces. It could be a 'little England', free of its imperial connections and divorced from Ireland, or it could be 'Great Britain', the hub of an empire.

London

Of Woolf's novels, all but *To the Lighthouse* and *Between the Acts* include at least a section set in London. Woolf was born there, brought up there, and lived there for most of her adult life; her periods of separation from it, including her exile in Richmond, allowed her to idealize it. Though Woolf's version of London is mediated by other texts, something of its history is an essential part of her context. Britain weathered the economic stagnation of 1873–96 (the 'Great Depression'), and the more acute agricultural crisis of 1878–80, by developing as a centre of financial services and shipping services.[37] The City of London became the financial centre of the world. The industries which had given the northern industrial cities their power went into decline, and the political influence of those cities declined with them. The population of Greater London grew: in 1884 one-fifth of all adults in England and Wales lived in London; its population was three times that of New York or Berlin, and greater than that of Ireland.[38]

The wealth of the City of London did not trickle down to those in other quarters. The poverty of the East End of London and of the 'rookery' districts had been a matter of concern and the object of sociological investigation since the 1850s, when Henry Mayhew had investigated them. However, a downturn in trade in the mid-1880s had created further poverty, and a new generation of polemical writings from investigative writers. Public rallies drew further attention to unemployment. A meeting held by the Social Democratic Federation in Trafalgar Square on 7 February 1886 had led to a small riot; another meeting there, on 13 November 1887, led to a much larger disturbance, with over a hundred people injured. Later protests, particularly those accompanying the London Dock Strike of 1889, were more peaceful, but equally focused attention on London poverty.

In 1888, London was governed by a mixture of 'boards' and authorities: responsibility for services such as paving, cleansing, lighting, and drainage was divided between local bodies called 'vestries', and the Metropolitan Board of Works; the Poor Law Boards handled charity, and the School Boards education. While the Board of Works had completed some major projects, it was often obstructed by the vestries, and lacked accountability.[39] The Local Government Act of 1888, as well as making county government more democratic, created the London County Council as a democratic successor to the Board of Works. Although the creation of the Council was not a direct result of the revelations about poverty, the social investigations of the period set the tone for the 'London Programme' of the 'Progressive' political grouping that came to power in the first elections of 1889: Sidney Webb, the leader of the Progressives, characterized the programme as one of 'high rates and healthy cities'.[40] The Council cleared the slum areas of the Old Nichol and the maze of streets between Holborn and the Strand. The Council's freedom of action was severely restricted by central government, but it could, over and above its actual achievements, create a new sense of civic pride. Webb wrote of attempting to create the kind of ' "Municipal Patriotism" which once marked the free cities of Italy'.[41]

Not only did the centre of the city expand, but the suburbs did too. Transport by train and tram made it possible to commute into work from the outskirts of the city: the verb 'to commute' took on this meaning (imported from the USA) in this period, and the noun 'commuter' was likewise naturalized in British English. 'Suburbia' was coined in 1895 as a noun to describe the suburbs: while 'suburbs' grants plurality and variety to the outer zone of the city, the singular 'suburbia' implies homogeneity and conformity. Woolf's use of 'suburban' as an adjective is often contemptuous, though it is more prevalent in the early novels, written when she was by her own reckoning 'a wretched illdressed inkstained Suburban' or 'shabby, self-conscious, [and] suburban'.[42] Ralph Denham's wish that his sister did not look so 'provincial or suburban' (*ND*, p. 28) significantly pairs and equates two terms: the phrase implies that anywhere outside central London is backward and drab.

Houses, Households, and Families

As the London County Council's slum clearance projects may suggest, standards of housing changed during Woolf's lifetime; so too did the definition of what constituted a 'household'. Woolf's own insistence on the need for a woman writer to have a room of her own partly reflects her own privileged upbringing, but expectations of domestic privacy were changing among all classes during this period. The rapid urbanization of the nineteenth century had been relatively unregulated by central government or local authorities, and had led to poorly built and poorly ventilated houses in cramped and irregular streets. Though clearance projects were permitted by the Housing of the Working Classes Act of 1875, and carried out to great effect in Birmingham, provision of the replacement housing was left to charitable organizations such as the Peabody Trust.[43] The many housing Acts which followed this one in the period 1882 to 1918 were not always effective because although they gave city councils the right to build houses, they did not make it a duty. Nevertheless, the legislation is revealing of the ideals of the time. The Housing, Town Planning, Etc., Bill of 1908 was introduced in response to conditions of overcrowding, primarily in Britain's major cities. Introducing the second reading of the Bill in May 1908, John Burns MP noted that in the previous twenty-five years 500,000 houses had been built in Greater London, yet, in spite of the demand for houses, there were 50,000 empty. His explanation was that basements and half-basements were becoming unpopular:

I do not wonder that in certain parts of London rich people cannot get servants. Why should people be interred in dark and often damp basements? They make the servants disagreeable, and they prevent that sanitation, light, and cleanliness which are so absolutely desirable, especially for people who are monotonously employed.[44]

Such buildings were blamed on 'unregulated plans and uncontrolled building'. The Act aimed to create, in Burns's words, 'the home healthy, the house beautiful, the town pleasant, the city dignified, and the suburb salubrious'.[45] The minister proposing the Housing of the Working Classes Act in 1912, Sir A. Griffith-Boscawen, similarly emphasized the importance of health, and not only 'physical health', but 'the whole question of mental and moral character'. Griffith-Boscawen justified the need in terms which recalled the 'national efficiency' debates: 'We cannot hope to bring up a great Imperial race in horrible slums, where no light and air can circulate, in insanitary surroundings, in places where children brought into the world have nothing to look at except what is squalid, horrible, and dirty'.[46] The belief that sunlight and fresh air were important to health are entirely characteristic of the period; diet and exercise were relatively neglected factors. The Assistant Registrar General, Dr William Farr, had claimed there was an exact mathematical correlation between overcrowding and mortality, and although 'Farr's Law' was disproved in the late 1890s, the ideals of lightness and spaciousness remained influential.[47] Woolf's own characterization of the Bloomsbury district in terms of light and spaciousness, by contrast with the darkness of Hyde Park Gate, draws on these assumptions. Griffith-Boscawen's suggestion that good health also rests on aesthetic factors, such as a beautiful environment, is more idiosyncratic, though Burns's earlier references to beauty and dignity indicate that it was not unique. The Garden City movement, begun by Ebenezer Howard in 1898, introduced the idea of building new towns, carefully planned to provide broad tree-lined avenues and open public spaces. The first was begun at Letchworth in 1903, and the second at Welwyn in 1919–20. The utopianism of such planning schemes is characteristic of the period's optimism about making a better future. Though the First World War partly undermined this optimism, it remained a characteristic of the modernity of the period.

Overcrowding within a house was also a concern. New houses increasingly aimed to provide separate rooms for cooking, eating, living, and sleeping. One indication of the norms is given in the Housing Act of 1935: counting all living rooms and bedrooms, and allowing for segregation of the sexes, a house was deemed to be overcrowded if there were more than two people per room. A survey of 1936 found that, by this standard, just below 4 per cent of working-class houses were overcrowded.[48]

The Housing Act of 1919 addressed the more immediate problem of the returning soldiers, and was altogether more successful than its predecessors.[49] The Reconstruction Committee created by Asquith in 1916 became a government ministry in 1917, headed by Christopher Addison; the Housing Act which he saw through Parliament became known as the 'Addison Act'. House building had virtually stopped during the war due to labour shortages, and the existing stock was in poor repair. The Act aimed to build 300,000 homes, 'homes fit for heroes'; it proved costly and in the event only 213,800 were built. Nevertheless, it represented a marked change in housing policy, demonstrating a more assertive attitude on the part of central government.

John Burns's argument about the difficulty in finding servants was not aimed solely at well-heeled MPs: many members of the middle class employed at least one servant, a cook being the highest priority. When Woolf contrasts the Victorian and Georgian eras by reference to 'the character of one's cook', her point of reference, though certainly class-specific, was not narrowly so ('Character in Fiction', in *EVW* iii. 422). In 1911 the census recorded 1.3 million women and girls in 'indoor' domestic service, and 54,260 men, out of a national population of 45 million.[50] However, the servant-keeping class was shrinking, suffering from the 'servant problem'. Since the late nineteenth century it had been widely noted that young women were increasingly unwilling to enter domestic service; Julia Stephen had written an essay on the topic, in response to several published in the periodical the *Nineteenth Century*.[51] Fewer young women were willing to make the sacrifice of independence that residential service required, or to accept the poor standard of accommodation in damp basements or cold attics. However, it seems too that their employers were less comfortable at the loss of privacy involved: 'the middle-class emphasis on domesticity was becoming increasingly expressed as a closeness and exclusiveness which could no longer tolerate an obtrusive stranger'.[52] It is notable that a significant number of servants—over 10,000—came from overseas, predominantly from France, Germany, and Switzerland; the Ramsays' 'Swiss girl' (*TL*, p. 14) is part of this pattern. The practice suggests that English women were increasingly difficult to find. Moreover, an increasing number of households employed a non-resident servant or 'daily' (though the word itself is not recorded in this sense until 1933). The number thus employed in 1911 was 126,061, a rise of about 12 per cent on the 1901 figure.[53] This practice supports the idea that families wanted greater privacy. By 1925, one booklet was recommending singing lessons for servants, on the grounds that 'the girl who has learned to control her voice is a much more desirable member of the household than one who has only the raucous shout of the East End factory hand'.[54] The First World War accelerated the trends of the pre-war period. Women who left service temporarily were introduced to 'conditions which had never before been even remotely contemplated', with regard to wages, accommodation, food, and leisure time.[55] After the war, they were unwilling to return. In the London commuter area, the number of servants per 100 families fell from 24.1 in 1911 to 12.4 in 1921; in the affluent West End of London the figure fell from 57.3 to 41.3 per 100.[56]

The average family size decreased during Woolf's lifetime. Between the 1870s and the 1900s the average number of children born to each marriage nearly halved, declining from just under six to just over three.[57] The Ramsays, with their eight children, would have been an unusually large family even in the late nineteenth century; still more so by 1913. The reasons for changes in family size remain obscure, and may have varied according to social and economic factors. Many historians have investigated the economic impact of children on a family. Among the working classes, legal restrictions on child labour after 1870 may have reduced the economic useful-ness of children. Among the middle classes, the rising cost of private education may have discouraged larger families. We see a glimpse of this in *Night and Day*, where the Denham family grapple with the problem of paying for Charles's education. In their case it is too late to limit the family size, but the discussion of Charles is couched in economic terms, where the financial risk of investing in Charles has to be weighed against the risk of investing in the stock market (*ND*, pp. 25–7). That Joan Denham considers reducing the number of servants indicates that for the middle classes, the relevant economic unit was the 'household' rather than the 'family' as such. A house-hold could be reduced both by the limitation of family size, and by making servants redundant.

The decline in the birth rate was a matter of concern in the period 1900 to 1914, not so much because of the decline of the total popula-tion, but because the rate of decline was sharply differentiated between social groups.[58] Sidney Webb in 1907 noted that the decline appeared to be 'much greater in those sections of the population which give proofs of thrift and foresight'.[59] While the majority of the population were limiting their families, he regretted that 'children are being freely born to the Irish Roman Catholics and the Polish, Russian and German Jews, on the one hand, and to the thriftless and irresponsible—largely the casual labourers and the other denizens of the one-roomed tenements of our great cities—on the other'.[60] Though his report distinguished these two groups to some extent, it predicted that the country would suffer either 'national deterior-ation' or 'the country gradually falling to the Irish and the Jews'. At the end of the report, both results are apparently combined in the idea of 'race deterioration'.[61] (The question this raises about the relation of 'nation' to 'race' is one to which we shall return.) Webb recommended that the state increase the appeal of child-bearing to the thrifty by reducing its economic burden. Such proposals were incorporated to a small extent in Lloyd George's 1909 budget, which included tax allowances for those taxpayers with children. They took another form after the First World War, in the idea of the 'endowment of motherhood', advocated by Eleanor Rathbone in *The Disinherited Family* (1924).[62] Such proposals, even when free of the language of 'race' and 'national efficiency', illustrate the increasing acceptance of the idea that the state has a vested interest in the economic well-being of the family. In this as in other ways, the boundary separating public from private had become more permeable.

The Impact of the First World War

The First World War is still a significant presence in British culture, and there is a danger of its overshadowing the significance of pre-war events and legislation. There are war memorials in even the smallest villages; the war poets occupy an important place in the literary canon, particularly in schools. The idea that the war was a turning point soon established itself, and by 1935 one influential historian felt that its significance should be reassessed. He felt that 1910 was the significant turning point: 'it was in 1910 that fires long smoulder-ing in the English spirit suddenly flared up. . . . That extravagant behaviour of the post-war decade, which most of us thought to be the effect of war, had really begun before the War. The War hastened everything—in politics, in economics, in behaviour—but it started nothing'.[63] As Woolf also saw 1910 as the pivotal year, the year in which all human relations had changed, several Woolf scholars have endorsed this view.[64]

Nevertheless, it is important to identify which changes the war hastened, as well as those which it directly brought about. The war claimed the lives of 750,000 men from the United Kingdom, and another 200,000 from elsewhere in the Empire. It left 1,500,000 men suffering the effects of wounds or poison gas.[65] However, the Government's management of the war was as significant as the mor-tality rates. Asquith's Liberal government had envisaged a short war, with little domestic impact. Within months of the outbreak of war in August 1914, it was clear that they were wrong. Asquith dissolved his cabinet in May 1915 and formed a coalition cabinet. The gov-ernment increasingly took an interventionist role in the management of industry, particularly munitions: the ideal of 'national efficiency' returned. However, intervention was particularly controversial in one area: army recruitment. In the early days of the war, there had been a large number of volunteers—Woolf represents Septimus Warren Smith as being among them (*MD*, p. 73)—though, problem-atically, the indiscriminate nature of volunteering caused skills shortages in vital industries. By June 1915, recruitment was falling. Conscription was anathema to liberals, but in January 1916 the Military Service Act came into force. It compelled single men to serve, unless they were priests, conscientious objectors, or workers in a vital industry. A second Act in April 1916 extended the draft to married men.[66] The power of the state had been an important political and philosophical question up to 1914, but conscription made the question a matter of life and death.

The war introduced technology into conflict on a scale not previously seen, most obviously in the form of poison gas, the machine gun, and the tank. Moreover, soldiers felt they had been treated as part of a machine: in one of Herbert Read's war poems, the soldier is '[a] cog in some great evil engine'.[67] The traditional martial vocabulary of 'honour' and 'glory', along with appeals to patriotic sentiment, began to have a hollow ring.[68] Similarly, to non-combatant pacifists, it seemed that terms such as 'national honour' or even 'the English nation' were meaningless abstractions.[69]

The first nine months of the war saw one-third of the male workforce leave their jobs for the army or war work. While the effects of this drain may have been offset by a reduction in emigration—before the war, 300,000 men had been leaving the country each year[70]—they left a gap to be filled, and it was filled by women. As Ray Strachey recalled in 1936, 'Middle-aged women who had been quiet mothers of families were suddenly transformed into efficient plumbers, chimney sweeps, or grave-diggers; flighty and giggling young girls turned into house-painters and electricians; ladies whose lives had been spent in the hunting-field turned into canal boatmen and ploughmen'.[71] Many took on clerical work: nearly 200,000 in government departments, 500,000 in private offices. Eight hundred thousand were recruited into engineering.[72] As a result of their contribution to the war, women were granted the vote, albeit on the terms noted earlier, and the Sex Disqualification (Removal) Act of 1919 opened all trades to them. In practice, the post-war period saw a reaction against women in work. Feminists noted with suspicion the revival of 'the cult of femininity'.[73]

Social Classifications

CLASS: THE TRIPARTITE MODEL

Woolf's awareness of distinctions of social class and her use of the
language of class have been neglected in critical discussions, certainly when compared to her awareness of gender difference. It is
true that she does not place class difference and social advancement
at the centre of her narratives. In this she broke not only from her
Victorian predecessors, but from near contemporaries like H. G.
Wells (whose *Kipps* (1905) is a comedy of social advancement that
owes much to Dickens's *Great Expectations* (1860–1)) and E. M.
Forster, many of whose novels rest on the difficulty of communicating between social classes. In rejecting the traditionally plotted
novel, Woolf was rejecting, among other things, the plot of social
advancement. Unlike George Orwell, who defined his own social
background as 'lower-upper-middle class', she was not ostensibly
interested in microscopic distinctions of class, not even for the purposes of satirizing the obsession.[74] Nevertheless, Woolf sometimes
uses markers of social class to place characters: most explicitly,
Sir William Bradshaw and Charles Tansley are marked as being the
sons of shopkeepers (*MD*, p. 81; *TL*, p. 18). Both are men who have
moved up the social scale by ability and hard work. Both seem to lack
the humanity that is 'proper' to their new-found class, and the reader
is left to speculate whether this is because their original class lacks
it, or whether they sacrificed it during their upward struggle. In
addition to such explicit references, Woolf used other, more subtle
markers of social class, the meaning of which derives from
now-obsolete systems of classification.

By the early twentieth century there were several competing
systems of social categorization available. The two main contenders
were a tripartite division of society into upper, middle, and lower
classes (with various subdivisions) and a bipartite division into the
'elite' and the 'masses'. It might at first appear that the 'elite' corres-
ponds simply to the upper classes, and that the two systems can be
reconciled; but the bipartite system made reference to different
characteristics, setting different criteria for membership of the club.

A crude division into three did not express all the nuances of
social distinction required by many writers, and there were several
variants. First, the terminology itself was open to variation: the

'upper classes' might also be termed 'the aristocracy', and the 'lower classes' the 'working classes'. The terms might appear to be merely synonyms for each other, but they include subtle distinctions. The satirical division of society into 'Barbarians', 'Philistines', and 'Populace', proposed in 1867 by Matthew Arnold, uses terms that are not exact synonyms for upper, middle, and lower classes. Membership of the 'aristocracy' implicitly rests on birth, marriage, or the conferment of a peerage, while membership of the 'upper classes' may be decided by a wider range of criteria, primarily wealth, and secondarily markers such as clothing and manners. The aristocracy is only one of several 'upper classes'. The derogatory term 'nouveau riche' had entered the language in the early nineteenth century, enabling the aristocracy to distinguish itself from other elements of the upper classes. In the late nineteenth century, the widely remarked phenomenon of impoverished male aristocrats marrying the rich daughters of North American industrialists made it more difficult to distinguish the two groups. The term 'upper classes' also differs from 'aristocrats', as does 'lower classes' from 'working classes', in acknowledging that classes are defined by their mutual relations, not by an innate quality or hidden essence.

As Orwell's reference to the 'lower-upper-middle class' implies, social commentators increasingly subdivided the middle classes. The most interesting subdivision is that of the 'lower middle class', a group which comprised two main groups, shopkeepers and small businessmen on the one hand, and 'the new white collar salaried occupations, most notably clerks but also managers, commercial travellers, school teachers and certain shop assistants' on the other.[75] In Marxist terms, these two groups are quite distinctive in their relations to the means of production: the former are self-employed and the latter are employees. The important distinction was between those who produced 'by hand' and those who produced 'by brain'.[76] The working class was perceived as using muscular force in their work, while, regardless of employment status, the lower middle class was sedentary, even if its members did not literally spend their working days seated. In *Sons and Lovers*, the miner Walter Morel ridicules the prospect of his eldest son becoming a clerk, 'a stool-harsed Jack': 'All he'll do is to wear his britches behind out an' earn nowt'.[77] His remark also serves as a reminder that class distinctions did not correlate exactly with income levels.

The two parts of the lower middle class were also marked by shared cultural characteristics. The 'mercantile clerk' and the 'small shopkeeper' were, according to Woolf's uncle James Fitzjames Stephen, characterized by a pretentious use of language which could be contrasted with the plain speaking of both the gentleman and the labouring man.[78] Such pretentiousness grew from the effort to avoid vulgarity. The class's concern 'with what was proper and respectable' featured strongly in satirical constructions of it.[79] The class placed a high value on the family and on domestic pleasures: ownership of a piano was an important class marker, as it enabled the family to entertain itself away from public houses and music halls. The value it placed on domestic privacy meant that it was strongly associated with 'suburbia', though the social composition of the actual suburbs was more mixed than this suggests.

Matthew Arnold's category of 'Philistines', introduced in *Culture and Anarchy* (1869), was to provide Woolf and her contemporaries with a powerful means of denigrating the middle classes.[80] The Philistines' defining characteristic is their obliviousness to the power of 'culture', but they are associated in Arnold's work with a cluster of epithets: they are 'mechanical' in their mental processes; they have an ideal of life which is unattractive, incomplete, and 'narrow'; they are 'hard' and 'vulgar'; they have turned the language of religion into a 'mere jargon'.[81] Woolf occasionally referred to people as 'philistine' in her diaries and letters: she characterized the Duckworths thus, associating this quality both with 'shrewd middle-class complacency' and with 'boorish' and 'rustic' qualities (*MB*, p. 107). She did not use the term directly in her fiction, but she often characterizes people using epithets associated with philistinism. For example, in *To the Lighthouse*, Charles Tansley's social class is defined not only by reference to his father, but also by the contrast between his use of 'ugly academic jargon' and Mrs Ramsay's appreciation of beauty (*TL*, p. 19).

The tripartite structure was complicated by the concept of the residuum. The term had first been used in the context of social class by the Radical Liberal MP John Bright during the debates on the 1867 Reform Act. Bright had campaigned hard for the widening of the franchise, but even he conceded that there was 'a small class' which lacked the necessary independence to use its vote wisely. This was 'the residuum . . . of almost helpless poverty and dependence' to

be found in almost every constituency.[82] As social investigators drew
urban poverty to public attention in the 1880s, some of those they
found fell more readily into the category of 'residuum' than the
earlier category of 'pauper' or its related condition, 'pauperism'.
One became a pauper voluntarily, by applying for Poor Law relief.
The concept of the residuum suggests a physical metaphor, in which
the residuum is an insoluble sediment in the fluid of mass society.
Though the residuum is in one sense a social category, the concept
implies that the group stands outside society and resists easy categorization. Moreover, the condition was seen as an involuntary one.
Some commentators on the residuum saw it in biological terms as a
distinct 'race', trapped by its biological inheritance; this view is one
aspect of 'social Darwinism'. However, Jose Harris has argued that
this outlook was by no means universal: a wide range of officials
'concurred in the view that the residuum could and should be elevated, improved, organized and regimented into conformity with
the rest of society'.[83] Another important and debated social distinction is embedded in the concept, that between the helpable and the
unhelpable; within the category of the helpable lie further arguments
about the best way of providing help. Clarissa Dalloway, thinking of
alcoholics who 'can't be dealt with' by Acts of Parliament (*MD*, p. 4),
is working within these categories.

Though the residuum was primarily understood as a class below
all others, there were other ways of conceptualizing it. As I have
mentioned, its abjection was so complete that it appeared to be not
below other classes, but outside the class system altogether. It could
also be understood as a quality of dependency and social immobility
that might be found, as John Bright said, 'in every class'. If the
conventional social categories of upper, middle, and lower might be
termed 'horizontal', then the residuum was, as Helen Bosanquet
said, a 'vertical' division: a 'trivial accident of birth or fortune' might
enable 'a true member of the Residuum' to conceal himself even
amongst the 'upper Barbarians'; that is, the aristocracy.[84] If the
plight of the middle- and upper-class residua had been ignored, it
was only because their families were able to bear the financial strain,
and they were not viewed as a threat to the health of the race.

The tripartite social model was capable of admitting many
subdivisions, the most important of which are seen in Charles
Booth's *Life and Labour of the People in London*. Booth and his

assistants made door-to-door interviews and observations, the most vivid summary of which is provided in Booth's map of London poverty. The map distinguishes seven social classes, and makes more distinctions at the bottom of the social scale. Thus the richest category, coloured yellow, combines the 'Upper-middle and Upper classes'. Though many friends of Leslie Stephen were concerned when his children moved from Kensington to Bloomsbury in 1904, believing they had moved to a disreputable area, it is notable that in Booth's terms, both 22 Hyde Park Gate and 46 Gordon Square were yellow. Both were 'servant keeping' areas. The next category, coloured red, encompassed the rest of the middle class.

The bottom category of Booth's social scale, a 'vicious', 'semi-criminal' class, was coloured black on his map; in his writings, which employed an eight-tier system from 'A' to 'H', it was labelled group 'A'. The category above, coloured dark blue, was labelled group 'B': 'Casual earnings, very poor'. His description of this category as 'a deposit' of those who were incapable of full-time work brings to mind the metaphor of the residuum as a sediment. It is interesting that Booth ascribes a passivity to group 'B' not found in the 'savage' group 'A': his system admits of distinctions even within the residuum.

The attention I have paid to these lower social groups may seem disproportionate to the attention that Woolf pays to them: her characters are predominantly upper middle class. However, it is important to recognize where her characters fit in the contemporary social spectrum. Moreover, the residuum is relevant to Woolf's continuing interest in eccentrics and outsiders. It would be fallacious to include such individuals within the residuum, but if the residuum is taken to be the group that defies conventional social categorization, they occupy similar positions within (or without) the social structure. More generally, the residuum offers a model for the marginalized position of women in Woolf's society. Indeed, John Bright's definition of the class as people with 'no independence whatsoever' who ought not to be given the vote could be taken as a definition of women in 1867, if one takes 'independence' to mean specifically financial independence. The daughters of educated men could not be classed as 'bourgeois', wrote Woolf, as they differed 'in the two prime characteristics of the bourgeoisie—capital and environment' (*TG*, p. 369).

CLASS: THE BIPARTITE MODEL

The bipartite model of the 'elite' and the 'masses' has a long history, but rose to prominence in the era of mass democracy and mass literacy, in the decades following the Reform Act of 1867 and the Education Act of 1870. Many critics have noted the influence of the German philosopher Friedrich Nietzsche on the model, but there were domestic precedents in the quasi-prophetic work of Thomas Carlyle.[85] In his *Past and Present* (1843) Carlyle had praised 'Nature' for bringing in the 'aristocracy' to conquer and so rescue the 'confused rabble'; without them the rabble was otherwise doomed 'to perish, of obesity, stupor or other malady'. This might seem to endorse hereditary privilege, but crucially, Carlyle traced 'aristocracy' back to its Greek origin, meaning the 'best', and, he claimed, the 'bravest'.[86] In this he paves the way for the idea of a 'natural aristocracy', a concept which combines elitism with a degree of meritocracy. Carlyle's term 'rabble' and the very similar term 'the mob' was, however, gradually displaced by 'the masses'. Though many of the qualities attributed to them were similar—for example, the belief that they were led by impulse and instinct rather than by intellect— the 'masses' were somewhat more docile. It might be said that the mob made its last appearance at the Trafalgar Square riots of 1886 and 1887. The rise of trade unionism meant that public demonstrations thereafter were far more orderly affairs.

'Mass society' soon became an object of intellectual curiosity, as seen in such works as Gustave Le Bon's *Psychologie des foules* (1895, translated as *The Crowd*), and Wilfred Trotter's *Instincts of the Herd in Peace and War* (1916). Trotter's work, some of which had been published before the war, was to widen the currency of 'the herd' as an alternative term for 'the masses'. The concept of the herd emphasized the element of instinctive reaction in the masses, and gave it a degree of scientific credibility.

The elite also went by other names, though some of them could be incorporated within versions of the tripartite model of social structure. The term 'intelligentsia' is the most striking innovation: imported from Russia, where it referred to the intellectual class, it was initially used (from 1907 to around 1910) to refer only to Russian society, but was soon naturalized and applied to British intellectuals. The First World War, and the pacifist position adopted by many intellectuals, was crucial in the crystallization of the 'intelligentsia' as a group. The British 'intelligentsia' was strongly identified with Bloomsbury. There had been no near-equivalent collective noun before this time. Figures like Leslie Stephen who specialized in non-fictional writing had often been termed 'men of letters', but this phrase does not give such writers a group identity. The term 'intellectual aristocracy' was coined by Woolf's cousin J. K. Stephen in 1891, referring to university-educated men, and she used it herself in her diary (*Diary*, iv. 250), but it achieved wider currency only after her death, following its use in an influential essay on Woolf's ancestry and social milieu.[87] Although the intelligentsia might be equated with the elite, and thus contrasted with the masses, the term was not always used this way. When Woolf first used it, in 'Cleverness and Youth' (1920), a review of a collection of short stories by Aldous Huxley, it was by way of complaining that he wrote too exclusively of 'the follies of the upper middle classes' and 'the unfortunate physical infirmities of the *intelligentsia*' (*EVW* iii. 176). In this utterance, the intelligentsia is one among many classes of society.

Elsewhere in Woolf's writing, intellectuals and thinkers seem to be a subdivision of the upper class: in a diary entry for 17 November 1936, she describes Lord Robert Cecil, member of an influential and aristocratic Conservative family, as a type of the English 'Governing class', and contrasts him with 'intellectuals' like Bertrand Russell and Aldous Huxley (*Diary*, v. 34). The contrast rests partly on the pacifist position of the latter, but also on Cecil's 'urbane' and 'hopeful' qualities. Here the intellectual elite is assimilated back into the tripartite model, apparently as a subdivision of the upper classes. In 'The Pargiters', Woolf's draft version of *The Years*, the narrator explains Kitty Malone's confusion on meeting the Robsons. She knew only one working-class family, and 'of the upper class' she knew 'only her own class, in the persons of some dons and professors, and the aristocracy, in the persons, for a time, of earls and a duke or two'.[88] This implies that academic families are a subsection of the 'upper class'; whether this is because of their intellectual abilities, or simply their affiliation to an 'ancient' university, cannot be determined. It is certain, though, that such families do not stand in a simple bipartite relation to the masses.

This account does not exhaust the possible systems of analysis and stratification. The increasing sophistication of statistical analysis meant that social scientists could group individuals on other 'vertical' criteria: for example, in examining the decline in the birth rate, Sidney Webb noted that it had declined among those 'where the inconvenience of having children is specially felt'. What this meant in practice was among classes where women worked in factories, but this group was by no means identical to 'the working class'. By examining claims of 'lying-in benefit' (a maternity benefit) from Friendly Societies, Webb also identified a decline in the 'sections of the population which give proofs of thrift and foresight'.[89] While these qualities were most strongly associated with the middle class, they were not its exclusive preserve. Webb's analysis suggests that the traditional forms of class analysis were reaching the end of their usefulness, and were being replaced by clustering according to attitudes and aspirations.

GENDER AND AGE

The biological distinction of male and female is simple: the cultural distinctions of masculine and feminine, 'girl' and 'woman', and 'woman' and 'lady' are more complex; they involve many hazy borderlines, and factors of age and class complicate the situation still further. As Denise Riley has argued, 'woman' is a historically variable category;[90] moreover, not only does it vary from era to era, but, at any given moment, different social groups will define it differently.

Virginia Woolf was acutely aware of the persistence of the Victorian stereotypes of adult femininity, the foremost of which she termed 'The Angel in the House':

She was intensely sympathetic. She was immensely charming. She was utterly unselfish. She excelled in the difficult arts of family life. She sacrificed herself daily. If there was chicken, she took the leg; if there was a draught, she sat in it—in short she was so constituted that she never had a mind or a wish of her own, but preferred to sympathize always with the minds and wishes of others. Above all—I need not say it—she was pure. Her purity was supposed to be her chief beauty—her blushes, her great grace. ('Professions for Women', in *CE* ii. 285)

Similarly, in 'The Pargiters', she noted the *Concise Oxford Dictionary*'s definition of 'womanly' qualities: 'modesty', 'compassion', and 'tact'.[91] Woolf may appear to be describing what we would call a 'housewife', but, while the 'Angel in the House' has some qualities in common with the housewife of post-1945 consumer culture, the upper middle-class woman of the early twentieth century was faced with quite unfamiliar demands. The presence of servants in the house, and the practice of paying for food 'on account', meant that women of this class found themselves in a role which was quasi-managerial, rather than practical: keeping accounts, directing servants, dealing with tradesmen, and ordering menus.[92] The exercise of 'compassion' was not merely a domestic virtue: the proper sphere of late Victorian and Edwardian women included education and philanthropy; the latter might take the form of being a Poor Law Guardian, or of independent charitable visiting of the sort Julia Stephen was remembered for in St Ives, and which Mrs Ramsay undertakes in *To the Lighthouse*. For the upper middle classes, the 'difficult arts of family life' included not only what went on within the family home, but also the maintenance of the family's social status within its class, through such practices as 'calling' on other families and dining with them, having 'at homes', and seeing that children were introduced to suitable marital partners.[93]

These roles were defined by contrast with the expected roles of the upper middle-class man: the woman's sphere was the domestic, the man's the public world. The exceptions, 'public' issues such as charity and education, could be accommodated into this scheme, though not without some strain, by being gendered as 'feminine' activities. Various rationales were advanced for this separation. Some believed that women were hormonally unstable to an extent that disqualified them from public activity (see the section 'Mental Health' in Chapter 6, below). Others advanced less biologistic arguments. One dominant argument in the period 1900 to 1914 gave women the role of protecting high ideals, unsullied by contact with the real world. Joseph Conrad's Marlow tells his all-male audience that women 'should be out of it'; 'We must help them to stay in that beautiful world of their own, lest ours gets worse'.[94] Similarly Richard Dalloway in *The Voyage Out* believes that Clarissa must preserve her 'illusions' (*VO*, p. 68).

Within Woolf's lifetime, the role of the upper middle-class married woman was changing. After 1918, the scarcity of servants, and the increasing emphasis on domestic privacy, meant that her managerial role was diminished. The title of a magazine introduced into Britain in 1922, *Good Housekeeping*, is symptomatic: while the woman of the 1890s was expected to concern herself with the rules of etiquette, so that she might safeguard and advance her family's social position, the ideal for the woman of the 1920s was more restrictedly domestic, as the 'guardian of her family's health and happiness'.[95] In theory, following the Sex Disqualification Removal Act of 1919, there were more opportunities for paid employment outside the home. In practice, many employers—notably schools—sacked female employees when they married.

These are, however, ideals rather than definitions, and as ideals they sprang from the upper middle classes. No doubt many women aspired to them, and felt oppressed by their unattainability, but they were not universally held, and still less were they universally achievable. It is true that many women aspired to emulate their social superiors, and it was often noted that on Sundays and holidays they 'moved up a class', exchanging 'their everyday habits for the clothes, food, spending patterns, resorts, and recreations of the class above them'.[96] This pattern was more common among women than men: domestic service brought many women into closer contact with other classes, and acted as a conduit for the diffusion of cultural ideals. The cook that Woolf sketches, coming in and out of the drawing room, borrowing a newspaper or asking advice about a hat, is one illustration of how this worked ('Character in Fiction', in *EVW* iii. 422). However, there were limits to this emulation, and different classes found other ideals, or at least interpreted 'self-sacrifice' very differently.

Although I have used 'woman' up to this point to denote all adult females, in Woolf's era it was also used as a class-specific term, an inferior position to that of the 'lady'. The position of the 'lady' was, however, precarious: it was founded not only on family background and breeding, but on signifiers such as clothing and manners. Anyone with sufficient money could buy the appropriate clothing, and, with the help of etiquette books and advice columns, could learn the correct manners. The identity of 'lady' was a performance. When Woolf categorizes someone as a 'lady', she very often describes her clothing or places her in a society event; by contrast, she more often supplements the category 'woman' with a description of bodily appearance, such as thinness or fatness, illness or health. The identity of 'gentleman' was equally vulnerable to impersonation, and anxiety about this emerges in several of Woolf's novels. To say that

someone is 'the very image of a noble gentleman' (*O*, p. 24) is to
assert that they possess the identity, but also to imply that the identity is merely a matter of image. In Orlando's case, even bodily
characteristics such as eyes, mouth, and nose are insufficient to
satisfy Queen Elizabeth; she, however, is capable of looking inwardly.
In *The Voyage Out*, Susan Warrington sees through Mr Perrott, the
son of a grocer, by the way he slightly exaggerates his performance:
'though practically indistinguishable from a born gentleman, [he]
showed his origin to keen eyes in an impeccable neatness of dress,
lack of freedom in manner, extreme cleanliness of person, and a
certain indescribable timidity and precision with his knife and fork'
(*VO*, p. 152). By locating gentlemanly qualities in 'indescribable'
differences of behaviour, those born to the status protect it: to
describe the proper qualities completely would be to enable a perfect
theatrical performance of them.

Womanhood and femininity can also be defined by their relation
to ungendered qualities such as 'humanity', and to double-gendered
qualities such as 'androgyny'. The distinction between the sexes was
often understood within an evolutionary framework. For some, the
human race was evolving towards a point where sexual differences
would be minimized; for others, a lack of sexual differentiation was a
quality of 'young' races, or of degenerate ones.[97] Within the political
sphere, as we have seen, suffrage campaigners were divided on
whether to demand the vote on the grounds of a common humanity,
or on the grounds that the distinctive qualities and needs of women
should be democratically represented. Following the partial success
of 1918, the division became more acute, and led to a distinction
between the 'old feminism' and the 'new feminism'. The old feminism insisted, as one of its advocates said, on 'the primary importance of the human being'. She declared: 'I am a feminist, and an Old
Feminist, because I dislike everything that feminism implies. I desire
an end of the whole business, the demands for equality, the suggestions of sex warfare, the very name of feminist'.[98] The new feminism,
by contrast, sought recognition of the specifically female qualities of
women, which in practice meant childbearing; the 'endowment of
motherhood' was a central part of the new feminist campaign. Both
approaches had potential weak points: the old feminism risked
accepting a definition of 'human being' that was based on male and
masculine norms; the new feminism risked defining 'woman' in

terms of her female characteristics to the exclusion of all else. As one critic of the latter said, it risked treating women 'as if they were permanently pregnant'.[99] In that regard, the new feminism risked being co-opted to the reactionary outlook promoted by many in the post-war era, and its conservative construction of gender difference.

Age was also crucially important in the definition of female categories. The transition from 'child' to 'girl' was acknowledged terminologically, as for example in Lytton Strachey's description of the stages of Queen Victoria's development: 'The child grew into the girl, the girl into the young woman'.[100] However, the age of transition is difficult to define. There were no socially defined rituals, probably because the beginning of girlhood was defined in relation to puberty. In *The Voyage Out*, the summary of Rachel Vinrace's upbringing uses the same categories as Strachey: when she was a 'child', her aunts were concerned with her health; when she became a 'girl' and a 'young woman', they turned their concerns to her morals (*VO*, p. 32). The boundary between girlhood and young womanhood was more distinct. Among the aristocracy and the upper middle classes, the ritual of 'coming out' at the age of 18 marked the beginning of the transition from girlhood to womanhood. For the aristocracy, coming out took the form of being presented to the monarch at court; for the upper middle classes it took the form of attending a 'society' gathering, and thereafter attending dances, balls, and parties.[101] The aim of the process was for the young woman to find (or be found) a suitable husband. Although 'coming out' was a clearly defined ritual, it did not prevent females of 18 and over being categorized as 'girls'. Though Rachel Vinrace is 24, her father still terms her a 'girl': he would like her voyage to transform her into a 'woman' (*VO*, pp. 92–3), and specifically into a hostess, a wife-substitute to assist his political career. The 'voyage out' is a version of 'coming out'. Though her aunt Helen finds her father's demand selfish and absurd, she adopts his categorization of Rachel (*VO*, p. 104).

A woman's thirtieth birthday was not marked by any special ceremony, but it was a culturally significant age. Until they were 30, women were supposed to be accompanied at dances by chaperones; afterwards they were not. The convention implies that women in their thirties were capable of defending their own honour, but also that they were undesirable. One conservative commentator of 1913 also remarked that 'After the age of thirty the average woman gets more "set" in her ways, is less adaptable, just as her body is less pliant'.[102] Her definition is not neutral, of course, but suited her purpose, which was to encourage pliant 'girls' of childbearing age to emigrate, marry, and strengthen the empire. A less formal age boundary is acknowledged in a Hogarth Press novel of 1924, where an unmarried woman in her thirties thinks ruefully of the period between the ages of 18 and 33 as 'the compliment season', the period when an attractive woman might expect to receive compliments on her looks.[103]

Like the terminology of class, the boundaries of these signs are often flexible, and the power to impose a category is a significant one. The category of 'young lady' was particularly contentious. On the face of it, the phrase might seem to represent class (upper or upper middle) and age (somewhere between girl and lady, presumably between the ages of 18 and 30). In actual usage, it was applied to a wider social range of women by their superiors, in a condescending way. Women working in clerical roles are regularly termed 'young ladies': one such person hands Peter Walsh his letters when he returns to his hotel (*MD*, p. 130); the businessman Louis in *The Waves* is cheered to have his entrance acknowledged by all the 'young ladies in the office' (*W*, p. 166). In *The Voyage Out*, Evelyn Murgatroyd is categorized by the narrator on her first appearance as a 'young lady' (*VO*, p. 142). But later, she rejects the term: Mr Perrott questions her utopian vision of the future, asking whether she would be content with 'the things young ladies like' such as 'pretty frocks'; sensing ridicule, Evelyn asserts that she is not 'a young lady' (*VO*, p. 151). Several of the female characters in *Mrs Dalloway* move between categories, even in the mind of the same observer. Rezia is variously categorized as 'a little woman', 'an Italian girl', 'a charming little lady', and 'a poor young woman' (*MD*, pp. 13, 78, 127). Unlike Evelyn Murgatroyd, she does not have an opportunity to protest.

EDUCATION

As the existence of the 'educated classes' implies, class and social mobility were closely linked to education. The most significant changes in educational legislation had occurred before Woolf was born, in a series of Education Acts from 1870 onwards, which put some form of elementary schooling within the reach of every child. The consequent demand for teachers necessitated that women be able to take teacher-training courses or university-level education. In the year of Virginia Woolf's birth, women were able to take London University degrees, studying at Bedford College, founded in 1849; at University College, which had accepted women on equal terms to men since 1878; or at one of the regional university colleges which entered students for London examinations.[104] King's College London established a 'Ladies' Department' in 1882, based in Kensington, but it did not enter women for degrees until 1899.[105] Virginia Stephen studied there in 1897, though her later remarks that she had never attended any college have tended to obscure the fact (*Letters*, v. 91). In her writings on education, Woolf tended to underestimate the importance of London and the 'provincial' universities, and was criticized by one contemporary for writing as if she had 'never heard of any but Oxford and Cambridge'.[106] There were, however, personal and cultural dimensions to her oversight: her brothers, her husband, and many of her male friends had been educated at Cambridge, and the cultural prestige of the 'ancient' universities meant that the status they accorded women was of particular national significance. The first women's colleges in Cambridge, Girton and Newnham, were founded in 1869 and 1871 respectively. In Oxford, Lady Margaret Hall was founded in 1878 and Somerville College in 1879; further colleges were founded in the 1880s and 1890s. Female students at Oxford and Cambridge were initially in the anomalous position of being members of their colleges, but not of the universities; of being permitted to attend university lectures and take university examinations, but not to receive degrees. The anomaly was tolerated initially, as supporters of women's higher education were more concerned to enable women to participate in university life than to take examinations that would allow entry to the professions.[107] Women were allowed to take degrees at Oxford from 1920 onwards (with the exception of theology degrees); the inequality was not fully rectified at Cambridge until 1948.[108] In Cambridge in 1890 Philippa Fawcett took her final honours degree in mathematics, and was placed above the highest placed male candidate. As a later historian of the suffrage movement noted, her achievement was important because it disproved the argument that women 'were incapable of advanced abstract thought'.[109]

Women's education did not advance unopposed. Some universities sought to divide university education along gendered lines: in 1908 the 'Women's Department' of King's College (successor to the 'Ladies' Department') introduced courses in 'home science'.[110] The University of London introduced a degree in 'Home Science and Economics' in 1911; the influential feminist journal *The Freewoman* derided it as a 'degree for housewives', and others questioned its necessity when the women's colleges at Oxford and Cambridge were so short of funds.[111] Other conservatives blamed women's education for the declining birth rate claiming that 'education and freedom' had unfitted advanced women for 'their divine function of motherhood'.[112] In a book-length anti-feminist polemic, Mrs Archibald Colquhoun criticized the pioneers of women's education for having adopted 'the theory of "equality" of man and woman' and for aiming at the 'intellectual approximation of the sexes' when they should have attempted to attain 'a greater perfection of womanhood'. Dissatisfaction among women was confined to 'educated women', she believed: she did not consider the possibility that this was because their education had broadened their perspectives; rather, it was because they had 'lost touch with reality'. Reality, for Mrs Archibald Colquhoun, was the reality of motherhood.[113]

In spite of these developments in women's education, universities were still largely populated by men from upper middle-class and upper-class backgrounds, educated almost exclusively at the fee-paying institutions known as 'public' schools. The public schools had an influence out of all proportion to the numbers who attended them: their ethos was imitated by other less exclusive establishments, particularly grammar schools; their products went on to take prominent public roles. Their ethos was established by Thomas Arnold in his reform of Rugby School from 1828 onwards: he had aimed to develop 'first, religious and moral principle; second, gentlemanly conduct; thirdly, intellectual ability'.[114] However, from the 1880s onwards, these ideals were supplemented and reinterpreted to accommodate the cult of athleticism, and an increasingly nationalistic and militaristic ethos. Public schools were predominantly boarding schools in which 'house masters' and their wives took on quasi-parental roles: this was a practical necessity for parents who were abroad in the imperial civil service. The dominance of the ethos was not total: private schools such as Abbotsholme (founded in 1889, and attended by Lytton Strachey) and Bedales (founded in 1893), attempted to establish a more liberal and progressive ethos; Bedales was a mixed school from 1898 onwards.[115]

Private schools for girls were a relatively recent development: in the mid-nineteenth century, better-off young females would have normally been taught by governesses. Such private tuition meant that the curriculum was widely variable, but the general expectation was that the pupils would learn 'accomplishments' rather than rigorous academic knowledge. The accomplishments listed by Anne Finch (Lady Winchilsea) in 'The Introduction' (1689) still held true in the late nineteenth century: 'Good breeding, fashion, dancing, dressing, play' (quoted in *ROO*, p. 76), though one might add those mentioned in *Night and Day*, namely, 'painting, gardening, [and] poetry' (*ND*, p. 211). However, private schools for girls had grown in importance from the mid-nineteenth century, with the foundation of the North London Collegiate School, a day school, in 1850, and Cheltenham Ladies College, a boarding school, in 1854. The girls' schools offered a more academic education than the governesses.

The late nineteenth century also saw changes in the nature of adult education for men and women of the working classes and lower middle classes. The Mechanics Institutes, the dominant institutions of the early nineteenth century, had begun to decline after 1860, displaced by Working Men's Colleges, such as the People's College in Sheffield (founded 1842), and the London Working Men's College (1854).[116] Whereas the Institutes tended to provide single unrelated lectures, the Colleges provided courses of study; whereas the Institutes had been oriented towards technical and craft-related knowledge, the Colleges were liberal and non-vocational, their ideals having been influenced by traditional universities. Like those universities, they tended to exclude women, though a London Working Women's College was founded in 1864. Morley College, where Virginia Stephen taught in 1905 and 1906, had 'emerged in the 1880s from a coffee tavern and working men's club within the Old Vic Theatre', was open to men and women, and provided non-vocational courses.[117] The Colleges were not the only option. Cambridge University began to deliver university 'extension' lectures in 1873; Oxford inaugurated a similar scheme in 1878, though it was relatively inactive until 1885.[118] The Workers' Educational Association (WEA) was founded in 1903 by Albert Stockbridge, and established

its first branches in 1904. Though inspired by the university
extension lectures, it departed from them in one important respect,
in that it organized tutorial classes, in which the students were
expected to be active participants and not passive recipients. Though
extension lectures and the WEA continued to be important throughout Woolf's lifetime, many of the more local and ad hoc institutions
were brought into the control of local authorities following the
Technical Instruction Act (1889) and the Education Act (1902).

Outside the schoolroom, there were numerous opportunities for
self-education from books in series such as the Everyman Library,
the Home University Library, and, from 1937 onwards, Penguin
Books' 'Pelican' paperback series. From 1923 onwards self-education
was additionally facilitated by the BBC, which broadcast many lectures on a wide range of cultural and scientific topics.[119] In Cornwall
in 1921, Woolf was left with profoundly mixed feelings after a conversation with a self-educated post office clerk, 'infected with books',
who had 'Everyman's Library entire' on his shelves; she was
troubled, it seems, by the way he closely resembled a Bloomsbury
intellectual, and yet read 'no moderns' and was happy to follow his
'own heart' as a guide to taste (*Letters*, ii. 464). In the manuscript of
Mrs Dalloway, Septimus's education at an institution resembling
Morley College is supplemented by Everyman books and the Loeb
series of classical authors.[120]

RACE

'Race' was a crucial word in national and international politics
throughout Woolf's life, but it was used in more diverse ways than at
the present day. Whereas now most writers would distinguish
between 'race' and 'culture', for most people in Woolf's generation,
as one contemporary noted, 'race', 'culture', and 'language' were
almost inextricably confused.[121] Patterns of behaviour which would
now be understood as learned behaviours were spoken of as if they
were a biological inheritance. However, this outlook was not universal: those within Woolf's liberal circle tended to distinguish 'race'
from 'culture' more sharply than conservative thinkers. Nevertheless, it is important to understand the ideas that they were rejecting.

The 'science' of ethnology claimed that there were three
European races, the Nordic, the Alpine, and the Mediterranean.
They were distinguished not only by physical characteristics, the

Nordic being blonde, the Alpine stocky and dark, and so on, but also by behaviour: the Nordic was alleged to be 'fond of fresh air and exercise and good living', and the Mediterranean was emotionally unstable.[122] Such classificatory schemes are almost always value-laden, and this one was very often linked to an idea of the superiority of the Nordic race. However, it was not the only scheme available. Those writing about the British Isles were more concerned with the distinction of 'Celt' and 'Saxon' elements in the British race. These manifested themselves not only in appearance, but also in psychology.[123] The Celt was understood to be more passionate and fiery-tempered than the Saxon. The distinction has a long history, going back at least to the mid-nineteenth century, and has been important in English literature as a shorthand means of characterization. The appearance and character of the eponymous hero of George Eliot's *Adam Bede* (1859) are ascribed by the narrator to his combination of Saxon and Celtic 'blood'.[124] In 1928 D. H. Lawrence explained that a 'little Welsh farm girl' in John Galsworthy's 'The Apple Tree' fell in love with the hero because she was 'a Celt and not a Saxon'.[125] Such classifications, because of their ability to make a character's appearance anticipate his or her psychology, are convenient for the realist novelist. Woolf, however, makes relatively little use of them. In *Mrs Dalloway*, Evans's surname suggests that he might be Welsh, and his red hair suggests that he might be classified as 'Celtic', but he remains so sketchy a character that he can neither confirm nor negate the stereotype. Woolf's avoidance of such means of characterization may have been motivated by a desire to present characters in terms of their individuality, and to avoid the stereotypes of the realists. The liberal circles in which she moved were relatively sceptical about the reality of race. As Leonard Woolf wrote in 1926, the idea of 'pure' race is meaningless: 'every person now living is a racial mongrel'.[126] Nevertheless, her avoidance of racial stereotypes in her novels may have been motivated by aesthetic rather than ethical concerns. Her diaries and letters have far greater recourse to the methods of realism, including racial characterization.

The idea of 'race' implies a narrative concerned with purity. To be meaningful at all, the concept of race requires that 'pure' racial characteristics can be identified within the actually existing mongrels, and it implies that pure races once actually existed. For writers who subscribed to the idea of pure race, the whole history of human contact and migration, with the inter-breeding that goes with it, was a history of contamination. Their ideas were part of a larger concern during Woolf's lifetime with 'degeneration'. Degeneration theorists were concerned that civilization was limiting the operation of Darwinian laws of the 'survival of the fittest', and was in fact allowing the proliferation of the 'unfit'. The threat of degeneration motivated the science of eugenics, which aimed to prevent the perpetuation of unfit traits and encourage the healthy ones.[127] While British eugenicists most often spoke of the 'nation' as the unit to be maintained, there was a strong tendency to identify race and nation; in Nazi Nationalist racism, the identification became complete.

In Britain, the relation of race and nation was particularly contentious in the period 1880 to 1905, because of the combined effects of the depression of the 1880s and the immigration of Jews fleeing pogroms in Tsarist Russia; Jewish immigration reached a peak in 1903–4.[128] Only a small percentage of the population were Jewish: 0.17 per cent in 1880, and 0.53 per cent in 1910, but the rise was steep.[129] Those arriving were mostly from poorer backgrounds, and tended to settle in poorer urban areas, particularly in the East End of London. Concerns about immigration motivated Balfour's Conservative Government to propose the Aliens Bill of 1905, which refused entry to diseased, pauper, or criminal 'aliens'. Anti-immigration groups favoured the idea that a nation should be racially and linguistically homogenous, 'comprising individuals speaking the same language and of the same racial origin'.[130] Speaking in the debate on the Aliens Bill, Major W. Evans-Gordon denied that Switzerland might be taken as a relevant precedent: it was not a nation 'in the true sense', but 'a confederation of three principal races of Western and Central Europe'.[131] (Evans-Gordon, as well as being MP for Stepney in the East End, was a prominent member of the anti-immigration organization the British Brothers League.)[132] Those opposing the Aliens Bill tended to emphasize the nation as a cultural entity, founded on tradition, and saw race as no barrier to cultural assimilation. One cited the case of a school in the East End where the Jewish children knew their English history better than the average English child; in America, he said, alien emigrants had been moulded into 'an essentially English race'.[133]

Racist slurs against Jews fell into two broad categories. The poorer Jews were accused of criminality, particularly involvement in the 'White Slave Trade', and of harbouring disease. Richer Jews, usually the families longer settled in Britain, were accused of secretly controlling international capitalist finance, and of having been the main financial beneficiaries of the Boer War and First World War; more mildly, they were constructed as vulgar and ostentatious. Describing Jewish acquaintances in her diaries, letters, and journals, Woolf often introduces racial stereotypes. In one instance, she employs the commonest cartoonists' caricature of the time, the representation of Jewish men as having large noses: a 'typical Jew' whom she met struck her as being 'a single nose' (*PA*, p. 259). This, however, is an isolated case. More often, she characterizes Jewish men and women as being ostentatious, not only as regards wealth, but also in the sense of being emotionally demonstrative. In both aspects, such a lack of reserve was considered bad form in upper middle-class English society.

In 1909, as a writing exercise in her journal, Woolf described Mrs Annie Loeb, the widow of a businessman in the City of London. From the outset, she undermines Mrs Loeb's social rank by characterizing her as a shopkeeper. She interprets Mrs Loeb's emotional demonstrativeness as deriving from financial motives: Mrs Loeb ingratiates herself; she fawns, flatters, and wheedles. The sketch of Mrs Loeb also includes an element of physical revulsion: 'Her food, of course, swam in oil and was nasty'.[134] While this piece of characterization mostly serves to reinforce the idea of Mrs Loeb's 'oily' manners, the revulsion also draws on the persistent idea that alien racial groups are unclean or diseased. Later in life, when she had married Leonard Woolf, Virginia continued to be uncomfortable with his family's displays of emotion—even with their 'talking incessantly' (*Letters*, iv. 222)—but did not attribute it to financial motives.

What makes these characterizations particularly shocking is the occasional intrusion of concerns from eugenics. As Hermione Lee notes, Woolf tended to exaggerate the numbers of Leonard's relatives at family gatherings, 'as a joke about how Jews do multiply (and "pullulate" and "copulate" and "amass")'.[135] Combined with such remarks is her isolated but disturbing comment that his eight brothers and sisters 'might well have been drowned' without the world being worse off (*Letters*, iv. 223). It is easy to extrapolate from such remarks and imagine Woolf's racism to have been central to her belief system. However, her anti-Semitic comments take on a different tone from when they are read as part of the full text of her diaries and letters. Woolf applies her venomous tone almost universally, without distinction of race, religion, or gender. Even her more affectionate sketches contain an element of caricature. She frequently sounds a note of physical revulsion similar to that seen in her sketch of Mrs Loeb. For example, hearing gossip of J. W. N. Sullivan (a popular science writer), Mark Gertler (a painter), and Sydney Waterlow (her one-time suitor), Woolf described herself as having gone to bed with 'gooseflesh': 'They have grease in their texture' (*Diary* ii. 149). Gertler was Jewish, but Sullivan and Waterlow were not. If social classifications motivated her distaste, class and not race was the important factor: of Waterlow she notes later in her diary that his grandmother was 'a ratcatcher's daughter' and his grandfather a printer's apprentice (*Diary*, ii. 191). Her characterization of Mrs Loeb as an ingratiating shopkeeper owes as much to her dislike of the nouveau riche classes as to racism. In many respects her remarks are typical of the ways that 'established' families represent those in possession of 'new' wealth, without any specific racial content.

Woolf became increasingly self-aware of her racism and that of others. In 1930 she follows her remark about the superfluity of Leonard's siblings with the reflection that the idea was 'ill natured' (*Letters*, iv. 223). In the same year she reflected on her marriage and her snobbery, recognizing that what had once seemed vulgarity was in fact vitality. 'How I hated marrying a Jew—how I hated their nasal voices, and their oriental jewellery, and their noses and their wattles—what a snob I was: for they have immense vitality, and I think I like that quality best of all' (*Letters*, iv. 195–6). Her self-awareness enters her fiction in *The Years*. There, in the 'Present Day' section, Sara Pargiter complains about 'the Jew', Abrahamson, who lives in the same building, and who will leave 'a line of grease' round the shared bath. Sara's racism, though shared by several characters, is not authorial: as David Bradshaw has argued, the novel emphasizes 'the continuous modern history of the Jews in London', and furthermore draws attention to the rise of racism and authoritarianism in Britain and Europe.[136]

Several of the themes touched on in this chapter coincide in Woolf's troubled thoughts about two men she met in Cornwall in 1921, one the self-educated clerk referred to earlier, the other a vegetarian theosophist. Cornwall is an interesting location for such an encounter, a place of escape and retreat from the metropolitan heart of the nation and empire. 'But can you explain the human race at all', she asked Lytton Strachey: 'I mean these queer fragments of it which are so terribly like ourselves, and so like Chimpanzees at the same time, and so lofty and high minded, with their little shelves of classics and clean china and nice check curtains and purity that I can't see why its all wrong' (*Letters*, ii. 464). The 'human race' is not being used here as a completely inclusive category: rather, it stands for 'the masses', something that Woolf would like to believe separate from and inferior to the Bloomsbury elite ('ourselves'). Elsewhere Woolf had attributed such elitism to a certain type of educated man, the type who elevates his mind 'to a very high tower' from which 'the human race' appeared 'like rats and mice squirming on the flat' (*VO*, p. 231). Here though, adopting the viewpoint herself, she is troubled by the possibility that 'the human race' in fact includes her, and that these Cornish eccentrics are in fact very similar to the London intelligentsia. Geographically out on the very furthest limb of England, Woolf questions whether she is culturally at the centre of the nation, or on its periphery.

CHAPTER 3

THE LITERARY SCENE

IN 'The Patron and the Crocus' (1924), Woolf confronts one aspect of the problem facing literature in the modern world: how it can aspire to being permanently valuable, when it is little more than a disposable commodity. It is a question which becomes thematic in her novels, particularly *Orlando*. More significantly, it is a question which informed the way she published her books, and her choice of genre and style. Woolf uses the 'crocus' as a symbol of literary inspiration and what the writer makes of it. She takes the 'patron' in a wide sense, meaning not just a rich benefactor with a personal relationship to the artist, but a whole range of pay-masters. The modern writer was faced with the problem of whom to write for:

For the present supply of patrons is of unexampled and bewildering variety. There is the daily Press, the weekly Press, the monthly Press; the English public and the American public; the best-seller public and the worst-seller public; the highbrow public and the red-blood public; all now organised self-conscious entities capable through their various mouth-pieces of making their needs known and their approval or displeasure felt. (*EVW* iv. 212–13)

High-minded literary experimenters fare badly in this sketch. They desire, says Woolf, 'a submissive public'. Her examples, Samuel Butler, George Meredith, and Henry James, each 'despised' the pub-lic, yet each 'desired a public', and each 'failed to attain a public'. Each 'wreaked his failure upon the public by a succession . . . of angularities, obscurities, and affectations which no writer whose pat-ron was his equal and friend would have thought it necessary to inflict'. Their crocuses 'are tortured plants, beautiful and bright, but with something wry-necked about them, malformed, shrivelled on the one side, overblown on the other' (*EVW* iv. 213). But conversely, those writers who write for the daily press produce crocuses that bloom brightly for only one day: 'the night comes and these flowers fade' (*EVW* iv. 214). Woolf can outline some of the qualities needed by a good patron, but can end only with further questions: 'But how to choose rightly? How to write well?' (*EVW* iv. 215).

Woolf implies that literary experimenters inflicted their 'angularities' and 'obscurities' on the public simply because they despised them, but to accept such an account as the whole truth would be to devalue much that is distinctive and rewarding in Woolf's work itself as well as in that of her modernist contemporaries. 'The Patron and the Crocus' asks why literature matters relative to other forms of writing, but the larger question, the one overshadowing all serious writers in the twentieth century, is why literature matters relative to other forms of knowledge. The modern world, in the form of commerce and science, values quantitative knowledge, but literature offers knowledge that is qualitative. The modern world values specialization and expertise in the production of knowledge. Many writers saw themselves as professionals, but the question of whether to equate the professional with the specialist was more fraught. To write in a distinctively 'literary' manner, for an audience of other specialists, is to risk retreating from the problems of the real world, and so to weaken literature's claims to be of any importance in that world. On the other hand, to write accessibly for a mass audience is to risk compromising the distinctiveness of literature, and so to destroy the separation from the world which gives literature the power to comment on it. In this light one can see the formal experiments of literary modernism as attempts to produce a literature which could engage with the world while maintaining a critical distance both from it and from mere literary entertainments; as attempts, in other words, to produce a literature that really mattered.

In times of political crisis these questions become questions of whether literature can make anything happen, and whether it should. On the one hand, one finds W. B. Yeats, looking back on the Easter Rising of 1916 and wondering whether his work had led young men to their deaths;[1] on the other, one finds W. H. Auden, writing 'In Memory of W. B. Yeats', expressing the possibility that Ireland still has 'her madness and her weather':

> For poetry makes nothing happen: it survives
> In the valley of its making where executives

Would never want to tamper, flows on south
From ranches of isolation and the busy griefs . . .[2]

Though the immediate context for Auden of things happening or not
was the imminent war with Germany, his inclusion of 'executives'
implies that the world of big business also presents a challenge to
literature. The problem for Woolf, as for Auden, is how to connect the
valley with the world, while preventing 'executives' from tampering.

Literature in the Marketplace

One chronic problem for literature is that it claims to embody
values that are above those of the marketplace, and yet, ever since
the invention of the printing press, it has been a commodity within
that marketplace. With the advent of mass literacy, literary production became mass production. If literature is viewed simply as part
of what we would now call the entertainment industry, then the
literary commodity is to be seen as one leisure product among
many. A newly published novel was, however, a commodity beyond
the reach of many purchasers. In 1898, Walter Besant estimated
that the minimum annual income on which someone might be able
to afford 'new and expensive' books was £250; but in practice,
'especially when there are children', the figure was £750.[3] He
estimated there were about 400,000 families (out of a population of
40 million) within the former income bracket; other near-
contemporary figures suggest there were fewer than 258,000 families within the latter. The typical novel in the period before 1918
had a cover price of 6s., though discounts meant that many would
retail for 4s. 6d. Even with the discount, most new novels were too
expensive for the majority of the population. Most families had
only a small surplus income. Publishers selling to a mass market
sought people with between 1d. and 3d. per week to spend, consumers who were more likely to buy a weekly or monthly magazine
than to save for a year to buy a novel.[4]

The effect of price is seen most starkly with Woolf's *Three
Guineas*, the political urgency of which was compromised by a
price—7s. 6d.—which prevented it reaching a mass market: several
readers drew the difficulty to Woolf's attention.[5] The first English
trade editions of her novels had the following prices:[6]

The Voyage Out (1915)	6s.
Night and Day (1919)	9s.
Jacob's Room (1922)	7s. 6d.
Mrs Dalloway (1925)	7s. 6d.
To the Lighthouse (1927)	7s. 6d.
Orlando (1928)	9s.
The Waves (1931)	7s. 6d.
Flush (1933)	7s. 6d.
The Years (1936)	8s. 6d.
Between the Acts (1941)	7s. 6d.

The price of *The Voyage Out* is typical of a novel before 1918: E. M. Forster's *Howards End* (1910) and D. H. Lawrence's *Sons and Lovers* (1911) had sold for the same price. After the war, there was a general increase, and the 7s. 6d. asked for the majority of Woolf's novels is again typical: Forster's *A Passage to India* (1924) and Lawrence's *Kangaroo* (1923) were priced identically. The higher prices of *Night and Day* and *The Years* were probably due to their greater lengths. The higher-than-average price asked for *Orlando* may be explained by the inclusion of illustrations; similar factors no doubt justified the price of the relatively short *Flush*.

The high price of novels in Britain was inflated by the existence of the circulating libraries. The circulating libraries were private businesses which, for an annual membership fee, allowed a reader to borrow an unlimited number of novels. By 1909 there were six major circulating libraries,[7] of which Mudie's Select Library was the most influential, and the one that became synonymous with the system. Mudie's minimum subscription in the period 1870–1914 was £1. 1s. 0d.: this entitled a member to borrow one volume at a time; for twice that sum, he or she could borrow four volumes at a time. The libraries required durable books for the purposes of circulation, which in practice meant that all first editions were produced as hardbacks. This was one factor in the high price of new novels, but was less important than the market conditions. The libraries bought in bulk, and were able to obtain good discounts from the publishers; however, it was essential to them to make new books available for lending at the same time as they were available for purchase, and this led the publishers to price as highly as possible. In France, where there was no lending system of any significance, new novels appeared in paperback at relatively low prices.[8]

The circulating libraries dictated the physical form and literary content of new novels. In the nineteenth century, they had preferred new novels to be published in the three-volume or 'three-decker' format. Publishers also produced single-volume editions for sale to the public, but only when the library sales had been exhausted. However, the single-volume market increasingly prevented the libraries from selling off their second-hand lending copies, and on 27 June 1894 the lending libraries declared that they were no longer prepared to pay the high price of three-decker novels; and that they would require publishers to wait for a year before publishing cheap reprints. Their change of policy killed the three-decker within a matter of three years.[9] The new dominance of the single-volume novel implied a certain maximum length for novels. When, in 1909, William Heinemann published William de Morgan's *It Never Can Happen Again*—at 300,000 words, an unusually long novel—he decided to produce it in two volumes, priced at 10s. rather than the usual 6s. The libraries objected to the two-volume format; then, when Heinemann agreed to produce an ungainly single-volume edition, they objected to the high price. As Heinemann recognized, the libraries were dictating the lengths of novels irrespective of 'artistic requirements'. In effect, a novelist with a narrative or theme that required 300,000 words would be discouraged from tackling it. The consequence of 'the limitations of space in the printed book' was, it seemed to the publisher and novelist Michael Sadleir in 1924, novels characterized by either 'greater compression' or 'lighter weight'.[10]

The circulating libraries were also cautious about controversial content: Mudie's full name was 'Mudie's *Select* Library', and the selection in question reassured subscribers that its books were morally unimpeachable. The caution of Mudie's influenced publishers, who in turn influenced authors. It was not the most draconian form of censorship, but it was one of the most significant. In 1909, the six major libraries formed the Circulating Libraries Association to exchange opinions about titles which might be considered unsuitable, and to force publishers to provide them with copies for vetting at least one week before publication. By these means, they sought to exclude any book 'which, by reason of the personally scandalous, libellous, immoral, or otherwise disagreeable nature of its contents' was 'likely to prove offensive' to 'any considerable section' of their subscribers.[11] Although the power of the circulating libraries declined during Woolf's lifetime, they were still a significant force. The prosecution of Radcliffe Hall's *The Well of Loneliness* in 1928 caused Boots Circulating Library to withdraw several other novels it deemed potentially controversial.[12]

Virginia Woolf was a Mudie's subscriber, and 'Mudie's Corner' on New Oxford Street was a regular port of call, particularly when she was living in Richmond. Nevertheless, she loathed the library and all it stood for. In 1917 she records a 'stout woman' in Mudie's choosing ten novels, seemingly unconcerned about artistry, stipulating only that 'she wanted no vulgarity, not much description, but plenty of incident'; she 'gulped down another mass of sweet sensation warranted not about the war, nor about drunkards' and then 'waddled off' (*Diary*, i. 61). Mudie's flourished, Woolf later wrote, by providing 'a sort of pap-slop—something made digestible and sweet for invalids' (*Letters*, iv. 24). In *Jacob's Room* the reliability of Mrs Norman, through whose eyes we see Jacob travelling to Cambridge, is implicitly called into question by the fact that Mudie's Library has provided her reading matter (*JR*, pp. 35–6). Though Woolf's observations betray some of the contempt for the 'masses' noted by John Carey, they also raise legitimate concerns about the role of literature which Carey tends to overlook.[13] She was concerned that literature was infantilizing the adult population, allowing it to escape from pressing social issues.

Virginia Woolf was unusual among contemporary novelists in that she did not employ a literary agent. The role of the agent had grown for two main reasons. First, changes in international copyright law had vastly increased the number of possible outlets for literary work. The Berne Convention of 1887 established international copyright; it was revised by conventions in Paris in 1896 and Berlin in 1910. The United States signed up to the convention with the Chace Act of 1891, the coverage of which was extended in 1909.[14] Domestic copyright was reformed by the Copyright Act of 1911, which extended copyright to fifty years after an author's death, regardless of the date of first publication.[15] (This Act governed copyright in the United Kingdom until 1956; in 1993 a European Union directive extended the period to seventy years. Virginia Woolf's works came out of copyright in 1992, only to go back in again on 1 July 1995.)

Secondly, another large market had appeared in the form of a new style of monthly periodicals publishing serialized fiction. The *Strand*, which first appeared in 1891, was one of the most significant models; costing 6*d*. per issue, it was affordable to those who could not buy new novels.

These new business opportunities required business and networking skills which not every author possessed, and so literary agents grew in their importance as intermediaries between authors and publishers. The Society of Authors carried out some such functions, but its role was inevitably impersonal. Joseph Conrad's agent from 1900 onwards, J. B. Pinker, advanced enormous sums to Conrad in the hope of future success, something the Society could never have afforded to do; by July 1913 Conrad owed Pinker £1,070. The immensity of the sum becomes apparent when one considers that a cook would have earned about £50 per year, and that less than 1 per cent of the population earned more than £750 per year. Conrad was, however, able to clear the debt by January 1915, owing to the financial success of *Chance*. The role of the agent was not purely financial, however: Conrad confided that Pinker 'kept me going as much perhaps by his belief in me as with his money'.[16] The old (and somewhat mythologized) personal relationship of author and publisher had been supplanted by the relationship of author and agent.

Woolf's position in the 'intellectual aristocracy', coupled with her father's reputation, gave her a network of contacts in the literary world as good as any that an agent could provide. The publisher of her first two novels was her half-brother; she and her husband, as the Hogarth Press, were the English publishers of the trade editions of all her subsequent novels. The Hogarth Press effectively acted as her agent in negotiations for American and other editions. Though it is possible that she failed to maximize her earnings through serialization rights, it is also clear that the kind of fiction she was writing was unsuitable for the mass-market periodicals that specialized in serialization. When T. S. Eliot enquired about including part of *Mrs Dalloway* in the *Criterion*, Woolf replied that it was too 'interwoven' to be segmented for periodicals (*Letters*, iii. 106). James Joyce had serialized *A Portrait of the Artist as a Young Man* and parts of *Ulysses*, but they had appeared in periodicals with a very small circulation, and he received no payment. The only work by Woolf to be serialized was *Flush*, which appeared in the American *Atlantic*

Monthly; the American journal *Forum* declined the serial rights for *To the Lighthouse*, and the American *Bookman* considered *A Room of One's Own* but never took it up. In all these dealings, Woolf was represented by her American publishers (*Diary*, iii. 127; *Letters*, iv. 71).

THE DIVIDED MARKET

The divisions in the world of literature were often described in the language of class, and the market was often divided in ways that seemingly corresponded to class divisions. In 1891, Edmund Gosse had claimed that there was an 'intellectual hierarchy' of authors: there were five or six men in each generation who represented 'what is most brilliant and most independent'; from them the hierarchy descended as a 'vast pyramid' down to 'the lowest and broadest class of workers', a 'broad and featureless residuum'.[17] Though it is unlikely that Woolf read Gosse's article, it embodies assumptions which would have been familiar to her.

Gosse's categories of production corresponded to categories of consumption and distribution. For many writers, a bipartite model was dominant. In a lecture in 1922, the poet and critic Robert Graves remarked upon there being 'a complete split between the publishers, bookshops and libraries that cater for "the people", and the literary press which caters for the intelligentsia'.[18] In 1927 Michael Sadleir argued that the division was due to literary agents, who had divided the relationship of author to publisher into two parts, 'the one personal and literary, the other formally contractual and financial'; this division was gradually repeating itself in the publishing trade, forcing publishers to choose 'between running a book-factory or catering exquisitely for the *intelligentsia*'; this was 'bad for the national mentality and bad for literature'.[19] It is unlikely that agents alone had the power to bring about such changes; rather, the increase in the potential financial rewards for an author had brought them about, widening the financial differential between success and failure. Nevertheless, and regardless of the true cause, many authors believed that there was a division in the market. Authors were conscious too of divisions in the literary elite: there were at any time several different intellectual elites, each with loyalties to particular publishers or literary journals. In the early 1920s there was a distinct split between John Middleton Murry's periodical the *Athenaeum* and

J. C. Squire's more conservative *London Mercury*; later, between Murry's *Adelphi* and T. S. Eliot's *Criterion*. All were minority publications.

What united the intelligentsia was their disdain for mass-market literature. It was commonly believed that works of mass-market fiction lacked distinctiveness; one was interchangeable with another. H. G. Wells gently mocked this in *Kipps*, where the former draper's assistant Arthur Kipps, having lost his inherited fortune, considers opening a bookshop:

I noticed when we used to go to that Lib'ry at Folkestone, ladies weren't anything like what they was in a draper's—if you 'aven't got *just* what they want, its [*sic*] 'Oh no!' and out they go. But in a bookshop it's different. One book's very like another—after all, what is it? Something to read and done with. It's not a thing that matters like print dresses or serviettes . . . They take what you give 'em in books and lib'ries, and glad to be told *what* to.[20]

The interchangeability of one book with another is illustrated in a later novel by Wells, where the very conventional Mr Stanley reads novels with 'chromatic titles' such as *The Red Sword*, *The Black Helmet*, *The Purple Robe*, *The Lilac Sunbonnet*, and *The Blue Lagoon*.[21] As Kipps's observation suggests, the circulating libraries were partly to blame. Michael Sadleir blamed the system whereby those who dealt with the libraries by post sent in long lists of alternative choices: such lists implied that all the items on them were effectively equivalent. The list system embodied the essential conservatism of the libraries, allowing them to 'blunt the demand for new publications'.[22] Subscribers, Sadleir believed, should insist on being given the particular book that they really wanted. The question of interchangeability is directly relevant to the distinctive qualities of modernist writing. Though Woolf's novels have certain family resemblances, each represents a distinct departure from each of its predecessors. Deliberately or not, Woolf and other modernists were creating works that would confound the list system, and would defy the expectations of booksellers like Arthur Kipps: *To the Lighthouse* and *Mrs Dalloway* are not interchangeable like *The Red Sword* and *The Purple Robe*. If literature matters at all, it matters considerably more than print dresses and serviettes.

In speaking of the intelligentsia and 'the people', Robert Graves also distinguished them as highbrows and lowbrows. The distinction has its origins in the nineteenth-century pseudo-science of physiognomy: a high-browed person (a person with a lofty forehead) was considered intelligent, and a low-browed person not.[23] The term 'highbrow', though first recorded in 1884 as an adjective, came into regular usage as an adjective and noun between 1908 and 1914, first in America and soon afterwards in Britain; 'lowbrow' came into regular usage at around the same time. Like the social class system, this class system included an aspirational element, and the term 'middlebrow' was coined by way of satirizing lowbrows who aspired to be highbrows: the middlebrow, announced *Punch*, was a new type discovered by the BBC; it consisted of 'people who are hoping that some day they will get used to the stuff they ought to like'.[24]

However, 'middlebrow' also took on connotations similar to 'middle class' and 'suburban', implying narrowness and philistinism, rather than dutiful cultural aspiration. These are the connotations it has in Woolf's essay 'Middlebrow', written in October or November 1932, though not published until after her death (*CE* ii. 196–203).[25] For Woolf, the distinction between 'highbrow' and 'lowbrow' is the distinction both between producers and consumers, and between minds and bodies: the former is 'the man or woman of thoroughbred intelligence who rides his mind at a gallop across country in pursuit of an idea'; the latter is 'a man or woman of thoroughbred vitality who rides his body in pursuit of a living at a gallop across life' (*CE* ii. 196–7). The two classes are, she claims, mutually dependent: the highbrow needs subject matter, and finds that everything that lowbrows do 'is of surpassing interest and wonder'. Her list of examples does not equate 'lowbrow' with any particular social class: it includes a stockbroker, an admiral, and a duchess as well as a prostitute, a bank clerk, and a dressmaker. The lowbrows need someone to represent their lives to them; they are so busy 'riding full tilt', living that is, that they cannot see 'what their lives look like'. Woolf's distinction is between the contemplative and the active life.

Within Woolf's scheme, the middlebrow is 'betwixt and between': not, as *Punch* would have it, a lowbrow aspirant to highbrow culture, but one who 'curries favour with both sides equally'. The problem is, Woolf argues, that lowbrows are far too willing to consume middlebrow culture, and far too willing to accept the sentimental middlebrow representation of their lives, a 'mixture of geniality and sentiment stuck together with a sticky slime of calves-foot jelly' (*CE*

ii. 200). What Woolf would like to see is a union of highbrows and lowbrows, joined in 'blood brotherhood' against the 'bloodless' middlebrow.

The paradoxical position of the writer, as producer both of durable truths and of perishable commodities, forms a significant strand in *Orlando*. Though the dominant themes of the novel concern biography and its relation to gender, the figure of Nick Greene allows Woolf to mock the literary establishment and expose the paradoxes of 'highbrow' literature. By the Victorian era, Greene has become a professional 'man of letters', someone for whom original composition has been supplanted by high-profile book reviewing; someone with many contacts in the publishing world who plays the role of an informal literary agent; someone with a concern for the public standing of the profession. The paradox is that someone so enmeshed in the 'business' side of contemporary literature has so little time for contemporary writing, harking back instead to the glories of a bygone age. Greene is a composite figure, based on several figures in the literary world. Several of Greene's opinions and phrases derive directly from *The Prospects of Literature*, a pamphlet by Logan Pearsall Smith published by the Hogarth Press in 1927. The pamphlet was the offspring of an argument between Woolf and Smith over the current health of English literature. In 1924, Smith had disagreed with Woolf's claim that her generation were 'trembling on the verge of one of the great ages of English literature' (*EVW* iii. 436); he had further objected to her writing for the fashionable journal *Vogue*.[26] In *The Prospects of Literature*, Smith argued that lucrative publishing deals and the immediate rewards of literary journalism were tempting writers away from a dedicated life of 'disinterested study'.[27] Smith's antithetical ideal for the aspiring writer was a 'life of toil and leisure' 'striving onwards towards a distant goal' to be 'crowned at last, if at all,' by 'enduring fame'.[28] Smith recognized that 'fame' was not a very adequate term, as it could mean both immediate celebrity and recognition by distant posterity. His suggestion that the English writer look to the French ideal of 'la gloire' directly informs Woolf's Nick Greene.[29] By putting Smith's high ideals in Nick Greene's all-too-human mouth, Woolf is highlighting their limitations, but not completely rejecting them: after all, Orlando's 400-year persistence with 'The Oak Tree' embodies the very dedication that Smith had advocated. Woolf is drawing attention to the difficulty of reconciling high idealism with the need to earn a living. Though some elements in the portrait of Greene may have been intended as coterie jokes for the consumption of Bloomsbury alone, Smith's pamphlet was reworking a familiar theme. Many others had distinguished between the seclusion of the writer's study and the public world of literary celebrity, and others were to repeat the distinction.[30] Woolf herself was to return to this conflict in *Three Guineas*. There, though she advocates the founding of 'an experimental college', in which 'learning is sought for itself' (*TG*, pp. 199, 201), she is aware that young women wish to obtain appointments and to earn their livings, aware that her idealistic scheme must confront everyday 'realities' (pp. 201–2). Later in the same work she stages a debate: the voice that wishes to protect intellectual liberty argues that to write 'for the sake of money' is a form of intellectual prostitution; but Woolf acknowledges that 'the daughters of educated men' may feel money to be 'desirable', at the very least, and 'fame' to be 'agreeable' (pp. 289–91). In its various forms, the conflict between being a worldly and an unworldly writer was to haunt Woolf's entire career.

Canon and Tradition

The specialization of knowledge affected both literary criticism and literary creation. Both T. S. Eliot and Ezra Pound insisted that to create serious poetry, the poet could not rely simply on inspiration, but must study earlier literature. In 1913, Pound justified this approach by explicitly referring to the specialization required of the scientist: 'The scientist does not expect to be acclaimed as a great scientist until he has *discovered* something. He begins by learning what has been discovered already. He goes from that point onward'.[31] T. S. Eliot echoed Pound in 1918, saying that it would be 'just as absurd' for a poet 'not to know the work of his predecessors or of men writing in other languages' as it would be for a biologist to be ignorant of the work of recent innovators in his specialized area.[32] Their views are founded on the assumption that literature is a continually evolving entity. To understand an author one must place him in relation to his literary ancestry. According to this view, an important role of literary criticism is to tell the 'story' of literature as a long, evolutionary narrative. Typically, such narratives would run from the works of writers in Old English up to the most recently deceased authors: the guide that Miss Allan is writing in *The Voyage Out*, from *Beowulf* to Browning, is entirely typical (*VO*, p. 368).[33] Narrative histories were important for the general public, the 'railway book-stall' market for Miss Allan's book, but also for the university courses in English literature that had grown up in the late nineteenth century.[34] University degrees were typically organized around the idea of a narrative history of literature.

Some modernist writers argued that their radical experiments were rooted in the history of literature. In 1918 Edwin Muir argued that if modernism were to be 'a vital thing', it would need to have 'its roots' in the past: 'in short it can only be a tradition'.[35] In 1919 T. S. Eliot said something very similar in 'Tradition and the Individual Talent': the poet must obtain, 'by great labour', a sense of tradition, and must write with a sense of the presence of past literature.[36] One might reasonably ask which literature the poet should read. Eliot is aware that one cannot digest the whole past indiscriminately, but he is vague about what constitutes 'the main current' of tradition. In other words, the appeal to 'tradition' is often based upon a specific and partisan tradition, a canon of great works.

Though Woolf greatly valued past literature, she was also acutely aware of the abuses of tradition; in *A Room of One's Own* she develops the idea of a tradition of women's literature. Woolf first delivered her lectures on women and fiction at the women's colleges in Cambridge, Newnham and Girton, in October 1928, but she greatly expanded them for publication. The date is significant: on 29 March 1928, the voting age for women had been reduced from 30 to 21, thus granting complete equality with men. *The Cause*, Ray (Rachel) Strachey's history of the suffrage movement, was published in the same year. A valuable work in its own right, *The Cause* may also be used to establish a context for *A Room*. Florence Nightingale's *Cassandra*, to which Woolf refers, had been published for the first time as an appendix to Strachey's work. It was clear to all feminists that winning the vote was only the beginning of their task: there were many other legislative battles to fight. Moreover, in her conclusion, Strachey noted that '[l]egal equality' was not 'the whole aim of the movement': 'There are aspects of it which are not suscep-tible to victory by law; there are changes of thought and outlook which even yet have not arrived'.[37] *A Room of One's Own* takes up this challenge, seeking to effect a change in our ideas of tradition and the canon. In this it draws on the pre-war suffrage campaigners: in 1908 the Artists' Suffrage League sought to establish a female canon, and its banners featured Jane Austen, Elizabeth Barrett Browning, and George Eliot, as well as female scientists.[38] In 1910, Strachey recalled, campaigners had 'paraded in costume . . . representing the professions and occupations of women, and the famous women of the past'.[39] Cicely Hamilton's *Pageant of Great Women* had established an alternative female canon running from Sappho to Jane Austen.[40] Woolf, in *A Room of One's Own*, sees women's literature as an evolving continuum: thus, Mary Carmichael's novel is 'the last volume in a fairly long series, continuing all those other books that I have been glancing at—Lady Winchilsea's poems and Aphra Behn's plays and the novels of the four great novelists. For books continue each other, in spite of our habit of judging them separately' (*ROO*, p. 104). The 'band of famous names' painted from 1907 onwards beneath the dome of the British Museum's Reading Room had established a male canon (*ROO*, p. 33), one which had irritated Miss Julia Hedge in *Jacob's Room* for excluding George Eliot and the Brontë sisters (*JR*, pp. 144–5). Woolf seeks to challenge its authority. She presents the heritage of women's literature more positively than Hamilton, who, in spite of her pageant, had said that while women had a 'good heritage' of the wisdom of their fathers, 'of the wisdom, the aspiration and the inspiration of our mothers (for some they must have had) there has come down to us practically nothing'.[41] For Woolf, there is a significant inheritance available, that allows a woman writing to think back 'through her mothers' (*ROO*, p. 127).

Literary Journalism

As Logan Pearsall Smith's *The Prospects of Literature* indicates, the financial rewards for literary journalism were tempting. Until the success of *Orlando*, Woolf depended on it to maintain her income. Many newspapers ran book review pages; there were many generalist reviews, which usually put political commentary at the front of the magazine and literature and the arts at the back, and literary reviews, which contained a combination of original work and book reviews. Some of the generalist and literary reviews had large circulation and could pay well; others were run on a more amateur basis. The *New*

Age, an influential generalist review before the First World War, was known by its editor as the 'no wage'.[42] Nevertheless, even when the financial rewards were not tempting, there were rewards in terms of 'career capital': appearing in the right pages could boost an author's reputation and increase sales of future books.

Much has been written in histories of modernism about the importance of the 'little reviews', short-lived literary and artistic journals that published original works and reviews, and that sometimes contained woodcuts or reproductions of modern artworks.[43] Some, like the *Egoist* (1917–19) and T. S. Eliot's *Criterion* (1922–39), were conservative in their physical format and typography; others, like Wyndham Lewis's *Blast*, were typographically confrontational and innovative. Though little magazines such as *Art and Letters* (1917–20), *Coterie* (1919–21), and *transition* (1927–38) were important to Woolf's modernist contemporaries, her association with them was minimal, and much of her output appeared in more conventional literary periodicals. As her name became better known, she was invited to write for an increasingly diverse range of publications, among the more surprising of which are *Vogue*, for which she wrote in the 1920s, and *Good Housekeeping*, which first published the essays of *The London Scene*.

As the portrait of Nick Greene implies, Woolf found the world of literary journalism repellent. She applied her pejorative label 'grocer' to several of the leading figures in the literary world: to Edmund Gosse; to Bruce Richmond, editor of the *Times Literary Supplement*; to J. C. Squire, literary editor of the *New Statesman* from 1913 to 1919, and editor of the *London Mercury*; and to John Middleton Murry, editor of the *Athenaeum*, and later of the *Adelphi*.[44] Nevertheless, the *Times Literary Supplement* (*TLS*) was the most important of her 'patrons' from 1905 to 1923. The *TLS*, a newspaper in its physical format, reviewed 'literature' in the broadest sense, including philosophy and science writing, criticism on music and the arts, literary criticism, original fiction, and poetry. All its reviews were anonymous, a practice that continued until 1974.[45] Its leading article, which covered the front page and part of the second, was usually a review-article, an essay, or an obituary essay of between 3,500 and 4,500 words. The reviews in the following pages were much shorter, usually between 1,000 and 2,000 words. Though the anonymity meant that reviewers did not directly enhance their reputations, many were able to use their leading articles as the cornerstones of collections of essays: Woolf did so in the two *Common Reader* collections, particularly the first, 1925 volume.

The literary and generalist reviews were also important patrons. The *Athenaeum* under Middleton Murry was, from 1919 to 1921, an important review for British modernist writers, providing a forum for T. S. Eliot and Aldous Huxley as well as for Woolf, though it was relatively conservative in appearance and content, and published very little new work. It was combined in February 1921 with the political review the *Nation* to form the *Nation and Athenaeum*. In 1923 a consortium of political liberals headed by John Maynard Keynes bought the title, and Leonard Woolf was made literary editor, a post he held until 1930. From this date onwards, the *Nation and Athenaeum* became Virginia Woolf's primary source of journalistic employment, and the *TLS* became less important to her. It should be noted too that these patrons themselves relied on wealthy patrons. The *Athenaeum* had been owned, indirectly, by the Rowntree Trust, a charitable trust which had the aim of promoting a broadly 'liberal' point of view through its subsidized publications. *Time and Tide*, a liberal news review with an important feminist slant, was subsidized by its editor, Margaret Haig (Viscountess Rhondda); *Art and Letters* was subsidized by Sydney Schiff, inheritor of a stockbroking fortune. However, unlike the owners of the daily press, these patrons did not expect a financial return on their investment, and so created a space in which literature was partly freed from the demands of the market.

Censorship

The 'approval or displeasure' of the public was not the only force that a writer had to reckon with: the displeasure of the state could also be expressed, primarily through the Obscene Publications Act of 1857. Publishers, wary of prosecution under the Act, often imposed their own censorship long before a novel reached the printer; the censorship of the circulating libraries was also a factor they took into consideration. Printers could be prosecuted for their role in publishing obscenity, and so sometimes raised their own objections. It was the printer of James Joyce's *Dubliners* who called for most of the changes, particularly to the story 'Counterparts'.[46]

Professional authors, wary of conflict with their publishers, were in turn capable of self-censorship, unless they felt that their subject matter demanded the breaking of a taboo. Publishers, printers, and authors would all have been aware of the particular kinds of writing that were vulnerable to prosecution. The terms of the Act itself were vague: it outlawed 'obscene' literature without attempting to define it. Definition had come with the case of *Regina* v *Hicklin* in 1868, in which Chief Justice Cockburn had formulated a test of obscenity: 'whether the tendency of the matter charged as obscenity is to deprave and corrupt those whose minds are open to such immoral influences, and into whose hands a publication of this sort may fall'.[47] The advent of the French naturalist novel in the 1880s and 1890s had also created a number of test cases for the Act, notably the prosecution of Henry Vizetelly in 1888 for publishing an English translation of Émile Zola's novel *La Terre*. During Woolf's career, the most significant British prosecutions were those of D. H. Lawrence's *The Rainbow* in November 1915, and of Radclyffe Hall's novel about a lesbian relationship, *The Well of Loneliness*, in November 1928. Woolf, along with E. M. Forster, wrote to the press protesting at the censorship of Hall's novel, and attended the trial.[48] When writing of lesbian relationships in *A Room of One's Own*, she gently mocks the censorship, asking whether the Chief Magistrate in the *Well of Loneliness* trial is concealed behind the curtains, and whether the Director of Public Prosecutions is lurking in the linen cupboard (*ROO*, pp. 106, 145); she mocks the Home Secretary for his readiness to find a sexual element even in a platonic relationship (*ROO*, p. 112). Woolf would have been aware too of the confiscation by the USA postal authorities of certain issues of the *Little Review* as it serialized *Ulysses* in 1919 and 1920, and of the '*Ulysses* trial' in New York in February 1921.[49] Joyce's novel had been offered to the Hogarth Press to publish in 1918, and they declined it, partly because of its length, and partly because Leonard was advised that no printer would be willing to be associated with it (*Diary*, i. 136; ii. 68 n. 11). In 1926, on the advice of a lawyer, the Hogarth Press decided not to publish Raymond Mortimer's pamphlet 'In Defence of Homosexuality'.[50]

Reviewers were an important part of the informal mechanism of censorship: a condemnation of a book on moral grounds was likely to bring it to the attention of the Director of Public Prosecutions. This

appears to have been the case with the prosecution of *The Rainbow*.[51]
There were other significant pressure groups, such as the National
Vigilance Association, founded in 1885, and the National Social
Purity Crusade, founded in 1901, which occasionally brought private
prosecutions against novels they considered offensive.[52] The reaction
against naturalism established a discourse of condemnation which
was to persist into the twentieth century, in relation to literature,
painting, and sculpture. Characteristically, reviewers contrasted the
sordid, base, or dirty world of the obscene writer against 'higher',
more beautiful and spiritual things; and they characterized the
obscene writer as looking with the eye of a medical student rather
than as a complete human being. This condemnatory discourse may
be found, for example, in criticism of Arthur Morrison's *A Child of
the Jago* (1896) and of James Joyce's *Dubliners* (1914).[53] Reviewers
also frequently invoked 'health'. In 1909, commenting approvingly
on the formation of the Libraries Association, a writer to *The Times*
cited a speaker at the Liverpool Sanitary Congress of the previous
year who had described obscene literature as 'dangerous to the
public health'.[54] In 1915, one reviewer of *The Rainbow* said that the
'sanitary inspector of literature' must 'notify' it, implying that it
was 'notifiable' like a transmissible disease.[55] To the censorious, the
removal of obscene literature was analogous to slum clearance.

In 1915 Leonard Woolf was required by the publishers of his
second novel, *The Wise Virgins*, to make revisions in thirty-six
places; despite pleading that 'the moral significance of the book'
required some of the scenes, he ultimately gave way.[56] Virginia Woolf
escaped the censors. As the Radclyffe Hall trial shows, she was prepared to stand up against them when necessary. Nevertheless, she
qualified her public praise for *Ulysses* with remarks that could have
come from the pen of a campaigner for moral purity, accusing Joyce
of 'the conscious and calculated indecency of a desperate man who
feels that in order to breathe he must break the windows' (*EVW* iii.
434). Her private remarks on *Ulysses*, though also mentioning
obscenity, made more of Joyce's class background: his being 'a board
school boy' and 'a self taught working man', and his book being
correspondingly 'underbred' (*Diary*, ii. 199, 189). Taken together,
these remarks suggest that Woolf's self-censorship was significantly
conditioned by her social background, rather than being an entirely
conscious attempt to avoid official censorship.

Mode, Genre, and Form

Though narrative writing forms the most important context for
Woolf's novels, the cultural standing of fiction relative to other
modes of writing is significant, and may have influenced the direction her writing took. Moreover, modernist writers spoke relatively
little of 'genre' and much more of literary 'form'; the impressionistic
metaphors they used to describe form were readily transferable from
one mode of writing to another. Poetry carried the greatest cultural
prestige, and for some critics was virtually synonymous with serious
literature. The study of poetry dominated the earliest university
degrees in English Literature. It is notable that the earliest critical
writings to recognize the existence of literary 'modernism' saw it as a
movement in poetry.[57] The novel was tainted by its function as entertainment, and its lack of precedent in classical culture; it was not
universally recognized as a serious art form. British drama had for
much of the nineteenth century been heavily formulaic, and also
regarded as entertainment rather than literature. The translation of
Henrik Ibsen's plays in the late nineteenth century had raised the
possibility of drama being taken more seriously, as had the plays of
George Bernard Shaw, but by the time Woolf began to write fiction,
that moment had passed. The prevailing view among the young of
the upper middle class is encapsulated by Hewet's response to
Rachel's reading:

'God, Rachel, you do read trash!', he exclaimed. 'And you're behind the
times too, my dear. No one dreams of reading this kind of thing now—
antiquated problem plays, harrowing descriptions of life in the East
End—oh, no, we've exploded all that. Read poetry, Rachel, poetry, poetry,
poetry!' (*VO*, p. 341)

We have earlier heard that Rachel has read a play by Shaw, *Man and
Superman* (1902), and several by Ibsen (*VO*, p. 259). Of course,
Hewet's view cannot be taken as objective: there are no objective
views in an area as contentious as literature. Nor can it be taken as
authorial: Woolf is satirizing his confident, university-educated attitude. Nevertheless, she seems to have internalized something of this
attitude towards the superiority of poetry. When W. B. Yeats's
anthology *The Oxford Book of Modern Verse* was published in
November 1936, she reflected in her diary: 'Am I jealous? No: but

depressed to feel I'm not a poet. Next time I shall be one' (*Diary*, v. 35). 'Next time' apparently means in her next novel; when Yeats's anthology appeared she was concluding her struggle with *The Years*. She had already written what she considered a 'poetical' work in *The Waves*, and was aware of the 'lyrical' qualities of her writing, for example in the 'Time Passes' section of *To the Lighthouse*.

There were several significant poets in Woolf's circle of acquaint-ance. She had first met T. S. Eliot in November 1918, finding him on first acquaintance 'a polished, cultivated, elaborate young American'; she was struck by his holding a 'very intricate & highly organised framework of poetic belief' (*Diary*, i. 218–19). At this time his *Prufrock and Other Observations* had already appeared; Leonard and Virginia Woolf were to print and publish his *Poems* in 1919, and an edition of *The Waste Land* in 1923. He was also to become an important critic and theorist of literature. Whether he affected Woolf's literary development is difficult to gauge. As recent criticism on Eliot and Woolf has so much emphasized his conservatism and misogyny and her feminism and radicalism, they can appear to be sharply contrasting figures. However, political differences are not identical to literary ones, even if they often correspond. Although Woolf never shared Eliot's estimation of Wyndham Lewis or Ezra Pound, he persuaded her to take James Joyce more seriously. In many of his *Prufrock* poems Eliot presented consciousness from within, in a fragmented form, suppressing the sort of explanatory and connecting material that readers had grown to expect. Like Woolf, he combined this large-scale fragmentation with a care for the lyrical qualities of individual phrases.

The Hogarth Press also published many new poets, and this kept Woolf in contact with changing views about the scope and function of poetry. Their most significant publications in this respect were the anthologies *New Signatures* (1932) and *New Country* (1933), both edited by Michael Roberts. The anthologies brought to prominence the so-called 'Auden Group', a group of poets of whom the central figures were W. H. Auden, Louis MacNeice, Stephen Spender, and C. Day Lewis; of them, Woolf was personally acquainted only with Spender. In his preface to *New Signatures*, Roberts drew attention to their modern subject matter and their role as politically radical leaders; their left-wing politics distinguished them from Eliot and Pound. They were united in their opposition to the fascist

Nationalists in the Spanish Civil War. The example of the Auden group may have been one factor in persuading Woolf that literature that took itself seriously as literature should attempt to address politically urgent issues, even though she believed that Auden's generation had failed to produce literature of lasting value ('The Leaning Tower', in *CE* ii. 162–81).

Not everyone considered the novel inferior to poetry, even if this was the dominant view: several writers were working to establish it as a serious art form. Although Hewet exhorts Rachel to read poetry, he himself would like to write a novel 'about Silence . . . the things people don't say' (*VO*, p. 249). His remark that the 'difficulty is immense' suggests that he has been pondering novelistic form much as Henry James had done in the prefaces to the 'New York' edition of his novels (1907–9): James characteristically discussed formal problems of point of view and of 'handling', rather than problems of subject matter.[58] Joseph Conrad's prefaces to his novels are less profound, but their very presence implies that the construction of the novels merits consideration. The attempt to establish the novel as a serious art form created some terminological difficulties: 'novel' was so strongly associated with linear narrative in a realist mode that many of the more ambitious experimental works did not appear to be 'novels'. T. S. Eliot, in an influential article on *Ulysses*, referred repeatedly to 'Mr Joyce's book', before declaring that 'the novel is a form which will no longer serve . . . the novel ended with Flaubert and with James'.[59] Woolf herself was faced with similar difficulties: as she began *To the Lighthouse* she considered inventing a new name for her books 'to supplant "novel" ', and thought of terming her current work an 'elegy' (*Diary*, iii. 34). These, however, are atypical perspectives: the works of Joyce and of Woolf were generally understood as novels, albeit novels that drew upon a wide range of literary resources.

How far the newly ambitious approach to the novel was a cause of the split in the literary market, and how far a consequence, is impossible to determine, but it is clear that the two trends were related. Fiction written for the mass market was written in a realist mode that would have been familiar to Victorian readers. The formal coherence of the realist novel was due to several combining factors: a recognizable narratorial voice, usually a 'third person' narrator, though sometimes 'first person'; characterization which assumed a natural relation between internal psychology and external appearance, and similarly between motivation and action; storylines which eventually, at the point of closure, made all major events and actions intelligible according to a commonly held world view. Not all 'upmarket' fiction departed from these rules, for it could also distinguish itself through its content. The Mudie's subscriber overheard by Woolf would have avoided even a realist novel, if it lacked 'incident', concerned the war, or depicted 'drunkards'. Nevertheless, much experimental fiction defied expectations in relation to some of the formal aspects of the novel.

Many of the literary experiments of the period sought to represent human consciousness as experienced from within. Such experiments are often grouped under the heading 'stream of consciousness', but the term conflates distinct literary methods. The idea that the mind contains a 'stream of consciousness' is a psychological hypothesis, first advanced in the late nineteenth century by William James. James claimed that even if, examining consciousness, we could isolate distinct images, they are meaningful only in relation to the conscious and semi-conscious ideas which flow around them.[60] 'Stream of consciousness' became literary terminology in 1918 when May Sinclair used it to describe Dorothy Richardson's technique in her long novel *Pilgrimage*.[61] As a literary term, it does not distinguish between the different kinds of consciousness and unconsciousness that various writers try to convey: some are concerned with the perceptual consciousness, some with intellectual consciousness, while others try to register the effects of the Freudian unconscious on our conscious mental life. Moreover, Woolf and her contemporaries were often aiming to represent not the perspective of a single consciousness, but of several distinct consciousnesses; and, at times, of consciousnesses that were several but indistinct, a 'group consciousness'.

The later terms 'free indirect discourse' and 'free direct discourse' are more accurate because they describe styles of writing. In Woolf's form of 'free indirect discourse' a character's thoughts are reported from a formally external, third-person position and in a narratorial perfect tense, but retain the characteristic vocabulary, syntax, and rhythm of that individual.[62] Joyce used free indirect discourse in *A Portrait of the Artist as a Young Man* (1916), but in *Ulysses* he used a wider range of styles, with free *direct* discourse predominating. In free direct discourse, thoughts are presented from a first-person perspective. In the earlier chapters of *Ulysses*, Joyce's actual practice is more complex: he often identifies a character from a third-person perspective, before giving truncated first-person utterances. The effect is very different from that of Woolf's method. For example: 'Mr Bloom reviewed the nails of his left hand, then those of his right hand. The nails, yes. Is there anything more in him that they she sees? Fascination. Worst man in Dublin. That keeps him alive.'[63] To translate this into free indirect discourse would require not only the insertion of 'he thought', and the alteration of verbal tenses ('she sees' to 'she saw', 'keeps him' to 'kept him'), but also more radical surgery to make sense of the verbless phrases such as 'The nails, yes'. Bloom's abrupt shift of pronoun from 'they' to 'she' would be still harder to convey. The different techniques for rendering consciousness have different strengths and weaknesses.

Free indirect discourse was not a completely unprecedented development—there are instances to be found in Jane Austen's novels—but Woolf's contemporaries used it to portray forms of consciousness that deviated from the rational adult norms further than the minds portrayed in earlier novels. The consciousness of a child creates limitations which are both severe and readily identifiable: Joyce adopts a child's perspective in the opening pages of *A Portrait of the Artist as a Young Man*, and again briefly in *Ulysses* to convey the experience of a recently bereaved boy.[64] May Sinclair's *Mary Olivier: A Life* (1919) employs some of Joyce's strategies in its opening section, 'Infancy'. Though the perfect tense separates the narrator from the protagonist, the pronouns intermittently adopt her perspective: 'In the dark you could go tip-finger along the slender lashing flourishes of the ironwork'.[65] The childish and informal 'you', rather than the more adult and formal 'one', places us in Mary's position. However, Sinclair employs a vocabulary far wider than that of a child, resulting in phrases such as 'slender lashing flourishes'. Further to create the illusion of a child's perspective, Sinclair occasionally withholds the name of a familiar object and instead describes it: Mary's father drinks from 'a glass filled with some red stuff that was both dark and shining and had a queer, sharp smell'.[66] The reader is left to guess the identity of the substance, presumably wine or port. Similarly, Sinclair sometimes names the object, but provides a parallel description: 'You saw the sun for the first time, a red ball that hung by itself on the yellowish white sky. Mamma said, "Yes, of course it would fall if God wasn't there to hold it up in his hands." '67

Woolf's renditions of a child's consciousness in *To the Lighthouse* and *The Years* are comparable in technique, though not identical. A more particular comparison may be drawn between Sinclair's description of the sun and the descriptive speeches at the opening of *The Waves*: Mary Olivier's perception of the sun as a 'red ball' anticipates Neville's seeing it as a 'globe' (*W*, p. 5). The clearest difference is that Neville's utterance is not presented as free indirect discourse, but as direct speech. The wide vocabularies and regular grammar of the speakers at the opening of *The Waves* implies that they are adults, yet their unsophisticated, unconceptualized perceptions imply that they are infants; the contradiction is sharper than in Sinclair. Unlike Sinclair, Woolf does not allow her characters to reveal what Neville's 'globe' actually is: it could be the sun, the moon, or any globular thing. Moreover, in Woolf's account, parents are completely absent, and those adults who are mentioned are remote.

Not every experimental writer wished to depict the world as seen from within. Contemporary with the mode of internal monologue, and sometimes combined with it, was a mode of external description, often caricatural and satirical in intent. Whereas realist descriptions of external appearance imply that there are depths of personality and complexity beneath the appearance, these external descriptions in their most extreme form implied that there was nothing other than surface. Foremost among those who objected to internal monologue was the painter, novelist, and theorist of modern culture, Wyndham Lewis. He used his novel *Tarr* (1918; rev. 1928) to advance his ideas about art: Tarr argues that art goes wrong in trying to capture the living qualities of human beings; rather, 'deadness is the first condition of art'.[68] The second condition, 'absence of soul', is really an extension of the first; Tarr means that good art is not concerned with the living interior of its subjects, but their external forms. As a consequence, 'good art must have no inside'. Though Lewis was the fiercest polemicist for this mode of writing, a caricatural approach can be seen in the work of other contemporaries of Virginia Woolf, notably Aldous Huxley. Some of its techniques, such as the comparison of humans to animals and inanimate objects, and

characterization by reference to a catchphrase, are recognizable from
the work of Dickens.

GENRE: EDUCATION, MARRIAGE, AND ADULTERY

We cannot read fiction without expectations: expectations, most
obviously, about what might plausibly happen to the characters, and
what would be implausible; and, more subtly, expectations about the
novel's range of vocabulary and range of intellectual reference; and
about what the narrator (if there is one) can tell us about the characters. We derive these expectations from our experience of everyday
life, but also from our prior experience of fiction. In fact, much of
our experience of everyday life is not direct, but mediated through
anecdote and news story: it may not be 'fictional', but it is narrated.
We may not be fully conscious of these expectations when we pick
up a novel, but nevertheless they condition our interpretations.
'Genre' is an important conceptual tool for thinking about readerly
expectations: it allows us to group together works which share a
family resemblance, and which arouse similar expectations. A novel
that begins by introducing a young unmarried woman, and then two
or more eligible bachelors, will raise expectations of plots involving
love, misunderstanding, and some form of consummation. The
novel may confound these expectations by allowing her to choose a
career instead of love, but, such is the cultural dominance of the
courtship plot, the meaning of that choice is defined in relation to
our expectations; it is a deviation from the norm. However, the
'courtship plot' is only a convenient category for grouping novels; it
has no deeper or essential reality. It is important to grant primacy to
expectations, because for an experimental writer like Woolf, genre is
something to be broken and rearranged. Though her novels sometimes raise expectations at the large-scale level of plots, the kinds of
expectation that matter are sometimes more local, temporary, and
nameless.

Take, for example, in *The Waves*, Percival leaving London to work
in India in a military or administrative capacity. Thousands of young
men did likewise, and readers would certainly have had expectations
about the likely outcomes, but there is no convenient genre label,
'the departure of the colonial administrator'. We can reconstruct
these expectations only by reading more fiction (and anecdote, and
news story). For example, in Sinclair's *Mary Olivier*, Mary's brother

Mark goes to India.[69] What is omitted is as significant as what is included: the narrator does not think it necessary to explain why he is going; that would be commonly understood. Likewise, when he returns on leave after five years, the negatives tell us as much as any positive statements: 'Five years without any fighting'; 'No polo. No fighting. Only a mutiny in the battery once'.[70] The negatives imply that the clichéd expectations were of a life of combat and sport. Mark returns to India, and some years later a telegram arrives informing the family of his death: he has apparently died of a heart attack while larking about with the other soldiers, carrying a man on his back. Mary reflects: 'He should have died fighting . . . There was the Boer War and the Khyber Pass and Chitral and the Soudan. He had missed them all'.[71] Mary's expectations give us an insight into the reader's expectations. To some extent, they derive from Mark's individual qualities (he was one of the healthier men in the family), but they also derive from his generic quality as 'a man who departs for India'. The bathos of his death, like that of Percival in *The Waves*, derives from an expectation of a more 'heroic' death in battle.

Expectations are not purely a matter of plot; nor are they held only by the reader. In Rose Macaulay's *Potterism*, a novel set in 1914 to 1919, and published in May 1920, Jane Potter contemplates writing a novel. She is in her early twenties and she wishes at all costs to avoid the example of her mother, a middlebrow novelist, and of her father, a newspaper baron, whose paper the *Daily Haste* expresses reactionary opinions about women and the war. Jane considers the options: writing a 'sarcastic, rather cynical' novel; or 'a serious novel, dealing with social or political conditions'; or perhaps 'an impressionist novel, like Dorothy Richardson's'.[72] These categories need not be mutually exclusive, but Jane appears to believe that they are, and her believing it is a small piece of historical evidence about modes of writing and about readerly (and writerly) expectations. Presumably a 'serious novel' must be somewhat earnest in its seriousness, to an extent that excludes sarcasm and cynicism; these qualities resemble Woolf's description of John Galsworthy, a compassionate observer of 'social iniquity' ('Mr Bennett and Mrs Brown', in *EVW* iii. 386–7). Presumably an 'impressionist' novel is taken to be so private that it cannot encompass social concerns. One could call upon *Mrs Dalloway* as the living disproof of that assumption, but to do so is not to dismiss this evidence: rather, looking at Jane Potter's map of the world of fiction in 1920 gives us some sense of how innovative *Mrs Dalloway* was in 1925.

Of the established genres, that of the *Bildungsroman* or 'novel of education' was particularly important for Woolf and many of her contemporaries. The genre concerns a man's growth from childhood to maturity, and how he overcomes the barriers to the full realization of his individuality.[73] In the sub-genre of *Künstlerroman*, that self-realization takes the form of his becoming an artist. The genre can be traced back to Johann Wolfgang von Goethe's *Wilhelm Meisters Lehrjahre* (1794–6), translated as *Wilhelm Meister's Apprenticeship*, and to Wordsworth's *The Prelude*, with one of the most important immediate precedents for modernist writers being Samuel Butler's *The Way of all Flesh* (written 1873–84; published 1903). The most widely read *Bildungsromane* by male modernists are Lawrence's *Sons and Lovers* and Joyce's *A Portrait of the Artist as a Young Man*.

For writers who wished to portray the growth of a woman, the male orientation of the genre rendered it problematic. While the hostility of the father, a constraining environment, and inadequate schooling were all too familiar to women growing up in the late nineteenth century, the possibilities of escape were far more limited, and the narrative component of sexual encounters were unthinkable in their *Bildungsroman* form. Moreover, the forms of 'success' open to women were more restricted, with marriage overshadowing all other options. *The Voyage Out* can be seen as a female *Bildungsroman*, but, like George Eliot's *The Mill on the Floss* (1860) before it, one in which the growth of the young woman is frustrated by the lack of available options, and which can only end tragically. There were, of course, many more options available to a young woman than marriage or death, but there were very few fictional precedents available to Woolf. Woolf returned to the *Bildungsroman* form in *Jacob's Room*, but again gave it a tragic ending, and questioned many of its assumptions.[74]

The childhood and youth of young males were narrated more formulaically in the genre of 'public school novel'. The genre might seem of peripheral importance to a female experimental writer, but Woolf was deeply interested in the ways that the rituals of male education shape the ethos of public life, and the schooling of Bernard, Louis, and Neville forms a significant portion of *The Waves*. Woolf would have learned much about male public school life from her brothers, but she also recalled her father reading to her the founding text of the genre, Thomas Hughes's *Tom Brown's Schooldays* (1857) (*EVW* i. 127–8). Many later memoirists took Hughes's classic as a point of reference in describing their actual experience; later examples of the genre became a point of reference in discussions of the public school ethos.[75] Typical narrative elements include the first day at school, subsequent scenes of bullying, of cricket and 'football' (meaning rugby football), of a day spent wandering in the countryside, a portrait of the headmaster and other memorable teachers, and narratorial disquisitions on themes such as discipline and the public school spirit. The element of narratorial commentary means that the genre overlaps with non-fictional discussions of the public school system, such as J. G. Cotton Minchin's *Our Public Schools* (1901), an imperialist defence of them, or L. B. Pekin's criticism published by the Hogarth Press, *Public Schools: Their Failure and Reform* (1932). Readers of the public school section of *The Waves* would have recognized the rituals, if only from fictional representations. In a late example of the genre, Arnold Lunn's *The Harrovians* (1913), the central character's experience of his last day at school is itself filtered through fictional representations: 'he knew that the sadness of leaving Harrow had been worked to death in sermons, novels, and boy essays. He felt vaguely that he and the monitors around him were behaving like a chapter out of a school story. "The last sad words of farewell as they fell from the lips of the dead old Head!" '[76] Although the summary of public school life in *The Waves* is given in Louis's voice, he appears to be paraphrasing the speech of the 'great Doctor': 'Some will do this; others that. Some will not meet again. Neville, Bernard and I shall not meet here again. Life will divide us. But we have formed certain ties. Our boyish, our irresponsible years are over. But we have forged certain links. Above all, we have inherited traditions' (*W*, p. 45). The rhythm of thesis and antithesis, and the weighing of gains and losses, derive from the tradition of fictional speech days.

The genre of 'family saga' incorporates the element of intergenerational conflict from the *Bildungsroman*, but, typically, narrates it over a longer timescale, usually over several generations, and therefore with a less exclusive focus on a single protagonist. Though the genre had been anticipated by Anthony Trollope and other Victorian novelists, it was essentially an Edwardian invention. Another important influence was Émile Zola's Rougon-Macquart sequence of novels (1871–93), and the social Darwinist theory they embodied concerning the genetic inheritance of flaws and defects. However, the British family saga mixed this essentially pessimistic world view with a belief in the countervailing exercise of personal will-power. John Galsworthy's 'Forsyte Saga', a sequence of novels set among the urban professional classes, beginning with *The Man of Property* (1906), remains the classic example; there were also many single-volume sagas. D. H. Lawrence's *The Rainbow* incorporates some elements of the genre, though the social class it depicts is not typical. The theme of intergenerational conflict was vitally important to Woolf, and she adapted the genre in writing *The Years*, retaining from Galsworthy the upper middle-class social context, but shifting the focus onto the daughters of the family.

Marriage plots were frequently criticized by writers of intelligent fiction for being formulaic and distant from actual experience. In 1905, Woolf had noted the limitations of the popular novelist W. E. Norris, 'the type of writer who regards marriage and the events that precede it' as the legitimate material of a novel, and who makes 'marriage bells' the point at which we depart, 'in a state of mild felicity' (*EVW* i. 36). In 1918, reviewing Hugh Walpole's *The Green Mirror*, she remarked that 'with our more thoughtful writers' the 'family theme' had replaced the 'love theme' (*EVW* ii. 215). In 1906 E. M. Forster too had criticized the courtship plot for implying that marriage was 'an end'. For the early Victorian woman, marriage was regarded as 'a final event': 'beyond it, she was expected to find no new development, no new emotion'. For the 'woman of today' and her husband, 'The drama of all their problems, their developments, their mutual interaction, is all to come. And how can a novelist of today, knowing this, end his novel with a marriage?'[77] It was easier to ask the question in theory than to answer it in practice: Forster's *A Room with a View* (1908) follows the classical courtship plot, though his *Where Angels Fear to Tread* (1905) is closer to his prescription. Woolf was to answer Forster's question very clearly in her novels, but she was not the first to do so: the portrait of marriage that she presents in *To the Lighthouse*, and the glimpses of awkward mutual interaction that we see in *Mrs Dalloway*, have their precedents in earlier fiction. A significant part of George Eliot's *Middlemarch* (1870–1), for example, is concerned with Dorothea's growing disillusionment with Casaubon. *Middlemarch*, which Woolf famously praised as 'one of the few English novels written for grown up people', can be seen as a precocious transitional novel (*EVW* iv. 175–6). Jane Miller has contrasted the nineteenth-century narrative pattern, in which the heroine's *Bildungsroman* is subsumed into a courtship plot, with the narrative pattern of many early twentieth-century novels, in which the marriage is 'a kind of delayed *Bildungsroman*': the 'mature heroines grow and come to understand themselves only after they have confronted the limitations of marriage and maternity'.[78]

The 'new woman' fiction of the 1890s had also set a precedent, allowing female characters to be motivated by desires for something other than domestic or sexual fulfilment, even if those characters were often placed in narratives that punished them for deviating from the norm. The 'new woman' novel had declined after 1895, but from around 1905 there began to appear a class of fiction known as the 'sex novel', the 'sex problem novel', or the 'marriage problem novel', which reprised some of its themes; both Keating and Miller identify and summarize a large number of them.[79] Like the 'new woman' novel, it was motivated by the increased opportunities for women in education and employment, and by a public debate about the 'nature' of womanhood and marriage. Its characters often responded in ways that, by the canons of conventional fiction, appeared perverse. The imaginary novel read by Miss Allan in *The Voyage Out* (*Maternity* by Michael Jessop) appears to be an instance: it is surely 'not natural', complains Miss Allan, for a husband to leave his wife 'because she happens to be in love with [him]' (*VO*, p. 432). The genre's narrators were tempted to generalize and to present their characters as typical of the contemporary situation. The novel read by Hewet in *The Voyage Out* concludes with the narrator hoping that 'in the far future, when generations of men had struggled and failed, woman would be, indeed, what she now made a pretence of being—the friend and companion—not the enemy and parasite of man' (*VO*, p. 346). Comparable instances could be found in many of the marriage problem novels of the period. The genre was controversial, and reactions to it were often hostile: Woolf noted how in 1909–10 H. G. Wells's *Ann Veronica* had been compared to diphtheria and typhoid (*EVW* ii. 129–30).

For novelists investigating a marriage problem in fiction, there was a continuing temptation to resolve the problem with a traditional plot. Resolving the problems of one marriage by launching the heroine into a second remained a notable possibility. For example, M. P. Willcocks's *Wings of Desire* (1912) presents a woman, Sara Bellew, trapped in an unhappy marriage, her career as a concert pianist stifled by her husband. Although the novel includes brief contrasting narratives of other women, Willcocks can resolve Sara's problems only by having her elope with a more sympathetic man, thus reducing her novel to a 'fairy tale'.[80] Elinor Mordaunt's *The Park Wall* (1916), admired by Woolf for being distinctively modern, sees its heroine, Alice Ingpen, married in the first chapter (*EVW* ii. 42–4). However, the deceitfulness of her husband is so unalloyed that the complex 'mutual interaction' hoped for by Forster does not develop; the husband spends so much time gambling and drinking that there are few occasions for interaction after chapter 10. The narrator remarks that the 'trials and troubles of lovers' interest us, because they are full of possibilities, but not those of married couples. She dismisses the contemporary 'fashion' for stories beginning with marriage as 'an affectation of taste': the 'dull, sordid inevitability' of an unhappy marriage is not suitable for narrative.[81]

In the period 1900 to 1920, novelists increasingly resorted to open-ended narrative structures, underscoring the 'unresolved nature of the marriage problem itself'.[82] Indeed, one factor in the modernist abandonment of traditional forms of narrative may have been the realization that traditional plots embodied outdated and questionable ideas about marriage.[83] If fiction was to matter in the modern world, it had to find forms which would allow it to engage with modern modes of life.

There was one long-established plot that dealt with life beyond the wedding day: the adultery plot, in which the heroine must conceal a marital infidelity or premarital indiscretion. Its converse aspect is the plot of unknown parentage, in which hero or heroine discovers that he or she is the offspring of an extramarital affair. Both plots were close to exhaustion by the 1890s: the extent to which they had become familiar may be gauged by the way that Oscar Wilde had exploited them in his dramas *Lady Windermere's Fan* (1892) and *The Importance of Being Earnest* (1895). Nevertheless, they still provided the framework of many popular novels, and so had the power to create readerly expectations even where none were intended. The dual focus of *Mrs Dalloway*—first on Clarissa, then on Septimus—suggests that the narrative will reveal some connection between them. That Clarissa begins by reflecting on her past, and specifically on the time before her marriage, suggests, misleadingly, that the connection will be found in her past; the reader looking to substantiate this connection may associate Clarissa's 'Bourton' with the town of Bourton-on-the-Water, only 23 miles distant from Septimus's home town of Stroud. It seems possible that Septimus is Clarissa's illegitimate child, or that, like Jo the crossing sweeper in Dickens's *Bleak House*, he holds the key that connects diverse characters. The connection between Septimus and Clarissa is ultimately revealed to be indirect (via Sir William Bradshaw), and analogical; but by hinting at the more stereotypical plot, Woolf encourages the reader to look for connections, and to think about what, other than marriage, connects the diverse elements in society. For Dickens in *Bleak House*, the adultery plot served the larger purpose of surveying a complex intermeshing society; in writing *Mrs Dalloway* Woolf not only alluded to the classic adultery plot, but shared the mid-nineteenth-century ambition to survey the 'condition of England'.[84]

BIOGRAPHY: *JACOB'S ROOM* AND *ORLANDO*

Biography was an important genre during the period, and a particularly important one for Woolf, given her father's role as first editor of the *Dictionary of National Biography* (*DNB*). A significant proportion of Woolf's early reviewing work consisted of biographies and works in the 'life and letters' mode, a biographical narration framing long extracts from the subject's letters; Frederic Maitland's biography of Leslie Stephen was written in this mode. Victorian and early twentieth-century biographers had adopted a reverential attitude toward their subjects; the underlying assumption was that biographies set an example for future generations. In Portman's *Hugh Rendel*, when it is suggested that the schoolboy will go on to a career in the Indian Civil Service, his house master promises to lend him a life of John Nicholson, and some of the 'Rulers of India' series.[85] The *DNB* consisted of relatively short and authoritative biographies which made less use of quotation than the 'lives and letters' style. Nevertheless, it too was reverential. As a project it embodied Thomas Carlyle's notion that history consists of the biographies of great men, an essay topic that troubles Jacob Flanders (*JR*, p. 48). To Woolf the *DNB* represented an official history, one that excluded women and other 'eccentric' figures (*EVW* iii. 38–41).

   The approach taken by biographers changed significantly during Woolf's lifetime, not least because of the approach taken by Lytton Strachey in his *Eminent Victorians* (1918) and *Queen Victoria* (1921). The most immediate surprise presented by these volumes was their size: in the first of them, Strachey had examined the lives of four great Victorian figures in half the space that would traditionally have been given to one. His tone too was different, ironic and at times mocking. In his Preface to *Eminent Victorians*, Strachey character-ized the traditional 'two fat volumes' of biography: 'who does not know them, with their ill-digested masses of material, their slipshod style, their tone of tedious panegyric, their lamentable lack of selec-tion, of detachment, of design? They are as familiar as the *cortège* of the undertaker, and wear the same air of slow, funereal barbarism'.[86] Woolf had read each chapter of *Eminent Victorians* as it was written, and *Queen Victoria* on its appearance, Strachey having dedicated it to her. She responded with very full praise (*Letters*, ii. 465). In a 1927 review she summarized the changes in manner of biography:

the author's relation to his subject is different. He is no longer the serious and sympathetic companion, toiling even slavishly in the footsteps of his hero. Whether friend or enemy, admiring or critical, he is an equal. In any case, he preserves his freedom and his right to independent judgement. (*EVW* iv. 475)

Strachey's method was not in itself modernist, but, as one contemporary noted 'in reinstating biography as an art', he had drawn attention to the 'formlessness' of literature in general; like modernist novelists and poets, he wanted his chosen genre to be taken seriously as art.[87]

   What Woolf took from him was not the seriousness, but the mock-ery of earlier biography. This first becomes apparent in *Jacob's Room*, which, as well as being a parodic *Bildungsroman*, can be read as a parodic biography. To read it this way, one needs to think of it as having a biographer narrator who has been set the task of writing a standard two-volume biography of Jacob as a 'great man': his child-hood, his education at Cambridge, his youthful exploits, his mature achievements in some area of literature or statesmanship, his public recognition, his happy old age, and perhaps his late second flowering. The difficulty for the narrator is that Jacob does not live beyond his youthful exploits. His life cannot be accommodated in the traditional narrative outline. The narrator, embarrassed by this exception to the generic rule, attempts as best he can to narrate Jacob's life in the traditional manner, generally suppressing his knowledge of what is to come, and making of Jacob a generic figure of the promising young man. He has assembled the source materials needed to write a biography, but, lacking a crowning achievement, cannot make the materials cohere. As a biographer, he weighs the evidence provided by the Mudie-reading Mrs Norman—'One must do the best one can with her report' (*JR*, p. 37)—and of the equally unreliable Mrs Papworth: 'where an inquisitive old woman gets a name wrong, what chance is there that she will faithfully report an argument?' (p. 138). (I gender the narrator as male not only because of the implicit misogyny of these and other remarks; elsewhere, because of the use of free indirect discourse, it is not always possible to disentangle the narrator's misogyny from Jacob's.) As a biographer, he sometimes fills gaps in the documentary record with conjectures and with generic scene painting. Thus, in the description of Mrs Flanders looking at Scarborough, we are told that the seasonal changes in the view '*should have been* known to her': the narrator cannot be sure that they were (p. 17; emphasis added). Much of what follows seems to be derived from sources other than Mrs Flanders herself: 'It was observed how well the Corporation had laid out the flower-beds', we are told, but we are not told who made this observation (p. 18). Likewise, the description of young men at Cambridge is self-confessedly conjectural and generic: 'Behind the grey walls sat so many young men, some undoubtedly reading, magazines, shilling shockers no doubt; legs, perhaps, over the arms of chairs; smoking; sprawling over tables, and writing while their heads went round in a circle as the pen moved—simple young men, these, who would—but there is no need to think of them grown old' (pp. 54–5). Not only do 'perhaps' and 'undoubtedly' betray the process of conjecture, but the images derive from generic depictions of male student life. As well as filling in missing information, the narrator also suppresses knowledge: in the passage just quoted, the knowledge of what happens to the young men; elsewhere, the knowledge of what Jacob did in the late evening in Paris (p. 174). Though Woolf is mocking the generic qualities of Victorian biographers, her mockery has a serious purpose. Biography sets an example to young men, and that example leads Jacob to his death.

The mockery of biography in *Jacob's Room* is tentative, and intermittent, and mixed with other literary experiments. The mockery in *Orlando* is far more complete, and helps to illuminate the earlier novel, though Woolf does not work to a consistent plan. Woolf works for local effect, sometimes mocking biography by adopting its conventions to excess, at other times eliminating them and commenting on the elimination, and at other times doing both together. Thus, in the catalogue of Orlando's purchases (*O*, p. 105) the biographer-narrator begins to present the 'ill-digested masses of material' lamented by Strachey, but also comments on the tediousness of such catalogues. In the opening description of Orlando's youthful appearance, the narrator describes his eyes and forehead, but admits his reluctance at having 'to admit a thousand disagreeables which it is the aim of every good biographer to ignore' (p. 15). By commenting on the landscape at one point as being 'a simple English kind which needs no description' (pp. 178–9) the narrator implies that such descriptions are usually so generic as to add nothing to our knowledge.

Orlando almost became a victim of its own mockery: soon after publication, the Hogarth Press received reports that bookshops were insisting on shelving it not with novels, but with real biographies. 'I doubt therefore that we shall do more than cover expenses', lamented Woolf (*Diary*, iii. 198). *Orlando* is a very private document: it is both a love letter to Vita Sackville-West, and a continuation of Woolf's war of words with Logan Pearsall Smith. At the same time, however, it was a public one, saying things about sexuality, biography, and history that were accessible to all. Moreover, it was a commercial enterprise, as Woolf the publisher was only too aware. More than any of her works, it demonstrates the tension between 'the patron' and 'the crocus'.

CHAPTER 4

PHILOSOPHICAL QUESTIONS

[P]hilosophic words, if one has not been educated at a university, are apt to play one false. What is meant by 'reality'? It would seem to be something very erratic, very undependable—now to be found in a dusty road, now in a scrap of newspaper in the street, now a daffodil in the sun. (*ROO*, p. 143)

IN her fiction and in many of her essays Woolf engages with abstract philosophical questions, but her mode of engagement is not always what one might expect. She addresses questions of aesthetics, particularly whether the value of a work of art resides in its reproduction of the real world, or in its formal qualities of pattern and rhythm. She engages with the question of whether reality exists independently of human perception, and the related question of whether clock time or psychological time is the more real. She inquires into the nature of the self: whether an individual's sense of self is a fixed quality, or something endlessly variable according to their environmental and social context. She draws on philosophical debates about ethics, particularly the problem of defining 'the good', the ultimate goal of all good action and conduct.

A nineteenth-century novelist might have engaged with such questions by having characters or narrators reflect on past incidents or future choices. Woolf, however, disliked the idea of art being a vehicle for philosophical instruction, particularly moral instruction. She criticized the late Victorian novelist George Meredith for failing in this regard. Meredith's philosophy obtruded: 'when philosophy is not consumed in a novel, when we can underline this phrase with a pencil, and cut out that exhortation with a pair of scissors and paste the whole into a system, it is safe to say that there is something wrong with the philosophy or with the novel or with both' ('The Novels of George Meredith', in *CE* i. 230). For a novel to consume a philosophy, it must incorporate it into the depiction of character and incident; it must form part of a seamless whole. Woolf's philosophy often underlies her ways of writing fiction, and for this reason essays

such as that on Meredith offer valuable insights, making explicit
ideas which are assumed in the fiction. However, even then, it is not
always possible to pin down Woolf's beliefs. As several critics have
noted, she did not write 'novels of ideas' in the conventional sense.[1]
Her novels are as much concerned to ask questions as to define a
position.

Representation and Aesthetics: *To the Lighthouse*

Fortunately, Woolf does not always achieve the standards she set for
George Meredith: certainly there are places in *To the Lighthouse*
where one can underline phrases concerning the nature of representation and of artistic perception. By returning to the works of
Woolf's contemporaries—above all, those of Roger Fry (1866–
1934)—one can illuminate the assumptions within those phrases. In
To the Lighthouse, William Bankes asks Lily to explain why she has
drawn a triangular purple shape in one part of her painting. It
becomes clear that Bankes values art for its ability accurately to
reproduce recognizable scenes. The 'largest picture in his drawing-
room' depicts 'the cherry trees in blossom on the banks of the
Kennet' (*TL*, p. 73). The definite article is important here, as is the
specificity of the name: not any cherry trees by any river, but those
particular ones. Secondarily, though poignantly, the widower Bankes
values the painting because he had spent his honeymoon by the
Kennet: that is, he values the painting not for its intrinsic qualities as
a painting, but for its personal associations. Lily proposes a different
approach. As Lily explains, Bankes realizes that a mother and child,
'objects of universal veneration', and a long established subject of
Christian painting, might be 'reduced . . . to a purple shadow without irreverence'. The lack of representational clarity is less important than the harmony that Lily establishes between the colours and
forms on the canvas: 'if there, in that corner, it was bright, here, in
this, she felt the need of darkness' (p. 72). Indeed, by concentrating
on the purple triangle, Bankes is still not quite understanding the
painting: he is taking it to be a painting 'of' the mother and child, but
it is not 'of' them in his sense; Lily concedes that it might be a
'tribute' to them. She is less concerned with imitation than with 'the
relations of masses, of lights and shadows'; she needs to 'connect' a
mass on one side of the painting with a mass on the other (p. 73).

When she returns to her painting ten years later, Lily is still concerned with structure, with 'the problem of space' (p. 231), and with finding 'shape' in the midst of 'chaos' (p. 218). She is conscious of a duality in her paintings: a surface lightness of paint, 'feathery and evanescent', and a deeper, carefully considered form, 'clamped together with bolts of iron' (p. 231).

Underlying Lily's discussion with Bankes is the question of what makes painting valuable, as painting. This question had been addressed influentially by Roger Fry in his 'Essay on Aesthetics' (1909). Fry begins by quoting an eminent painter as saying that 'The art of painting is the art of imitating solid objects upon a flat surface by means of pigments'.[2] While the definition admirably demystifies the art, it still gives a central place to imitation. Fry comments that 'if imitation is the sole purpose of the graphic arts, it is surprising that the works of such arts are ever looked upon as more than curiosities'.[3] As a contemporary noted, 'the Imitation theory of art' had been 'killed by the invention of photography'.[4] If a photographer can produce a reliable imitation of a scene, then the artist must aim to produce something more than an imitation, or must break completely with the representational tradition. Fry concludes his essay with the idea that art is an expression of the imaginative life; it aims not at imitation of nature, but at creation. Fry's theory of art was *formalist*: it was more concerned with the formal qualities of a work of art than with what it represented. For Fry the French painter Paul Cézanne exemplified a mode of painting in which form was as significant as subject matter. Fry also valued Chinese art for its formal qualities, and this provides one explanation of Lily Briscoe's 'Chinese eyes' (*TL*, p. 212): they imply that she has a formalist artistic 'vision'.[5]

In the actual paintings of Woolf's contemporaries, Fry's emphasis on form corresponded to several different, but related practices. The majority of paintings by Vanessa Bell and Duncan Grant are representational, but even in these, the colour often has a 'flat' quality, with little differentiation of shade. Its flatness reminds the viewer of its existence as a pigment on a flat surface. In Duncan Grant's collages *Still Life* (*c.*1915) and *Interior at Gordon Square* (1915), the principle of flatness is taken further, producing a semi-abstract quality in the latter.[6] If one sees the painting without knowing its title, one is aware of the strong vertical lines purely as vertical lines before

Studland Beach,
c. 1912, by
Vanessa Bell

Self-portrait,
1928, by
Roger Fry

one can decode them as walls, doors, and window frames; one is aware of the bright blue triangle at the centre as a triangle, and not as a representation of an armchair. The title of Vanessa Bell's *Composition* (*c.*1914) gives no clues as to what it might represent, if anything.[7] The relative sizes of the two dark lines at the top right, and the blue square behind them, give some sense of pictorial depth, but this is denied by other elements in the composition. It is a pleasurable composition to contemplate not because of any representational content, but because of the balance of the blue-grey square in the top left and the ruddy-brown forms at the bottom of the composition; and because of the unbalancing, somewhat sinister effect of the dark verticals.

To the Lighthouse is concerned not only with Lily's justification of her practice, but also with her need to find the right state of mind for creation and for artistic vision. She resents Bankes's intrusion at first, because it breaks her concentration. When he asks her what she wished to make of the scene in front of them, she has to detach herself once more. In exploring Lily's psychology, Woolf echoes Fry, but does not follow his theory to the letter. For Fry 'imaginative life' is distinguished from 'everyday life' because of its detachment from action. In everyday perception, many details in the things we see escape our attention, because the mind naturally selects those elements which are most relevant to our continued survival.[8] Jane Harrison gives an extreme example: 'If we watch a friend drowning we do not note the exquisite curve made by his body as he falls into the water, nor the play of the sunlight on the ripples as he disappears below the surface'. We cannot: 'our whole being is centred on acting, on saving him'.[9] But, as Fry says, if we look at a representation of everyday life, or even look at everyday life framed and reflected in a mirror, we cease to be 'actors' involved in events, and become true 'spectators'; the scene acquires 'the visionary quality'.[10] We are free to notice not only individual details, but similarities between them: the way that one shape resembles another; the way one large 'mass' of colour is 'balanced' by another. The artist, unlike the photographer, is free to alter the relative positions and proportions of the elements in her painting, and thus to create a more pleasing form. (Those advancing such arguments gave little or no consideration to the extent to which photographers take care to frame their shots, and thus give 'form' to a composition.) The things we notice in a

painting are not wholly detached from everyday life: Fry is anxious
to explain that our aesthetic experience of 'mass' is governed by our
bodily experience of massive objects that resist movement.[11] Nevertheless, aesthetic detachment leaves us free to experience such
feelings regardless of practical considerations.

The state of mind which Lily needs to achieve is more complex.
In 'The Window' she apparently wishes to achieve detachment from
gender, 'subduing all her impressions as a woman to something
much more general' (*TL*, p. 73). In 'The Lighthouse', the situation
becomes more complex: at first, the problem is not to achieve
detachment, but in fact to feel some sense of 'attachment' to the
house; until this is achieved, everything seems 'aimless' and 'cha-
otic' (p. 198). Though she needs attachment in this regard, she also
needs to detach herself from Mr Ramsay, whose intrusiveness
threatens her creativity. After the expedition has departed, and she
settles down to her painting, Lily achieves the right degree of
detachment, subduing the 'impertinences and irrelevances' that had
distracted her (p. 213). She needs to escape 'gossip', 'living', and
'community with people' (p. 214). As Lily achieves the necessary
detachment, she reflects that the house has an 'unreal' appearance
(p. 258). She has freed herself from habitual, economical 'sight', and
has achieved a more 'vivid' vision (pp. 258–9). To paint, Lily needs
to be 'attached' to her feelings, but she needs also to be detached
from the people around her. Only then can she have her vision.

Woolf does not restrict the vocabulary of aesthetics to the painter
in the novel. The richness of *To the Lighthouse* derives from the way
that Woolf establishes similarities between Lily's concerns and those
of Mrs Ramsay. Mrs Ramsay's organization of the dinner party is an
expression of her imaginative life: she needs to connect disparate
elements, balancing one guest against another. At first she feels
unsuccessful: 'Nothing seemed to have merged. They all sat separate. And the whole of the effort of merging and flowing and creating
rested on her' (*TL*, p. 113). Later, though, when the candles are lit,
'the faces on both sides of the table were brought nearer by the
candle light, and composed . . . into a party round a table' (p. 131).
The crucial word is 'composed': the dinner party is an artistic composition. It is not until after Mrs Ramsay's death, though, that Lily
recognizes the analogies between their respective spheres of activity:
Mrs Ramsay 'brought together this and that and then this', diverse

elements formed into a pattern or composition, 'making of the moment something permanent' (pp. 217–18). By extending the language of aesthetics into the domestic sphere, and thus establishing analogies between Lily and Mrs Ramsay, Woolf is able to suggest that Lily has escaped the restrictions of Mrs Ramsay's life, and yet is simultaneously able to recover something valuable from Mrs Ramsay's life: it is not dismissed as 'merely' homemaking, but is recuperated as an expression of an otherwise frustrated imagination. Mrs Ramsay gave 'form' to the chaos of her family and friends.

Lily's ideas about her paintings, and Fry's ideas about aesthetics, help to illuminate the aims and assumptions of all Woolf's novels. Above all, they illuminate her disregard for the conventions of realist representation and plotting. She is as much concerned to create a satisfying formal *pattern* as to create recognizable characters. 'Pattern' is a key word for her: although she sometimes uses it dismissively, when referring to a visual decoration mechanically reproduced (the pattern that Lily sees on the tablecloth, for example), she also uses it more positively, to refer to a more vital and vibrant form, emerging from the chaos of perceptions and modern life. 'Pattern' in this second sense takes the place of traditional 'plot'. Woolf described her aims in writing *The Voyage Out* as being 'to give the feeling of a vast tumult of life, as various and disorderly as possible, which should be cut short for a moment by the death, and go on again—and the whole was to have a sort of pattern, and be somehow controlled' (*Letters*, ii. 82). Patterns emerge in her novels through repetitions of imagery and vocabulary, and less frequently, repetitions of action.

Perception and Reality

The questions that *To the Lighthouse* raises about artistic representation open out into larger questions about the nature of perception and reality. Mr Ramsay's philosophical work concerns, as his son puts it, 'Subject and object and the nature of reality'. When Lily Briscoe asks for a further explanation, Andrew asks her to 'Think of a kitchen table . . . when you're not there' (*TL*, p. 33). Andrew's suggestion alludes to the philosophical tradition of taking tables and chairs as typical real objects.[12] There are many philosophical questions about subjects and objects, but they tend to touch on two main themes: the question of how far an individual's personal, subjective knowledge of those objects is reliable; and, more searchingly, whether we have any grounds for saying that there are real objects 'out there' in the world beyond our perceptions. If we are in a room, and we can see and touch a table in front of us, then, if we can trust the evidence of our senses, we are warranted in believing that the table exists. But if we leave the room, or simply turn our backs on the table, on what basis can we assert that it still exists? It is true that tables are relatively durable and relatively static, but such relative tendencies do not give grounds for philosophical certainty. From such questions, some philosophers reached a position of subjective idealism: the world exists only as an idea in the mind of each of the subjects who perceive it. The philosophers who opposed such a position are often referred to as 'realists' or 'materialists'.

The philosophical questions raised by Andrew are not incidental pieces of local colour: they illuminate the whole of *To the Lighthouse*, and much else in Woolf's fiction. Through its presentation from a series of distinct perspectives, *To the Lighthouse* dramatizes questions about the limitations of knowledge. Moreover, in its concern with mortality and loss, the novel repeatedly presents people thinking about other people in their absence. The first concern is created simply by the dramatis personae and their different modes of thinking: the novel asks whether Mr Ramsay's way of thinking, systematic and linear, is more real and reliable than Lily's artistic way of thinking. Even Bankes, whose scientific work involves his taking 'sections' of potatoes (*TL*, p. 35), presumably to examine through a microscope, has his own distinct way of seeing, a scientific form of detachment that allows him to remain open to Lily's art in spite of his prejudices. The lighthouse is seen differently by different characters, and even by the same character at different times: some times it is 'a silvery, misty-looking tower', at others it is 'stark and straight' (p. 251). When James finally reaches the lighthouse, the reader might momentarily think that the novel has made a definitive statement: 'So it was like that, James thought, the Lighthouse one had seen across the bay all these years; it was a stark tower on a bare rock' (pp. 273–4). But it immediately becomes apparent that this is merely James's perspective, not the whole truth: 'It satisfied him. It confirmed some obscure feeling of his about his own character' (p. 274). James is not so much seeing the lighthouse, as seeing his own reflection; or, at least, he is selecting from the lighthouse those elements that confirm his own sense of self as stoical and manly. It is easier to recognize the limitations of James's knowledge because of Lily's reflections a few pages earlier on the impossibility of knowing Mrs Ramsay: no single perspective is sufficient, and even 'fifty pairs of eyes' are not sufficient to see her properly (p. 266).

The recollection of absent objects, and, more significantly, people, informs 'The Lighthouse'. Lily recalls the past so vividly that, even as she paints, 'she seemed to be sitting beside Mrs Ramsay on the beach' (*TL*, p. 231). Woolf's mode of presentation, through Lily's consciousness, makes it impossible to tell whether Mrs Ramsay's questions and her hunting for her spectacles are Lily's recollection of an actual incident, or her imagination of an ideal one. It is unclear whether there is a real Mrs Ramsay beyond Lily's imagination. To the extent that Lily is involuntarily haunted by Mrs Ramsay, there would seem to be; but to the extent that the dead are at the mercy of the living (pp. 235–6), it would seem that she is contained within consciousness. Lily also recalls her own phantom table, the one from the dinner party in 'The Window', and recalls the decisive moment when she moved the salt cellar. In the moment of recollection, such subjective memories are as vivid as present perceptions of the object-ive world. This is true not only for Lily: *To the Lighthouse* is scattered with recollected moments in the form of sharply visual, almost photographic scenes: for example Mr Ramsay noting a hen protecting her chicks (p. 30), or Paul and Minta repairing their broken-down car (p. 235). It is also scattered with small moments of revelation where the present forms the seeds of such memories. James, on the opening page, belongs to 'that great clan' which allows 'future prospects' to alter their perception of 'what is actually at hand' (p. 7). It is implied that he will remember the refrigerator in the catalogue for the rest of his life, because of his mother promising the journey to the lighthouse; his task of cutting out images from the catalogue is a paradigm for the way that memory works in the novel.

Philosophers attempted to reconcile the subjective and the object-ive elements of reality by arguing that language filters our percep-tions. There are real things 'out there', feeding our five senses with information, but the mind and body work selectively on this infor-mation. As one influential philosopher wrote, language takes the 'fluid' world and constructs a 'rigid', mosaic-like picture of it, 'at a sacrifice of exactness and fidelity but with a saving of tools and labor'.[13] Human beings have evolved so that they select those sense impressions which will help them to survive and reproduce, and ignore all others. The mind was commonly spoken of in metaphors and similes of sieves, nets, and meshes; in one popular account, it was like a machine used in a quarry for sorting different sizes of sands and gravel.[14] More sophisticated human activities, like the physical sciences, work on a similar basis, though they are not concerned with immediate survival. If concepts such as 'force' or 'energy' allow for a concise description of the world as observed by science, then they should be used, but, as Leslie Stephen argued, there is no reason to believe that 'force' or 'energy' have any real existence beyond our minds.[15]

The modernist experiments in the presentation of consciousness seen above in Chapter 3 share many assumptions with this area of philosophy. The consciousness of a child was interesting to both artists and philosophers because children were believed to lack sophisticated adult concepts, and so to be closer to the real world of sense impressions.[16] However, adults too sometimes lack the appropriate concepts: Lily cries, thinking of Mrs Ramsay, but she experiences the sensation of her eyes being 'full of a hot liquid' before she thinks of tears (*TL*, p. 242). Woolf, in one of the most frequently quoted passages from her essays, also sees reality as a chaos of sense impressions. Like a philosopher, she invites her reader to imagine 'an ordinary mind on an ordinary day': 'The mind receives a myriad impressions—trivial, fantastic, evanescent, or engraved with the sharpness of steel. From all sides they come, an incessant shower of innumerable atoms'. The essence of Woolf's argument is that if we free ourselves from the tyranny of fictional convention, and attend to the actual 'impressions', we can see that modern life does not follow the patterns employed by realist writers like Bennett, Galsworthy, and Wells: 'the accent falls differently from of old' ('Modern Fiction' (1925), in *EVW* iv. 160). Her argument is concerned primarily with the structural conventions of the novel, but it extends down to the conventions of language and the ways that it filters experience.

Her arguments about the novel also draw on a basic philosophical distinction. She terms Bennett, Galsworthy, and Wells 'materialists': they are excessively concerned with describing the surface details of the material world, and too little concerned with the internal details of consciousness. Philosophically, it would be usual to contrast materialism with idealism, but Woolf says that James Joyce, her typically modern writer, is more 'spiritual'. Her use of the word, with its suggestions of spiritualist religion, might suggest that a philosophical context is of little relevance, but she shares this terminology with her father. He had once contrasted materialism, 'the doctrine that matter is the ultimate reality', with what he called 'spiritualism', 'the doctrine that mind is the ultimate reality', that '[n]othing really exists except thought in its various modifications'.[17]

With her first piece of experimental fiction, 'The Mark on the Wall' (1917), Woolf began to create a fictional world in which the contents of consciousness are as important as the external objects. At the start of the piece, the narrator begins with her sensations of 'the fire', the 'yellow light', and the 'chrysanthemums', and infers from them that 'it must have been the winter time'. We know of the mark itself only through visual impressions: it was 'a small round mark, black upon the white wall, about six or seven inches above the mantelpiece' (*MW*, p. 3). The piece, with its immobile narrator, can scarcely be termed a story: it is as much an essay on the nature of reality, in which are weighed the values of impersonal, non-human reality, of social reality, and of imaginative reality. Woolf is interested in the difference between the 'real standard things' which stabilized Victorian social life, and those which attempt to stabilize the present day; but she is also interested in the continuities between the Victorian point of view and the 'masculine point of view' which dominates the present. The Victorians' supposed love of 'generalizations' recalls the Generals of the present: 'The Mark on the Wall' is explicitly a story set during wartime. Unlike the philosophers, Woolf does not argue a case, but what emerges from her narrator's reflections is a distinction between a hierarchical world, in which every sense impression is judged against normative standards, and a liberated but more private world, in which the norms have been destroyed.

The later piece 'Kew Gardens' (1919) also challenges established perspectives. It appears closer to conventional fiction in one respect, its use of a third-person narrator, but its sudden and unexplained changes in perspective, from a human scale to a snail's-eye view, suggest a connection with philosophical writing on the reliability of the senses. By imagining the world as it would be viewed by various non-human organisms, such as seagulls, parasites, *ephemerides*, or microbes, philosophical writers forced their readers to realize that their own seemingly natural concepts were merely mental constructs.[18] By presenting the '[b]rown cliffs with deep green lakes' that confront the snail, Woolf questions the importance of the humans who walk around the gardens; this questioning appears more explicitly in the contrast between the 'irregular and aimless movement' of the humans and the determination and 'definite goal' of the snail (*MW*, pp. 16, 13).

Clock Time and Psychological Time: *Mrs Dalloway*

Clocks and time take on a life of their own in *Mrs Dalloway*, and their way of marking time stands in contrast to the characters' experiences of time, particularly in its relation to memory. The contrast is not purely a philosophical one, because it has political implications, but a significant background for it may be found in the work of the French philosopher Henri Bergson (1859–1941). When Big Ben first chimes, in the opening paragraphs, it appears an almost benign presence, and certainly a revered one, if we can believe Clarissa's account of the 'hush' of 'solemnity' that greets it (*MD*, p. 4). However, as the novel unfolds, it creates an association between Big Ben and centralized authority. It also hints that clock time is an arbitrary measure, most obviously through its account of St Margaret's chiming a few minutes after Big Ben: 'like a hostess who comes into her drawing-room on the very stroke of the hour and finds her guests there already. I am not late. No, it is precisely half-past eleven, she says' (p. 42). Who, one is left asking, is to dictate the correct time? This theme is spelt out still more explicitly in the sketch of the clocks of Harley Street, '[s]hredding and slicing, dividing and subdividing' time, upholding 'authority', and echoing Sir William Bradshaw's advocacy of 'proportion' (p. 87). Woolf chose for her authoritarian doctor a surname that was synonymous with timekeeping: in the early twentieth century, a 'Bradshaw' was a railway timetable.

　Bergson argued that clock time falsifies the real nature of time, and that we need to distinguish between clock time (or *temps*) and 'psychological time' (or *durée*). He began by considering the paradoxes of the ancient Greek philosopher Zeno of Elia (fifth century BC).

For the present purposes, the paradox of Achilles and the tortoise will suffice. The renowned athlete Achilles has agreed to enter a race with a tortoise. To make the race more fair, Achilles has agreed that the tortoise be given a head start of, say, 10 metres. Common sense tells us that Achilles will quickly overtake the tortoise and win the race. Zeno, however, describes the race in a way which seems plausible, and yet which makes it appear that Achilles will never actually overtake his rival. By the time that Achilles has reached the tortoise's starting point, the tortoise has moved on to a new position. By the time that Achilles reaches that position, the tortoise has moved to a new position further on. One can repeat the process infinitely: it seems that the tortoise has always moved on, and Achilles can never reach him. Zeno's paradox poses a challenge to philosophers: what is wrong with his description of the race? It employs apparently everyday concepts, yet denies our everyday experience of time and movement.

Bergson argued that the paradox was due to the human intellect imposing a false conception of time onto its experience. By picturing the race of Achilles and the tortoise as if it were a series of photographs, Zeno is failing to understand the real nature of time and movement. He is making a continuous phenomenon into a series of discontinuous moments, just as a cinema film does. When we speak of something happening 'at' a certain time, we are imagining times as if they were places. We are 'spatializing' time. A cinema film does this quite literally: on the celluloid one frame is spatially adjacent to the next. A clock likewise divides the period of twelve hours into physically distinct segments, '[s]hredding and slicing', as Woolf would have it.

Bergson's idea of a personal, psychological time which was more real than publicly agreed clock time was attractive to many novelists. It seemed to endorse the idea of a private consciousness which was free of the constraints and conventions of a mechanized, regimented mass society. The central concepts of Bergson's philosophy did not demand any knowledge of technical philosophical terms. In May Sinclair's *Mary Olivier*, the young Mary thinks about the continuity of time for herself, without any guidance from Bergson, though we may be confident that her author was not so innocent: 'You couldn't really tell when the twenty-third [hour] ended and the twenty-fourth began; because when you counted sixty minutes for the hour and sixty seconds for the minute there was still the half second and the half of that, and so on for ever and ever'.[19]

There is little critical consensus about the extent to which Woolf was influenced by Bergson, in part because it is unclear to what extent she was familiar with his ideas.[20] In 1932, in response to an enquiry, Virginia Woolf said that she had 'never read Bergson' (*Letters*, v. 91), and after her death Leonard Woolf denied that he had influenced her work.[21] However, it is not impossible that she was familiar with Bergson's ideas through popular accounts or through conversations. Jane Harrison later recalled that the experience of discovering Bergson was one shared 'by every thinking man in Europe' in the pre-war period.[22] 'Man' here is apparently inclusive of women; indeed, many of Bergson's ideas appealed to feminists and suffragists in the pre-war period.[23] Following the success of Bergson's public lectures at University College in October 1911, there had appeared many non-specialist articles and books on his work, including one by Sydney Waterlow, Woolf's one-time suitor. Certainly Woolf attended a more specialist paper on Bergson by Karin Costelloe (later her sister-in-law) on 3 February 1913.[24]

As well as hinting at the Bergsonian concepts of *temps* and *durée* in *Mrs Dalloway*, Woolf introduces similar ideas into several other novels. Towards the end of *Orlando*, as the protagonist tries to deal with her complex accumulation of memories, the narrator discusses the concept of time. Picking up a handbag, Orlando recalls the 'bumboat woman' from the Jacobean era; stepping out into Oxford Street, she recalls the sights, sounds, and tastes of Turkey, India, and Persia (*O*, pp. 290–1). The narrator claims that there are 'sixty or seventy different times' beating simultaneously 'in every normal human system'. Some people manage to synchronize them, so that 'when eleven strikes, all the rest chime in unison'. Clearly Woolf treats systematic philosophy ironically and mockingly: the figures of sixty and seventy are plainly arbitrary, each indicating the arbitrariness of the other. Nevertheless, alongside the ironic treatment is a serious proposition, that clock time and calendar time do not tell the whole truth about time as humans experience it. Rare is the person who can synchronize their sixty or seventy internal times with the clock striking eleven; 'The true length of a person's life, whatever the *Dictionary of National Biography* may say, is always a matter of dispute' (*O*, p. 291).

Woolf also attempts to convey the discrepancy between *temps* and *durée* in the form of her writing, so that we not only apprehend it intellectually, as a concept advanced by the narrator, but also experience it as readers. Clocks do not necessarily appear explicitly: often the distinction of *temps* and *durée* manifests itself as a distinction between the life of the body and the life of the mind; the body, being material, must conform to clock time, while the mind escapes it. Mary Ann Gillies has argued that Woolf's attempt to convey intense 'moments of being' is, in effect, an attempt to convey pure moments of Bergsonian *durée*.[25] The phrase 'moment of being' is one which Woolf expounds in her autobiographical 'Sketch of the Past': they are moments of life lived with great vividness, and particularly moments of minor revelation. They prove to Woolf 'that one's life is not confined to one's body and what one says or does' (*MB*, pp. 83–6). Certainly in Woolf's narratives such moments are often contrasted with everyday physical reality, but they are not the only contrasting element.

Woolf's exploration of psychological time begins with her early sketch 'The Mark on the Wall'. It conveys a set of thought associations which, we can imagine, may have occupied no more than a few seconds. The contrast between psychological time and clock time is established in part by the contrast between time required to read the piece, and the time it conveys. The contrast is moreover hinted at by the tapping of a tree branch on the window pane (a natural equivalent for the ticking of a clock), and by the change of pace that occurs when the narrator's reverie is interrupted.

There are more developed instances in *To the Lighthouse*. Woolf creates a sense of the duality of forms of time, using dialogue and descriptive writing to mark clock time in the material world, but interpolating these descriptions with the characters' internal thought processes. Thus, in conventional speech, and a conventional novel, the opening conversational exchange might take place quite rapidly:

'Yes, of course, if it's fine tomorrow,' said Mrs Ramsay to her son. 'But you'll have to be up with the lark,' she added.

'But,' said Mr Ramsay, stopping in front of the drawing-room window, 'it won't be fine.'

'But it may be fine—I expect it will be fine,' said Mrs Ramsay, making some little twist of the reddish brown stocking she was knitting, impatiently.

'It's due west,' said the atheist Tansley, holding his bony fingers spread so that the wind blew through them.

'Nonsense,' said Mrs Ramsay, with great severity. (adapted from *TL*, pp. 7–10)

Between the lines of dialogue, Woolf interpolates the thoughts of the main characters. James's thoughts in particular have the appearance of an instantaneous revelation, one that endows the pictures in the mail-order catalogue with 'heavenly bliss' (p. 7). Later in the same novel, Mrs Ramsay asks whether Nancy had gone to the beach with Paul, Minta, and Andrew (p. 100). There is no indication that Prue paused for any time before replying in the affirmative (p. 107), but within this instant Woolf interpolates a long description of the expedition to the beach.

Just before this section, there is an instance of the duality of time in which a moment of being is contrasted with material reality. Lily and Mr Bankes are on the lawn talking, while Prue plays with a ball, and Mr and Mrs Ramsay look on. Mr Bankes's question is interrupted by the sudden image of the Ramsays: 'So that is marriage, Lily thought, a man and a woman looking at a girl throwing a ball. That is what Mrs Ramsay tried to tell me the other night' (*TL*, pp. 98–9). A narratorial voice goes on to describe the process whereby an ordinary scene can become 'symbolical'. While this process lasts, thinks Lily, for 'one moment, there was a sense of things having been blown apart, of space, of irresponsibility as the ball soared high' (p. 99). Conventional time, as measured by the time it would take for the ball to return, appears to have been suspended. When Prue catches the returning ball, 'the spell' is broken (p. 100). The scene not only illustrates Woolf's technique, but might be taken as a symbol of the narrative juggling at which Woolf is so adept: throwing a conventional narrative ball high into the air—one line of dialogue, for example—she undertakes a more detailed psychological description, before catching the returning ball, and completing the conventional narrative.

Bergson and Multiple Selves: *Mrs Dalloway* and *The Waves*

Throughout her novels, Woolf is aware that each individual contains several distinct selves. At times Sigmund Freud's distinction between the conscious and the unconscious (the ego and the id) comes into play: for example, in James's murderous rage against his father in the opening pages of *To the Lighthouse*. However, elsewhere the different selves are distinguished by other means, and these are better contextualized by reference to Bergson. For example, in *Mrs Dalloway*, Clarissa sees herself in her dressing-table mirror and feels 'an imperceptible contraction'. This contraction has its visible equivalent in her pursed lips:

She pursed her lips when she looked in the glass. It was to give her face point. That was her self—pointed; dart-like; definite. That was her self when some effort, some call on her to be her self, drew the parts together, she alone knew how different, how incompatible and composed so for the world only into one centre, one diamond (*MD*, pp. 31–2)

The distinction she draws between her private and public selves develops her earlier reflections about being both 'Clarissa' and 'Mrs Richard Dalloway' (p. 9); the idea of composing the disparate elements of the self into a unity is an artistic question that anticipates Mrs Ramsay's later composition of the unified dinner party.

Woolf had explored the same idea in relation to herself, in 1922, as she was beginning work on *Mrs Dalloway*. Her working routine had been interrupted by a visit from Sydney Waterlow, and she needed to ease her way back into writing. She distinguishes between being 'very, very concentrated, all at one point' (a phrase which anticipates Clarissa's 'pointed' self), and having to draw on 'the scattered parts of one's character'. She also distinguishes between the sometimes artificial role of 'Virginia', and the mode of being 'merely a sensibility' when she is writing (*Diary*, ii. 193). It may seem that Woolf was using her diary to invent ideas of the self which she would later employ more confidently in her novels. However, she may have been not so much inventing as recollecting.

Bergson was understood by many to have championed 'intuition' at the expense of 'intellect': intellect was the bad faculty, unnaturally distorting time into a spatialized form. However, he conceded that intellect was a valuable mode of consciousness: although it sliced reality into somewhat arbitrary segments, its doing so allowed the human organism to manipulate its environment and so survive. Intellect and intuition each have their uses. Sydney Waterlow's 1912 exposition particularly emphasized Bergson's doctrine 'that in each of us there are two different selves, one which we reach by deep introspection, and another, more superficial, which is its "spatial representation" '.[26] Unlike the two forms of time, which are absolutely distinct, the two selves are opposite ends of a sliding scale:

At one end of the scale is the state of things that occurs when I react to an imminent danger, as to a sudden blow threatening my eye. Here there is no memory but a close approximation to pure perception; my mental life is narrowed down to a point and consists solely of a reflex action caused by my brain-process. . . . At the other end of the scale is the diffused mental state which, when we merely remember or are sunk in reverie, includes no perception of a present object; and, by a process which he [Bergson] describes as one of dilatation and contraction, our minds range through all the stages between these two extremes.[27]

An organism whose mental life consisted only of reflex actions could never form a larger picture of the universe: it would be almost an automaton. Conversely an organism whose mental life consisted solely of reverie would be destroyed by the first 'sudden blow' that struck it. The two mental states are complementary. The relation of the body to the mind, argues Bergson, is not what we usually imagine. The mind needs the body not in order to provide it with sense data, but in order to filter out perceptions: 'what needs explanation is not why we perceive anything, but rather why we do not in practice perceive everything'; 'the function of the body is to limit the life of the mind, and that with a view to action'.[28] The body, to use an image which Woolf favoured, is a hard shell covering a vulnerable, soft interior.

Sitting in front of her mirror, Clarissa suddenly contracts from a diffused mental state to the more pointed form of being 'Mrs Dalloway'. While her role as a society hostess is not, for her, a matter of life and death, it nevertheless requires her to focus sharply on the external world, at the expense of the inner person. Putting this passage in the context of Waterlow's account of Bergson allows us to recognize the sense in which 'Mrs Richard Dalloway' is an automaton, operating simply by reflex.

Woolf explores similar ideas in *The Waves*. Walking through London, Bernard reflects on the relation between the two selves, contrasting a diffuse, reflective state of mind with a more action-oriented one:

I will let myself be carried on by the general impulse. The surface of my mind slips along like a pale-grey stream reflecting what passes. I cannot remember my past, my nose, or the colour of my eyes, or what my general opinion of myself is. Only in moments of emergency, at a crossing, at a kerb, the wish to preserve my body springs out and seizes me and stops me, here, before this omnibus. We insist, it seems, on living. (*W*, pp. 92–3)

Similarly as the friends sit in the restaurant waiting for Percival, Neville sees a knife-blade simply as 'a flash of light' and not as 'a thing to cut with' (p. 97). Were such a state of detached contemplation to persist, Neville would starve, but when Percival arrives, knives are restored to their practical function (p. 100). Percival has this effect either because, as a matter of manners, the group would not begin eating until all seven members had arrived, or, more symbolically, because Percival is a man of action, and his influence transforms people's perceptions.

Language also channels and focuses perceptions: linguistic categories subdivide reality just as clock time subdivides *durée*. The characters in *The Waves* are highly self-conscious about the attractions and limitations of language. Bernard's facility with 'phrase-making' is seen both as a strength and a limitation. During the farewell meal with Percival, Bernard asks what deep and shared emotion has brought the group together. It might be convenient to call the emotion 'love', but 'love' is 'too small and particular a name'. Their emotions have a greater 'width' and 'spread' (*W*, pp. 103–4). Bernard implies that language would contract their emotions. Similarly, Neville, sitting by a river in the autumn sunlight, asks 'Why discriminate?' To name what he is experiencing in the present moment would be to change it (p. 65). Such processes can also apply to other people: at one point, Bernard expresses irritation at being 'contracted' into a 'single being' by Neville, whose hard, dry intellect has undermined his pretentions to complexity (pp. 71–2). Likewise Neville, echoing Mrs Richard Dalloway, resents the way that he appears to be 'merely "Neville" ', when to himself he feels immense and immeasurable (p. 178).

The theme of expansion and contraction is important not only to several of the individual characters, but also to the group as a whole. Their oscillations between unity and separateness provide the novel with its distinctive narrative pattern, and provide one of many possible explanations of the title: *The Waves* concerns the rhythmical gathering together and breaking apart of the group. When an individual contracts into him- or herself, he or she finds it more difficult to join with the rest of the group. When the group first reunite at Hampton Court, Neville remarks that the 'edges of meeting are still sharp'; there is always someone who refuses to submerge his or her own identity (*W*, p. 177). As the edges are smoothed away, the group itself can contract into a unity. Woolf frequently uses 'globe' and its cognates in *The Waves*, as one way of trying to describe that unity. She even, unusually, employs 'globe' as a verb: near the end of the farewell meal, Louis wishes to prolong 'the thing that we have made, that globes itself here'; Bernard regrets that ideas 'break a thousand times for once that they globe themselves entire' (pp. 119, 129). ('Breaking' again recalls the omnipresent metaphor of waves gathering and dispersing.)

Percival, while he is alive, greatly helps the group focus itself. In the restaurant, once he has arrived, the group relax and lose their edges. Their senses widen, and they become receptive to 'far-away sounds' (*W*, p. 110). Objects in the external world blur into a single 'roar'; all sounds are 'churned into one sound' (p. 111). In this state of group unity, attempts at self-definition ('to say, "I am this, I am that" ') are false (p. 112). However, Percival is not essential. Indeed, the novel's philosophical concerns with individual and collective consciousness are also political themes: with the death of Percival, the six remaining friends must learn to live without a leader.

Time too in *The Waves* follows patterns of dilation and contraction: it is often imaged as gathering to a drop, gradually, and then abruptly falling away. Bernard's recollection of a long conversation with Neville brings together a Bergsonian idea of time with the novel's more dominant theme of expansion and contraction. In Bernard's account of their conversation, the two were relaxed and intimate, immersed in each other's ideas. Then, suddenly, they heard 'a clock tick', and their state of unity and state of consciousness changed:

We who had been immersed in this world became aware of another. It is painful. It was Neville who changed our time. He, who had been thinking with the unlimited time of the mind . . . poked the fire and began to live by that other clock which marks the approach of a particular person. The wide and dignified sweep of his mind contracted. He became on the alert. (*W*, p. 228)

Things become 'definite' and 'external'. Neville, it would appear, is expecting another visitor. Their intimacy is lost, and Bernard leaves.

Here, the 'sudden blow threatening the eye' of which Waterlow had written becomes something more subtle: the intrusion of the external world into the private space that the two men had created for each other, and the intrusion of clock time, as the outside world's measure of publicly agreed time. The clocks of Harley Street have become something less grotesque, but equally painful in the way they intrude on personal relations, dividing the united being of Bernard and Neville into its component parts.

Alternatives to Plot: *To the Lighthouse* and *The Waves*

For many readers, one of the more disconcerting characteristics of Woolf's approach to fiction is her apparent lack of interest in incidents, actions, and moral choices. As the philosopher Jaako Hintikka has remarked, her fiction is less concerned with 'our duties and values', and more with 'rather basic metaphysical and epistemological themes'.[29] In their lack of interest in duties and values, her novels contrast sharply with the 'great tradition' defined by F. R. Leavis. Leavis's 'tradition' consists of Jane Austen, George Eliot, Henry James, and Joseph Conrad, writers whose mastery of literary form incorporates 'moral seriousness'. Leavis does not define 'moral seriousness' or how it ought to manifest itself, but the novels included in his tradition are characterized by a psychological realism that allows the novelist to create believable characters who are 'moral agent[s]'; as moral agents they must necessarily make moral choices, albeit choices constrained by circumstances.[30] This definition applies most clearly to Leavis's criticism of Eliot and James; less so in relation to Austen and Conrad. The pivotal moments of moral reflection and moral choice to be found in Eliot and James are generally absent from Woolf's novels. So too are the choices of marital partner that one finds in courtship narratives, which, in their more elevated forms, are also moral choices about the kind of life the heroine envisages for herself. The climactic moment of *Night and Day* (chapter 31) is the closest that Woolf comes to the tradition, echoing Dorothea's climactic choice in Eliot's *Middlemarch* (chapter 80). Lily Briscoe's struggle with the persistent influence of Mrs Ramsay echoes it more faintly: the obvious difference from earlier novels is that her decision has no obvious consequences for any of the living characters.

Woolf, like many of her Bloomsbury contemporaries, was familiar with the work of the philosopher G. E. Moore (1873–1958), and his idea of ethics sheds light on Woolf's approach to moral questions in her novels. In everyday English 'ethics' denotes the principles of conduct in ordinary life or some specialized sphere of it. In his *Principia Ethica* (1903), Moore defined it rather differently: the distinctive quality of the discipline 'Ethics' was not the investigation of 'human conduct' or actions, but the investigation of 'the term "good" ', and its opposite 'bad'.[31] Clearly the term 'good' can apply to more than conduct alone; if we were to examine conduct alone in order to clarify our understanding of 'good', we would achieve only a limited understanding.[32] (As we shall see, Woolf's own insistent questioning of common assumptions shares something with Moore's tenacious interest in the definition of terms.) An examination of conduct is inadequate because we must distinguish between means to an end, and ends in themselves. Good actions are merely means to an end; 'good' is the end in itself. Good actions are not worthy of philosophical attention, because an action which might have a good effect in 'one particular age and state of society' might not have the same effect in another.[33] Moore did not altogether exclude questions of conduct—the fifth chapter of *Principia Ethica* was titled 'Ethics in Relation to Conduct'—but, as John Maynard Keynes recalled in 1938, Bloomsbury read Moore selectively: it tended to overlook this chapter and concentrate on the sixth and final chapter, 'The Ideal'.[34]

In contextualizing Woolf's work, there is a danger of assimilating her to a 'Bloomsbury' with which she was not always sympathetic. We know that Moore influenced many male members of Bloomsbury, through their membership, at Cambridge, of the select intellectual society known as 'the Apostles': Moore had become a member in 1894.[35] This would not in itself make Moore's work a relevant context for Woolf's, but there is evidence that she soon became acquainted with it. It is likely that the *Principia Ethica* lay behind her discussions of 'the nature of good' with Clive Bell in March 1905; it is certain that, at Bell's suggestion, she read the book itself in August 1908.[36] She later depicted Helen Ambrose reading it in *The Voyage Out*; she did not name it, but the passage quoted by Richard Dalloway is distinctively Moorean (*VO*, pp. 77–8).[37]

Rather than depict moral choices leading to good (or bad) actions, Woolf attempts to enable her readers to experience the idea of good in itself. Woolf's depictions of groups often show them achieving what Moore would term an 'organic unity', in which the whole is more than the sum of the parts. Bernard articulates what it means to be part of an organic unity at the start of the restaurant scene, just after he has rejected 'love' as an adequate description of the group's emotion. The 'red carnation' in the vase, says Bernard, was 'a single flower as we sat here waiting', but now the group has become unified, it is 'a seven-sided flower, many-petalled, red, puce, purple-shaded, stiff with silver-tinted leaves—a whole flower to which every eye brings its own contribution' (*W*, p. 104). Each contribution is valuable in itself, but the whole is more valuable than the sum of its parts. The scepticism about language in *The Waves*, discussed earlier, arises because language cannot articulate the sense of wholeness that the friends feel.

In the final chapter of *Principia Ethica*, Moore defined his ideal of the good as consisting of certain states of consciousness: 'By far the most valuable things, which we know or can imagine, are certain states of consciousness, which may be roughly described as the pleasures of human intercourse and the enjoyment of beautiful objects'.[38] These states of consciousness consisted of organic unities. Take our consciousness of a beautiful object: the object on its own, if no one is conscious of it, 'has comparatively little value, and is commonly held to have none at all'.[39] The other part of the state, consciousness, is also of little value on its own: indeed, it is difficult to imagine consciousness in itself, as consciousness is always consciousness *of* something. The value of this state of consciousness cannot, therefore, derive from simple addition: the difference in value must be attributed to the organic unity of the two elements. Moreover, the enjoyment of beautiful objects is complex because a full response (in Moore's opinion) includes both an emotional and a cognitive element: either on its own is comparatively worthless. The same is true of the pleasures of 'human intercourse' and 'personal affection': in Moore's ideal form of human relationship, one appreciates the 'mental qualities' of one's fellow human, but simultaneously one appreciates 'the appropriate *corporeal* expression of the mental qualities in question'.[40]

It is worthwhile reconsidering Bernard and Neville's intimate conversation in this light. The materials of their conversation have, in Bernard's account, little value in themselves: he has 'a vast

accumulation of unrecorded matter' in his head, and occasionally he
will 'break off a lump': it may be 'Shakespeare' (perhaps a token of
value), but, less promisingly, it may be 'some old woman called
Peck' (*W*, p. 227). The 'lumps' of small talk that Bernard and
Neville bring to the conversation are not valuable in themselves: it is
the process of sharing, and of setting each 'in a better light' (p. 228)
that is valuable. In Keynes's summary of Moore, 'Nothing mattered
except states of mind . . . These states of mind were not associated
with action or achievement or with consequences. They consisted
in timeless, passionate states of contemplation and communion,
largely unattached to "before" and "after" '.[41] Bernard and Neville
achieve such a state of mind, but when the clock ticks, the idea of
time reasserts itself. In this scene Woolf combines Moorean
and Bergsonian ideas about states of consciousness and moments of
transition between them.

Woolf's novels often appear to raise questions without providing
answers, either through a narrative voice or the voice of a character.
This quality has seemed a weakness to those who wish to obtain
some sort of positive message from a novel, and as a strength to those
who like to reach their own conclusions. Woolf's questioning
approach is in itself philosophical, and resembles the characteristic
methods of Moore and his generation of Cambridge philosophers.
Moore placed great value on analysis and definition. Most of the
'difficulties and disagreements' in philosophy, he wrote, were due to
a 'very simple cause': 'the attempt to answer questions, without first
discovering precisely *what* question it is which you desire to answer'.
The work of 'analysis and distinction' was an essential preliminary to
answering any question.[42] As Keynes recalled, ' "What *exactly* do
you mean?" was the phrase most frequently on our lips. If it
appeared under cross-examination that you did not mean *exactly*
anything, you lay under a strong suspicion of meaning nothing
whatever'.[43]

Woolf quickly absorbed this mental discipline. In a letter to Clive
Bell, written as she was nearing the end of *Principia Ethica*, she
adopts a distinctively Moorean approach: 'You ask me whether I like
your letters. In what sense do you mean, I wonder?' Having analysed
the differences in their letter–writing modes, she returns to the matter of defining the question: 'But I tremble as I write! After all, you
may have meant me to answer quite a different question. I often

think that we are most unlike in the values we attach to things; you will take seriously what is frivolous to me, and vice versa' (*Letters*, i. 361, 362).

Such a concern with precision informs the following fragment of dialogue in 'Kew Gardens':

> 'Lucky it isn't Friday,' he observed.
> 'Why? D'you believe in luck?'
> 'They make you pay sixpence on Friday.'
> 'What's sixpence anyway? Isn't it worth sixpence?'
> 'What's "it"—what do you mean by "it"?'
> 'O anything—I mean—you know what I mean.' (*MW*, p. 15)

The second speaker takes the idiom of the first one literally, and implicitly criticizes his irrational belief in 'luck'. The first speaker retaliates in an equally Moorean manner by demanding a definition of 'it'. The 'it' which the second speaker refuses to define is presumably the pleasure of walking in the gardens. Underlying this exchange is Moore's most fundamental question, 'What is the good?' Is 'it', the experience of walking in the gardens, good in itself, or good merely as a means to an end?

Although in this extract Woolf appears to have absorbed Moore's characteristic question of 'what exactly', she also keeps her distance from it: the concern with definition belongs to the characters, not to the author; it manifests itself in an ill-tempered, pedantic combativeness. It may be that this habit of mind made only a negative contribution, ensuring, as Leonard Woolf suggested, the absence of 'humbug' from Virginia's novels.[44] To see whether the question of definition made a more positive contribution to the novels, we would need to think of them as doubly interrogative: asking questions, and then asking further questions about the terms of the question. For example, *Mrs Dalloway* may be taken as asking the question 'Is the war over?', and then asking 'What *exactly* do you mean by "over"?' The question is hinted at in the opening pages:

For it was the middle of June. The War was over, except for some one like Mrs Foxcroft at the Embassy last night eating her heart out because that nice boy was killed and now the old Manor House must go to a cousin; or Lady Bexborough who opened a bazaar, they said, with the telegram in her hand, John, her favourite, killed; but it was over; thank Heaven—over. (*MD*, p. 4)

The logical turn—'except'—makes the reader double back and ask what 'over' really means. We are returned to a Bergsonian question of whether time is continuous or discontinuous. It is not an abstract philosophical issue, but one of human importance to Septimus, for whom the war is not over.

To the Lighthouse also makes use of such interrogatives. A concise and localized example occurs in Lily's discussion with Mr Bankes. 'But the picture was not of them, she said. Or, not in his sense' (*TL*, p. 72). The underlying questions here are, first, 'Is this a picture of Mrs Ramsay and James?', and secondly, 'What *exactly* do you mean by "of"?' Is the word meant in the sense understood by mimetic art, or by post-Impressionist art? The interrogative mode goes more deeply into the novel's concern: the novel's implicit question is hinted at by Mrs Ramsay's explicit one, 'what have I done with my life?' (p. 112). The question also preoccupies Mr Ramsay, who wonders what will happen to his work and to his reputation after his death, and who also thinks of his children as 'a good bit of work' (pp. 50, 94). Their questions lead the reader to ask, 'What exactly do you mean by "doing"?', or perhaps 'What exactly do you mean by "achievement"?' Should we accept Mr Ramsay's values, and believe the writing of books to be significant, or should we accept Mrs Ramsay's, and take the raising of children and the making of marriages to be the more important? Weighing Lily's values against Mrs Ramsay's, should we take the achievement of a perfect and memorable evening to be more significant than that of a canvas which may well be ignored or destroyed? Woolf asks a question about 'the good', but provides no direct answers.

CHAPTER 5

SOCIETY, INDIVIDUALS, AND CHOICES

IN 1961, the chapter on Woolf in a guide to modern literature was subtitled 'The Theory and Practice of Fiction': it emphasized her formal experimentation at the expense of her thematic interests. It summarized *Mrs Dalloway* as if it were primarily the story of Clarissa and Peter; Septimus's narrative was dismissed as a 'macabre . . . episode'.[1] More recent accounts have given Septimus far greater centrality, but it would be possible to overcompensate: foregrounding Septimus makes the novel more obviously a polemical novel, addressing the contemporary question of the social conditions endured by ex-soldiers. Near the conclusion Richard Dalloway and Sir William Bradshaw recognize that Septimus's case, illustrating the 'deferred effects of shell-shock', is relevant to an unspecified parliamentary Bill (*MD*, p. 155). It would, however, be misleading to describe *Mrs Dalloway* as being a novel 'about' shell shock or more generally 'about' ex-soldiers; it would be a mistake to allow the parliamentarian and the doctor to determine its final meaning. Septimus's mental health is important, but only when one considers his relation to the other elements in the novel: his literal relations to his doctors; and analogical relations, the connections of similarity and difference that are established between him, Clarissa, and Peter. When Woolf addresses social questions in her work, they appear obliquely. She creates a fragmentary network of associations, hints, and connections, but leaves the reader to make the final connections.[2] Identifying the politically charged keywords in the networks requires a thoroughly textual form of contextualization, one that refers as much to contemporary books and pamphlets as to real events.

Authoritarianism and Individualism: *Mrs Dalloway*

The debate over 'national efficiency' which followed the Boer War had raised the question of how far the state should be allowed to exercise its authority over the individual. Though many Liberals were opposed to the ideas of the efficiency movement, Lloyd George's People's Budget of 1909 demonstrated that they were increasingly sympathetic to the idea of the state as a community in which the work of one individual benefited all, and were willing to accept the consequences regarding taxation. The debate over conscription during the First World War had sharpened the question, and had been particularly divisive for Liberals. *Mrs Dalloway* raises the questions of how far the power of the state radiates, and by what means it is transmitted; it asks who exercises power and who it is exercised over; and it asks how far it is possible to resist or evade the state's authority. The chimes of Big Ben spreading across London, and the 'leaden circles' dissolving in air repeatedly draw attention to the theme of the radiation of power. The novel represents authority as an institution that enforces conformity. It does so most explicitly in its imagery, for example in the passage that connects 'proportion' with 'the clocks of Harley Street' (*MD*, p. 87).

When Woolf began work on *Mrs Dalloway* in April 1922 it was as a short story, 'Mrs Dalloway in Bond Street', which she completed in October (*CSF*, pp. 152–9).[3] By August, she had realized that this story would lead to others, and by 6 October 1922, she was projecting a sequence of eight stories.[4] On the same day she began work on the second, 'The Prime Minister'. Septimus makes his first appearance in this story, insane, though not explicitly an ex-soldier, and planning among other things to 'kill the Prime Minister' (*CSF*, p. 333). By 14 October Woolf was planning 'a book' that would be 'a study of insanity & suicide: the world seen by the sane & the insane side by side' (*Diary*, ii. 207). By June 1923, she had given her novel the working title 'The Hours', one which survived until at least May 1924; in August 1924 she reverted to 'Mrs Dalloway' (*Diary*, ii. 248, 301, 310). On 19 June 1923 she imagined a greater scope for the novel: she claimed that 'I want to give life & death, sanity & insanity; I want to criticise the social system, & to show it at work, at its most intense—'. She conceded that in making such claims she might be 'posing', and this often-quoted passage from her diary certainly needs to be understood in context: she was defending herself against the criticism that her published work lacked 'deep feeling' and a substantial sense of reality (*Diary*, ii. 248). She completed her first draft on 9 October 1924, and revised the novel in the following months. She had sent the manuscript to the printers by 6 January

1925, and had received the proofs by 24 January. The novel was published on 14 May 1925.[5]

The novel's three central characters, Clarissa, Septimus, and Peter, are all, to different extents and in different ways, outsiders, all resistant to the patterns imposed by authority. Septimus is most obviously an outsider because of his insanity. The contrast of sane and insane views of the world forces the reader to ask which is the more true, and how authority attempts to impose its view of the truth onto the world.[6] Septimus's pre-war employment as a clerk places him outside the culturally dominant classes. Like Leonard Bast in E. M. Forster's *Howards End*, he has made efforts to 'improve himself' (*MD*, p. 72). The transformation has been far from complete, though, and in several places the narrator draws attention to details that distinguish Septimus's culture from those above him: his idea of 'England' is very limited; lacking a classical education, he reads Aeschylus in translation (pp. 73, 75). In terms of his gender identity, Septimus is also an outsider: physically, he was 'weakly' before the war, though he 'developed manliness' during it (p. 73); sexually, his affectionate relationship with his officer, Evans, suggests a 'homosexual' element in his character.[7]

In class terms, Clarissa is an insider, but her role as a politician's wife, 'Mrs Richard Dalloway' (*MD*, p. 9), places her just outside the circle of authority. As a hostess, she facilitates the workings of political society, yet wields no actual power. By creating Clarissa through a combination of free indirect discourse and external reports, Woolf is able to convey both Clarissa's loneliness in this role, and her complacent acquiescence in it; the novel is simultaneously sympathetic and satirical. Her acquiescence is echoed, less sympathetically, in the brief account of Lady Bradshaw's having 'gone under', surrendering her will to that of her husband (p. 85). The restrictions on Clarissa are as much ideological as legal: she could have stood for election to Parliament, and the first female MP, Constance Markievicz, had been elected in December 1918. However, Clarissa's perception of her place in the world is too deeply ingrained for her to change. The possibility of a change in mentality is embodied in the next generation, in Elizabeth Dalloway.

Peter Walsh is both inside and outside. As a colonial administrator, he has helped govern a district 'twice as big as Ireland' (*MD*, p. 41), yet his role has placed him geographically far from the centre of the

Empire. He sees London, or at least its externals, as if he were an outsider (p. 60). Peter's actions establish connections between colonial and patriarchal power: having paused to admire the statue of General Gordon, hero of the siege of Khartoum, he starts to follow the 'young woman' from Trafalgar Square to Oxford Street, 'stealthily fingering his pocket-knife' as he goes (p. 45). The implications of sexual violence are undeniable, though they are not the only available reading. The pocket knife moreover connects him with the clocks of Harley Street, '[s]hredding and slicing', and thus with Sir William Bradshaw. The passage on 'proportion' and 'conversion' conversely directs the reader's attention to similarities between Bradshaw's power over his patients and the power of the Empire over its subjects (pp. 84–5).

However, this is a one-sided portrait of Peter. The habit of playing with his knife appears to Clarissa as the sign of silliness and weakness rather than a genuine threat (*MD*, p. 39). There is something distinctly unmanly about Peter Walsh. As he strolls through Regent's Park, enchanted by the richness and greenness of London, he reflects: 'This susceptibility to impressions had been his undoing, no doubt. Still at his age he had, like a boy or a girl even, these alternations of mood; good days, bad days, for no reason whatever, happiness from a pretty face, downright misery at the sight of a frump' (p. 60). 'Susceptibility' and 'impressions' are the keywords. 'Susceptibility' is implicitly contrasted with a martial and masculine invulnerability. Sensitivity to 'impressions' was, in the gendered psychology of the time, a feminine quality of mind. The idea dated back at least to the mid-nineteenth century, but was still endorsed by writers in the early twentieth: for Mrs Colquhoun, in *The Vocation of Woman*, the female mind 'takes more impressions' than the male, but leaps to hasty generalizations.[8] For these reasons, the 'impressionist' novel was taken by some to be a 'feminine' mode of writing. As if these keywords were not enough, we are later told more explicitly that Peter was 'not altogether manly' (*MD*, p. 132). Of course in both cases the analysis of Peter's character derives from his own consciousness, and it is possible that he is deceiving himself as to his own femininity.[9] However, if it were self-deception, we might expect the perceptions of other characters to expose it, just as they do his self-deception as to his youthfulness.

Many of Peter's characteristics correspond to those of the 'intermediate sex' or 'Uranian', a type defined and defended by Edward

Carpenter in the pre-war period.[10] Carpenter argued that the distinction of masculine and feminine was not absolute, but that the two shaded into one another; so too did love and friendship. As Carpenter recognized, this approach had immense significance for gender relations: 'Women are beginning to demand that Marriage shall mean Friendship as well as Passion; that a comrade-like Equality shall be included in the word Love.'[11] Carpenter defined the male Uranian as 'by no means effeminate', but 'sensitive in temperament and artistic in feeling'; he tended to be of 'a rather gentle emotional disposition—with defects, if such exist, in the direction of subtlety, evasiveness, timidity, vanity, etc.'. His quotations from Otto De Joux are particularly relevant to Peter: Uranian men 'are often . . . overcome with emotion and sympathy at the least sad occurrence'; 'Their sensitiveness, their endless tenderness for children, their love of flowers, their great pity for beggars and crippled folk are truly womanly'.[12] The ubiquitousness of flowers in the novel means that Peter's thoughts about them provide uncertain evidence, but there is a brief instance of his tenderness for children, when he ('the kind-looking man') comforts Elise Mitchell (*MD*, pp. 55–6). He is not unique in his sympathy for beggars—Rezia Warren Smith and Richard Dalloway both express similar feelings—but he contemplates the beggar woman at great length, and gives her a shilling (pp. 68–70). In many respects, Peter fits the type. It is possible that he knows it. In describing the male Uranian, Carpenter was concerned to defend the Uranian from the accusation of 'morbidity': 'morbid' was often used as a coded and pejorative term for same-sex desire, and carried implications of 'disease and degeneration'.[13] Carpenter also defended the Uranian from accusations of sensuality and libertinism: he conceded that if the male Uranian did have a fault, it was '*not* sensuality—but rather *sentimentality*'.[14]

In this light, Peter's concern that his reaction to the ambulance might be 'morbid' or 'sentimental' (*MD*, p. 128) becomes rather interesting. In the immediate context of the passage 'morbid' suggests an excessive concern with death. However, in combination with 'sentimental', in the light of Peter's other characteristics, and in the light of Carpenter's text, it may also mean 'homosexual'. There is an echo of Peter in the minor character Mr Bowley, 'who had rooms at the Albany and was sealed with wax over the deeper sources of life, but could be unsealed suddenly, inappropriately, sentimentally' by such things as the passage of the 'Prime Minister's car' (p. 17). Mr Bowley's address, in apartments for bachelors, had carried homosexual associations since the 1890s.[15] Peter's concern at his response to the ambulance is a kind of self-policing, betraying a concern that his 'Uranian' side is coming to dominate his personality. Authority in *Mrs Dalloway* depends on there being clear dividing lines between categories: Peter's Uranian qualities blur the boundaries.

The most clearly defined upholders of authority are the doctors, Holmes and Bradshaw. Woolf's satirical account of their practices can be read as biographically inspired, but if we identify Bradshaw as the type of the 'expert' or 'specialist', he has a significance that goes beyond the simply personal. Bradshaw's fundamental principle of 'proportion' ought to require him to take a balanced and circumspect view, but the principle appears to have taken on an obsessive quality. The word 'proportion' is repeated mantra-like through the passages describing Bradshaw (*MD*, pp. 80–7), and the obsessiveness cannot be attributed solely to Septimus. Moreover, the narration forcibly reminds us that 'proportion' is a euphemism for far more coercive methods. The depiction of Bradshaw is marked by the distrust that many in British business and government felt for those who possessed specialist technical knowledge. There was a deeply ingrained preference for the gentlemanly amateur who possessed 'all-round' knowledge. In the wake of the Boer War, those politicians who promoted the ideal of 'national efficiency' began to argue that experts should be given a more prominent role in business and in government; similar arguments were recapitulated during the First World War, but in neither case did they prevail. As G. R. Searle says, the specialist 'was seen as a monomaniac, whose enthusiasms made him incapable of judging a situation from a general, all-round point of view'.[16] *Mrs Dalloway* undermines the authority of Bradshaw by the view it takes of his expertise.

By juxtaposing Bradshaw's 'sane' version of the truth with Septimus's 'insane' version, the novel implicitly asks whether any single truth is sufficient. This is not simply a philosophical question about the nature of truth, but it is also a political question about the power to impose an ideology or a view of the world. Thinking of Bradshaw's requirement that he and Rezia be separated, Septimus asks, ' "Must", "must", why "must"? What power had Bradshaw over him? "What right has Bradshaw to say 'must' to me?" ' (*MD*,

p. 125). To many Liberals in the post-Boer War period, it had seemed that the long-established political principles of 'popular rights and free discussion' were in danger of being displaced by doctrines of force, disguised as an appeal to efficiency.[17] The question of compulsion was repeated during the First World War, particularly in relation to conscription and censorship.

Mrs Dalloway is more successful at presenting a vivid image of centralized authority than it is at suggesting solutions to the problem. How might one escape the centralizing state, and what alternatives might there be? One alternative is glimpsed in Bourton in the 1890s. Bourton is presented as a place and time of freedom and possibilities, an Edenic location free from the authoritarian categories of present-day London. Its freedom is imagined particularly as a sexual freedom, seen in Clarissa's intimate friendship with Sally Seton (*MD*, pp. 28–31), and in Clarissa's freedom to choose between possible male partners. The summer at Bourton is not dated precisely, but Peter refers to 'thirty years' having elapsed (p. 65), so we may date it to the summer of 1893: this is, significantly, before Oscar Wilde's trial for 'gross indecency' in 1895; it implies the comparative sexual tolerance of that period, and not the more repressive atmosphere that prevailed after Wilde's 'fall'.[18] A similar freedom is also imagined further back in the past, in a comparison of Rezia's loneliness to the country seen at midnight, 'when all boundaries are lost', 'as the Romans saw it, lying cloudy, when they landed, and the hills had no names and rivers wound they knew not where' (*MD*, pp. 20–1). The novel contains what we might call an 'under-narrative', an implied account of human history: once, when the Romans arrived, and again following the prosecution of Oscar Wilde, identities became fixed and choices became restricted; an imperialism of the spirit set in. While such a narrative enables the reader to see the categories of the present day as something artificially imposed, it is implicitly nostalgic and anti-rational: nostalgic because, by locating the period of greater freedom in the past, it implies a narrative of decline in which we can only look back on lost freedom, rather than look forward to future freedom; anti-rational because, by conflating the imposition of names with naming itself, and by conflating the misuse of reason with reason itself, it implies that a world without boundaries, physical or conceptual, is superior to one with them. The under-narrative is not the only narrative in the novel—we are given the more optimistic sketch of Elizabeth's emancipation—but it is the dominant one.

The only characters within the novel's present day time-frame who completely escape authority are Septimus and the several beggars mentioned throughout the text. Septimus falls outside the social system on account of his insanity; the beggars by being members of the residuum. Clarissa's view of the alcoholic 'dejected miseries' sitting on doorsteps is typical: they 'can't be dealt with . . . by Acts of Parliament' (*MD*, p. 4); they have escaped the authority that echoes throughout the novel. The ascription of a symbolic value to beggars was by no means uncommon, but it was not the only way of writing about them. Treating them as symbols of liberty tends to obscure their humanity and to erase the lives they led before becoming vagrants. Clarissa's parenthetic remark—'drink their downfall'—suggests the possibility of enquiring into causes, but its full implications are masked by the easy alliteration; the phrase is swept along in the tide of Clarissa's rhapsodic and lyrical account of London. One contemporary investigative writer on female vagrancy romanticized the 'unconquerable spirit' and 'artistic' qualities of some of her subjects, seeing it as 'innate', and arguing that 'no social system could cater for them'.[19] In Mary Fulton's novel *Blight* (1919), an incidental figure in the glamorous crowds of central London, an 'old man in rags' selling newspapers, is 'Indifferent, calm, motionless as a seer'.[20] Richard Dalloway, seeing a female vagrant in Green Park, makes her sound more like an independent scholar than a homeless alcoholic; he imagines that she had 'flung herself on the earth, rid of all ties, to observe curiously, to speculate boldly, to consider the whys and the wherefores, impudent, loose-lipped, humorous' (*MD*, p. 99). The descriptions of beggars derive in part from Woolf's own observations (e.g. *Diary*, ii. 47), but she interpreted those observations within a framework of ideas which were not her own.

Peter Walsh's account of the female beggar opposite Regent's Park Station does not directly make her a symbol of individual liberty (*MD*, pp. 68–70), but a carefree attitude is implied in the line of her song that runs 'if someone should see, what matter they?' His transformation of the beggar into a figure who has stood in the same spot for millions of years could be seen as an extravagant reworking of the cliché 'the poor are always with us'; it also serves, like the idea that vagrancy is innate, to prevent us from asking how she came to be there. Rezia's view of the woman, by contrast, is far more practical and sympathetic, and while it does not seek to explain how the woman came to her present wretched state, it does at least acknowledge that she had seen 'better days': 'Suppose it was a wet night? Suppose one's father, or somebody who had known one in better days had happened to pass, and saw one standing there in the gutter? And where did she sleep at night?' (p. 70). We are left to infer that Rezia's sympathy might reflect her anxiety about her own future, and so to ask whether this woman was once as Rezia is now. Contemporary readers might reasonably have wondered whether the beggar's condition was due to the war. At about the same date, Stephen Graham identified four main causes of homelessness: drink, 'immorality', the Great War, and finally the prison system, which gave inmates little preparation for life outside.[21] While these are not entirely adequate as explanations—one would need to ask *why* someone might turn to drink, for example—they do at least undermine the idea that vagrancy is natural or inevitable. They suggest that vagrants, though they might be outside the 'social system', are nevertheless produced by it. If one of the alternatives to social conformity that *Mrs Dalloway* proposes is a defiant individuality, it is not altogether an adequate alternative. The character who takes this 'defiance' to its furthest limit, escaping the 'corruption, lies, [and] chatter' of social life is, after all, a tragic suicide (*MD*, p. 156). To say that there was 'an embrace in death' is to say that we are all tragically alone in life; there is no possibility of a social system which is not oppressive.

The choice between lonely individualism and oppressive socialization is a pessimistic one. The classic realist novel of the Victorian era resolved the problem by reference to the family as a social unit, but for Woolf the family can be as oppressive as the 'social system'. In the novel most directly concerned with family life, *To the Lighthouse*, the family is shown to be disintegrating. In *Mrs Dalloway*, the classic Victorian plots of family connection survive as possibilities that are never realized. The novel leads the reader to expect Clarissa and Septimus to be brought together in some way: this is a generic expectation that arises as soon as the novel moves its focus from one character to another. The expectation is created by immediate precedents such as *Ulysses*, which unites Stephen Dedalus and Leopold

Bloom, and by Victorian precedents. The ways in which they might be united are restricted by class differences. It is possible to imagine a 'comic' conclusion to *Mrs Dalloway*, in which the relation between Septimus and Clarissa is ultimately revealed to be a family relationship: that, for example, he is her long-lost son. A 'tragic' variant on this would allow the revelation to emerge only after Septimus had died. Another variant would be for Septimus to have been Clarissa's lover: there is a small precedent for this in Leonard Bast's relationship with Helen Schlegel in *Howards End* (1910). In another variant, Septimus might know the secret of Elizabeth's parentage, and the mystery of her Chinese eyes (*MD*, p. 104), just as Jo the crossing sweeper knows the secrets of the aristocratic Lady Dedlock in *Bleak House* (1854). All four imaginary plots depend upon adultery, and all four use it to unite characters across class divisions. In the plot of the classic realist novel, closure occurs when the family unit is reunited, and when transgressors are punished for their misdemeanours. By the early twentieth century, such plots no longer seemed valid to writers of 'highbrow' fiction. Families in Woolf's novels are often oppressive. Instead, the connection between Clarissa and Septimus is one of analogy: Septimus is, as Woolf later wrote, Clarissa's 'double' (*EVW* iv. 549); she feels 'somehow very like him' (*MD*, p. 158).

To resolve the choice between isolation and socialization, Woolf introduces the 'group': people who experience a sense of intimacy that does not necessarily depend on the usual mechanisms of language or physical proximity. In a very general sense her interest in forms of associative life other than the family resembles that of her contemporaries, in a nation where clubs, unions, guilds, and societies were rapidly multiplying. However, unlike those kinds of associative life, Woolf's 'groups' are not formal institutions; they do not have to meet or converse to experience a sense of union. Formally constituted groups, such as the suffrage organization in *Night and Day*, are often the objects of Woolf's satire.

There are several precedents for Woolf's interest in such forms of contact. Many sociologists and psychologists had written about group consciousness and the crowd: Gustave Le Bon, in *Psychologie des foules* (1895), translated as *The Crowd* (1920); Wilfred Trotter in *Instincts of the Herd in Peace and War* (1916); and Freud in *Group Psychology and the Analysis of the Ego* (1921; trans. 1922). Woolf referred familiarly to Trotter's ideas in her diary (*Diary*, i. 80). Her aunt, Caroline Emelia Stephen, had written about the forms of religious communion familiar to the 'Quakers', or Society of Friends.[22] The French school of writing known as unanimism, which enjoyed a short-lived celebrity in Britain from 1912 to 1914, attempted to create a literary vocabulary for group consciousness.[23] (The 'un-' prefix in its name denotes unity, not negativity, and is pronounced like the 'un-' in 'union'.)

Woolf explicitly advances a theory of group consciousness in *Mrs Dalloway*. Peter Walsh recalls Clarissa as a young woman having a theory that her being was not confined to her physical location; her circle of sympathy was not restricted to people she had actually met. In Peter's recollection, the theory compensated for their shared feeling 'of dissatisfaction; not knowing people; not being known'. Clarissa had felt her self to be 'everywhere', so that 'to know her' one would have to 'seek out' the people who 'completed' her, and likewise the places. 'Odd affinities she had with people she had never spoken to, some woman in the street, some man behind a counter—even trees, or barns' (*MD*, p. 129). It is a theory of visible 'apparitions' and invisible selves that spread widely beyond their immediate location (pp. 129–30). Recalling Clarissa's theory, Peter Walsh uses it to explain the durability of his own relationship to her. Their actual meetings were infrequent and often 'painful'. They formed a 'sharp, acute, uncomfortable grain', 'yet in absence, in the most unlikely places, it would flower out, open, shed its scent, let you touch, taste, look about you, get the whole feel of it and understanding, after years of lying lost'. Her having 'come to him' while abroad suggests a kind of a haunting (p. 130). As well as allowing Peter to interpret his own relationship, Woolf's introduction of the theory allows the reader to understand what Clarissa means when she feels 'somehow very like' Septimus Warren Smith, even though she has never met or spoken to him.

Woolf implicitly advances a theory of group consciousness through her characteristic vocabulary and imagery in *Mrs Dalloway* and elsewhere. One function of Woolf's ubiquitous water imagery is to immerse her characters in a medium in which invisible connections become imaginable to the reader. Thus the Prime Minister's car creates a 'slight ripple', a 'vibration' (*MD*, p. 15); the 'tremors' of Big Ben, its leaden circles dissolving in air, likewise create a rippling motif (p. 42). Clarissa becomes a plant on the riverbed (pp. 25–6), and Lady Bruton's 'grey tide of service' is set rippling by Hugh Whitbread (p. 91).

Caroline Stephen's analysis of religious communion outlines similar ideas, but other sources are needed to contextualize Woolf's characteristic imagery. 'Loneliness', Caroline Stephen wrote, 'is certainly not identical with the mere absence of human beings'.[24] She analysed the multiple layers of human contact: 'We meet each other in many different planes as well as at many different points. Two human beings may be cut off from all interchange of word or thought (as for instance by the illness of one of them) while yet physically they are in each other's immediate presence, and fundamentally they are absolutely one in heart. The intermediate union is destroyed, while the most superficial and the deepest are alike intact'.[25] Such a paradoxical combination of absence and presence could characterize *The Waves*, where the characters scarcely ever address each other directly: although they very often perceive the same places and objects, and appear to be within earshot of each other, they only very rarely echo each other's vocabulary.[26] Though the narrator—the most minimal narrator in all fiction—insists that the characters 'said' their words, the lack of cohesion gives the impression that their words are private thoughts. The book consists almost entirely of spoken words, and yet produces an effect of silence.

The terminology of 'ripples' and 'vibrations' is nowhere to be found in Caroline Stephen's very abstract account, and seems to derive from unanimism. For a group to be 'unanimous' in this sense is for it to be possessed of one 'spirit' or 'mind'. Such a sharing of spirit may occur even between those who do not formally know each other: between members of a large crowd, and even those who are physically separated. The unanimist writers sought to describe such forms of unity. Doing so forced them to evolve new narrative forms and new narratorial vocabularies, some of which Woolf adopted. The unanimists were widely discussed in the years immediately preceding the First World War: F. S. Flint wrote about them in the *Poetry Review* in August 1912; Jane Harrison read a paper about them to the 'Heretics' society in Cambridge in November 1912; Leonard Woolf reviewed a novel by the most important of the group, Jules Romains, in August 1913. 1914 saw the appearance of *Death of a Nobody*, a translation by Woolf's friends Desmond MacCarthy and Sydney

Waterlow of Romains's *Mort de quelqu'un*; the novel was prefaced with a dedicatory letter from MacCarthy to Roger Fry, and a band around the cover described it as 'A POST-IMPRESSIONIST NOVEL'.[27] Unanimism was an idea that appealed to pacifists and feminists: Florence and Ogden contrasted the militarist, breeder of 'rankling hatred', with 'woman', 'the sympathetic, the unanimist, the creator'.[28]

The 'plot' of *Death of a Nobody* is very simple: the 'nobody' of the title, Jacques Godard, a retired engine driver living in Paris, dies; the novel then shows how the news of his death spreads outwards, touching people who never directly knew him. At the end of the novel, after Godard's burial, Romains gives a sustained account of a young man's thoughts on mortality: the young man had not known Godard, but is invisibly touched by the feeling generated by his death. The novel portrays the physical means by which the news spreads, and complements this with vocabulary and imagery that attempt to describe the invisible influences at work. In this vocabulary, 'vibrations' spread outwards, 'expanding' and 'dilating'; the image of ripples created by a pebble dropped into a pool is used at several points.[29] Godard's 'soul' or 'existence' becomes an active agent, splitting into fragments, multiplying itself and taking possession 'of a hundred living frames'.[30] The souls of other people 'oscillate' and try to reach a 'centre' or an 'equilibrium'.[31] People and impersonal forces both 'swarm' and form 'waves'.[32]

The vocabulary of unanimism emerges in other novels by Woolf, most notably *The Waves*, where it conveys the sense of simultaneous separation and connection that the six friends feel. From the very outset, and into her adult life, Jinny ripples and quivers: physical movements, perhaps, but ones with important metaphorical associations (*W*, pp. 8, 83). Neville conceives his life as being a moving ripple (p. 18). Bernard, travelling to London, feels a 'unanimity' with the fellow occupants of his train carriage (pp. 91–2), much as one character in *Death of a Nobody* feels with strangers in the public stagecoach.[33] Though Bernard's sense of individuality reasserts itself as they leave the station, he soon feels 'strange oscillations and vibrations of sympathy' with the crowds (*W*, p. 93). He is conscious that his existence as a 'private being' does not describe the totality of his life. Likewise Neville later insists that his name describes merely 'the narrow limits' of his life, while to himself he is 'immeasurable; a net whose fibres pass imperceptibly beneath the world' (p. 178). The image of fibres has a precedent in *Death of a Nobody*, where the village is 'linked together by a mesh of fine elastic nerves that throbbed beneath the strokes of the midday chimes'.[34] Some elements in Woolf's vocabulary of the group may have come from other sources: Bernard's reference to the 'magnet' of his friends' society (*W*, p. 175) echoes metaphors used by Le Bon ('the magnetic influence given out by the group') and adopted by Freud.[35] Nevertheless, Le Bon's vocabulary and Romains's broadly resemble each other, in that both employ metaphors of invisible forces, derived from physics, to describe social phenomena.

The vocabulary of unanimism and the idea of the 'group' allowed Woolf to conceptualize units of society other than individuals and families, and allowed her to describe their interactions. It allowed her to imagine a utopian form of community free of conflict. The vocabulary has its shortcomings. It provides a shortcut, allowing a writer to avoid describing the real material activities and institutions that connect social groups. The vocabulary of unanimism, which has much in common with the vocabulary of contemporary spiritualists and mystics, could be said to be mystifying real social relations. However, the classic realism of the Victorian era was equally inadequate to the modern world. Woolf's recourse to the vocabulary is forced upon her by the complexity of social and economic relations in her time. The problem was expressed very concisely by John W. Graham in his pacifist work *Evolution and Empire* (1912): the credit economy that had evolved in the nineteenth century formed a global 'spider's web'. The owners of a large country house in England 'do not live on a share of the produce of the neighbouring fields' as they might have done in the Middle Ages, but instead depend 'on Argentine railways or Alaskan gold, or land increments in New York City'.[36] It is notable that Graham himself has to resort to metaphor to describe these relations: his image of the spider's web anticipates similar images in Woolf's works. The problem for the novelist is clear: the material relations between people, in the sense of *economic* relations, could no longer be readily apprehended by closely observing their immediate physical environment. Even when modernist writers were not conscious of the problem in exactly this form, many had an intuitive sense that realism was inadequate to describe the complexity of the modern world.

Career Narratives: *Night and Day*

The early years of Virginia Woolf's life saw a great expansion in the kinds of work open to women. This expansion of possibilities undermined the generic expectations that had long sustained narratives about women, but the problem of fashioning a story around a woman's relationship to her work remained a difficult one. Such narratives are not an isolated literary matter: they form part of the discourse of social debate and social policy. We constantly tell ourselves stories that make the raw fact of employment into a meaningful narrative; politicians and employers tell stories too. Choosing a career is a matter of choosing a narrative; surviving a dead-end job is a matter of telling oneself stories about where it, or the money earned, will lead. Woolf's narratives are illuminated by comparison not only with contemporary novels, but also with contemporary non-fictional stories and analyses of work.

The life narrative of an educated man's daughter in the nineteenth century had been extremely limited, at least in Virginia Woolf's account. It was a matter of entertaining visitors; visiting the sick and teaching the poor; studying history, literature, and music; learning the piano and other accomplishments. The end of this education was marriage, and as one of Woolf's sources says, 'it was not a question of *whether* we should marry, but simply of *whom* we should marry' (*TG*, p. 206). Although this plot allows many twists and embellishments, at root it is very simple. Marriage, as Woolf says, was the only 'profession' open to the daughters of educated men. Consequently, it was natural for even 'the most enlightened of men' to conceive of all women as 'spinsters', 'all desiring marriage' (*TG*, p. 381). It is clear that by the early twentieth century the question of *whether* to marry, and the question of the conditions under which one *might* marry, had become possible narratives. However, as Woolf found narratives of choice uncongenial, it is important also to consider the states of mind that were engendered by the new career narratives, the mental adjustments that men and women had to make. As Ray Strachey noted, concluding her history of the campaign for women's suffrage, there were aspects of equality which 'are not susceptible to victory by law', but which required 'changes of thought and outlook'.[37]

Woolf's account in *Three Guineas* is a simplification for the purposes of her polemic. Her contemporary and friend Molly MacCarthy, also born in 1882, recalled the period in her girlhood when she was 'full of vague aspirations and questionings' as to what she was to do in life. In *The Englishwoman's Year Book* she read an article on 'The Stage' which was 'discouraging', and one on 'Sick Nursing' which was 'inspiring'. She announced to her mother that she intended to be a sanitary inspector, and was rebuffed: she would have to resign herself 'to being an English lady'. '[S]ervice and sacrifice' were the ideals.[38] While MacCarthy's account broadly confirms Woolf's, it indicates that a young woman of the upper middle classes was not totally blinkered: she could read about professions other than marriage, and imagine herself in them, even if the accounts she read were discouraging.

The new areas of employment open to women were mostly 'clerical' in character. According to an article in 1888 that coined the term 'glorified spinster' to describe the new working woman, such women found employment as 'teachers, nurses, accountants, clerks, librarians, [and] heads of certain business-departments'.[39] In 1912 a short series of articles in the feminist journal *The Freewoman* on 'Where Women Work' covered teaching in two articles, and clerical work in the third.[40] Women in clerical roles formed a small percentage of working women, but given the social bias of Woolf's fiction towards the middle classes, they are the most relevant to her fiction. They were, moreover, a rapidly rising percentage of the female workforce. In 1901, most employed women, 42 per cent, were in some form of domestic service, while only 7 per cent were in commercial and financial work, another 7 per cent were in professional and technical work (mostly teachers and nurses), and 1 per cent were 'clerks, typists, etc.'. Over the following decades, the numbers in domestic service gradually declined, reaching 35 per cent in 1931. The numbers in the professional and technical group remained roughly static; the numbers in commerce and finance rose gradually to 9 per cent in 1911, 10 percent in 1921, and 11 per cent in 1931. The numbers working as clerks and typists accelerated more rapidly, reaching 2 per cent in 1911, 8 per cent in 1921, and 10 per cent in 1930. Over this period, women formed a near constant percentage of the total labour force, between 29 and 30 per cent.[41]

What statistics cannot indicate are the career narratives that applied to women. In both the working classes and the middle classes, there was a widespread expectation that women would withdraw from the workplace on marriage. In schoolteaching and many of the 'higher professions', this was formalized as the 'marriage bar': women were forced to resign their jobs on marriage.[42] In consequence, for many women, paid work was merely an interlude before they embarked upon their 'real' careers of wifehood and motherhood. There was an air of unreality about it. In 1886, the anonymous commentator on the 'glorified spinster' had insisted that such women need not anticipate marriage 'as their ultimate destiny'; nor need they count themselves as 'Old Maids', 'cruelly deprived of their natural sphere of work and happiness' (that is, marriage), unable to make 'a full and satisfactory life for themselves'.[43] The 'glory' of the glorified spinster lay in her ability to refuse the narratives that other people were writing for her. However, the optimism of the anonymous commentator was not fully realized in practice.

Virginia Woolf's adaptation of the genre of courtship novel makes questions about marriage and work prominent in *Night and Day*. Relatively little is known about Woolf's progress in writing it. In July 1916 she mentioned to Vanessa that she was considering writing a novel 'about' her, and, given that Katharine Hilbery in many ways resembles Vanessa, she was certainly gestating *Night and Day* (*Letters*, ii. 109). From the surviving section of manuscript, it is clear that she was writing what was to be chapter 11 on 6 October 1916. At this time the novel was called 'Dreams and Realities'. She continued writing during October and November of that year, and on 5 January 1917 began what was to become chapter 16.[44] The manuscript for the later chapters has not survived, and she makes little mention of its progress in her letters or diaries; but from a letter to Vanessa, it is clear that she was writing about Katharine's blue dress on 22 April 1918.[45] She completed the first draft on Armistice Day, 11 November 1918 (*Letters*, ii. 290). She spent the following months revising and typing the manuscript, which she gave to Leonard Woolf to read at the end of March 1919, and took to her publisher, Gerald Duckworth, on 1 April 1919 (*Diary*, i. 259, 261). *Night and Day* was published in Britain on 20 October 1919, and received mixed reviews. Though many were favourable, those who were familiar with Woolf's recent experimental prose pieces such as 'The Mark on the Wall' were surprised by the traditional form of the novel.

Katharine Mansfield saw *Night and Day* as a ship that had been on a long voyage, unaware of recent turmoil, and surprisingly lacking any 'scars': ostensibly she meant the turmoil of literary experimentation, but implicitly she meant the turmoil of the First World War.[46]

Normally a contextual reading of a historical novel would refer primarily to the period of its composition and publication, and not the era in which it is set, but the 'history' that Woolf represented in *Night and Day* was so recent as to be relevant to its contextualization. At the same time, its representations attempt to preserve the memory of the political optimism and radicalism of the pre-war years. The idea of analysing marriage as a pseudo-profession dates from this era, and had been most thoroughly realized by Cicely Hamilton in *Marriage as a Trade* (1909). Virginia Woolf was apparently aware of its terms of reference. In the letter in which she in effect accepted Leonard Woolf's proposal of marriage, she had weighed up her contradictory thoughts and feelings. Her statement of the advantages anticipates the cautiousness of the characters in *Night and Day*: 'Anyhow, you'll be quite happy with him; and he will give you companionship, children, and a busy life'. Immediately, by contrast, she realizes how limiting such a life would be: 'then I say By God, I will not look upon marriage as a profession' (*Letters*, i. 496). Twenty-six years later, in *Three Guineas*, the idea of marriage as a profession, and 'an unpaid profession' at that, was still central to her analysis of patriarchy (*TG*, p. 236). The phrase and its variants run through *Night and Day*.

Cicely Hamilton looked at marriage as a trade not merely to criticize it, but as an ironic and witty way of analysing contemporary relations between the sexes. Her fundamental aim was to argue that the supposedly 'natural' qualities of women were in fact due to their being educated for the trade of marriage. While for men, marriage is one among many career options, and is a 'career' that can be conducted in parallel with others, for women it was close to being compulsory. To conduct her analysis, she adopts the language of social investigation and industrial reform: she is interested in the economic 'conditions' that prevail in this industry; she criticizes the 'sweated trade element' in marriage; and she speaks of women becoming 'class-conscious', meaning conscious of 'woman' as a class.[47] She also adopts the language of national efficiency, regretting that the lack of training for marriage creates 'that habit and attitude of mind which is known as amateurishness'. The impossibility of knowing the profession and character of the future husband make 'a thorough and businesslike training' impossible; the 'spirit of amateurishness . . . makes for inefficiency'.[48]

Woolf introduces the questions of marriage and work early, in an exchange between Katharine Hilbery and Ralph Denham. Denham is visiting the Hilbery family for the first time, and Katharine is showing him the relics associated with her grandfather, the poet Richard Alardyce. Denham assumes that she is the one responsible for writing the biography of Alardyce:

'You've got it very nearly right,' she said, 'but I only help my mother. I don't write myself.'

'Do you do anything yourself?' he demanded.

'What do you mean?' she asked. 'I don't leave the house at ten and come back at six.' (*ND*, pp. 14–15)

Katharine's demand that Denham clarify his question encourages the reader to ask what it means to 'do' something, to be usefully employed. Clearly for Katharine, 'work' need not require one to leave the house. Woolf implicitly questions her culture's separation of the world into 'work' and 'home'. Such spatial distinctions further reinforced the distinctions between masculine and feminine activities, and forced women to focus more exclusively on marriage as a trade.[49] Katharine is aware that, to Denham and others like him, her work appears to be merely a leisure activity. As the narrator later comments, she is a member of 'a very great profession, which has, as yet, no title and very little recognition . . . She lived at home. She did it very well, too' (*ND*, p. 41). The namelessness of her trade diminishes Katharine's authority: although she is conscious that she 'does' something, she feels that she cannot assert herself in a crowded room because she does not have 'a profession' (p. 56).

The novel also draws attention to the analogies between marriage and the professions with the apparently digressive story of Cassandra Otway's father, a colonial civil servant who had been passed over for promotion. As the narrator says, this disappointment 'had poisoned the life of Sir Francis much as a disappointment in love is said to poison the whole life of a woman' (*ND*, p. 214). The comparison invites the reader to consider the respects in which marriage is a career for women. The comparison emerges more directly when

Katharine Hilbery visits Mary Datchet, and admires the independence that her flat represents: 'in such a room one could work—one could have a life of one's own', thinks Katharine, in a phrase that anticipates Woolf's later study. Mary's relationship with her work is an 'exalted' form of engagement, thinks Katharine, 'which had no recognition or engagement ring' (p. 284). Mary herself later makes the point that 'you can't limit work' to a narrow range of activities: 'No one works harder than a woman with little children' (p. 375). Mary's views on the idea of marriage itself as a profession are harder to gauge. When her associate Mr Basnett asks Katharine if she is 'on the look-out for a job', Mary interjects, saying that 'Marriage is her job at present' (p. 376). While Hamilton had been sympathetic towards women who pursued the 'trade' of marriage, arguing that they had little choice, Mary subordinates the idea to a more barbed and personal criticism, implying that Katharine could have chosen otherwise.

Mary's point about the work involved in raising children was one that sociologists and feminists had been making for some time, and continued to make in the 1920s. In 1907 Sidney Webb, concerned about the falling birth rate in the middle classes, had argued that the 'profession' of motherhood needed to be placed 'upon an honourable economic basis'.[50] Ellen Key, in her influential book *The Woman Movement* (1912) had argued that the 'service of mother' must receive 'the honour and oblation' that the state currently gave to military service, and her point was partially endorsed by the pacifists Florence and Ogden.[51] Both suggestions are double-edged for feminists: while acknowledging as never before that the role of mother and housewife counts as work, they risk implying that it is the only work appropriate to women. In the post-war period the campaign for the 'endowment of motherhood' raised the same problems.[52]

Katharine's remark about the difficulty she has in asserting herself because of her lack of a profession is characteristic of Woolf's approach to social questions. Here, as elsewhere in *Night and Day*, Woolf examines the states of consciousness that shape her characters' experiences, in the worlds of work and of marriage. As the novel's title itself suggests, duality is a crucial theme, and several of the characters display an ambivalence and detachment towards both marriage and work. The description of Mary Datchet's daily routine implies a lack of authenticity about her, a persistent self-consciousness about the life she leads. As she leaves her flat 'she *said to herself* she was very glad' not to be leading a life of leisure; in the street 'she *liked to think herself* one of the workers'; and 'she *liked to pretend* that she was indistinguishable from the rest' (*ND*, pp. 75–6; emphases added).[53] The root of her self-consciousness may be 'that she was, properly speaking, an amateur worker' (*ND*, p. 76), unpaid and dependent on a private income, but the narrator does not explicitly interpret the irony this way. It seems as likely that Woolf is exploring the self-consciousness felt by anyone deliberately adopting an unusual and unprecedented lifestyle. It is not Mary's amateur status that matters, but her being a woman in the predominantly male world of formal 'work'. Cicely Hamilton had analysed the peculiar mental state that characterized the modern woman:

Where the man can be single-hearted, the woman necessarily is double-motived. It is, of course, the element of commerce and compulsion that accounts for this difference of attitude; an impulse that may have to be discouraged, nurtured or simulated to order . . . can never have the same vigour, energy and beauty as an impulse that is unfettered and unforced.[54]

Hamilton brilliantly inverts the patriarchal cliché that women are out of touch with the real world, living in a 'beautiful world' of ideals,[55] and suggests that quite the reverse is true: when it comes to love, men are the sentimental romantics, and women are the pragmatic realists. The author of 'The Glorified Spinster' had argued something similar: although in her view the majority of women probably were romantic, the glorified spinster had lost 'the power of idealising human beings', and consequently for her 'falling in love is almost impossible'.[56] Hamilton's is the more subtle account, in that it acknowledges the coexistence of two contradictory modes of consciousness in the 'double-motived' woman.

Katharine displays a similar double consciousness in relation to love. Receiving a love letter and sonnet from William Rodney, Katharine 'could see in what direction her feelings *ought* to flow, supposing they revealed themselves' (*ND*, p. 107; emphasis added). She is conscious, in other words, of traditional courtship narratives, and can conceive herself as a character in one, but she does not authentically feel those feelings. She is conscious of love as a social convention, a theatrical performance, 'a pageant' (p. 107), an 'illusion'

(p. 509), or a convenient fiction. When she does think of romantic love, it assumes the form of parody, 'a magnanimous hero, riding a great horse by the shore of the sea' (p. 108), a ludicrous figure who anticipates _Orlando_'s Shelmerdine (_O_, p. 239). Rather than having a secret engagement, as a character might in a romantic comedy, she keeps secret her having broken off her engagement to William Rodney (_ND_, p. 424). Katharine's self-consciousness and self-control are echoed in Ralph Denham. When the couple finally reach an understanding (pp. 517–20), the characters retain a sense of their fundamental isolation; Katharine 'had now to get used to the fact that someone shared her loneliness'.

By placing two such characters at the centre of a courtship novel, Woolf undermines the central idea of romantic fiction, the idea of spontaneous and authentic self-expression. Of course in conventional romantic fiction, characters cannot always immediately achieve spontaneity—it may be blocked by social convention or personal reticence—but it is presented as the ideal to be pursued. When Katharine, by contrast, 'burst[s] out' passionately at William Rodney, it is to berate him for talking so much about feelings (_ND_, pp. 250–1). Henry recognizes Katharine's inauthenticity, and anticipates a narrative of self-realization for her: 'Katharine hasn't found herself yet. Life isn't altogether real to her yet' (p. 213). Katharine, however, does not think of her self-consciousness as a problem, but as a clear-sighted realism. She has 'found herself' more completely and more consciously than Henry would wish.

Woolf's focus on her characters' self-consciousness anticipates what in the theatre Bertolt Brecht was to call the 'alienation effect', a style of acting which continually reminded the spectators that an illusion was being created, so allowing them to think critically about the events portrayed. Just as the Brechtian actor 'does not allow himself to become completely transformed on the stage into the character he is portraying',[57] so Woolf's mode of narration does not allow Mary to be completely transformed into a working woman, or Katharine into a woman in love. We are made aware that the roles they occupy are socially created, that they might have made other choices, and that they might yet create entirely new roles. If Katharine's self-discovery involves an element of inauthenticity, that is because her society does not give a name to her 'profession' of living at home, or acknowledge its worth. _Night and Day_ has often been seen as an anomaly in Virginia Woolf's *oeuvre*, a regression to a conservative form of novel before the great advances of the 1920s. However, *Night and Day* may be closer to *Jacob's Room* than is usually recognized: *Night and Day* is an anti-novel, parodying the conventions of romance just as *Jacob's Room* parodies those of the *Bildungsroman*. By placing sceptical rationalists in a genre that requires spontaneous passionate types, Woolf undermines the genre's central assumptions. Moreover, in its questioning of what it is to 'do' something, and its reassessment of women's professions, *Night and Day* anticipates *To the Lighthouse*. There, as we have seen (in the section 'Representation and Aesthetics' in Chapter 4), Lily reassesses Mrs Ramsay's work as a wife and mother in terms which assimilate it to her own work as an artist. As *To the Lighthouse* recognizes, the changing social circumstances of women not only necessitated new narratives, but new states of consciousness. Men and women needed to find a way of rethinking the past that could improve on its 'old-fashioned ideals' while retaining what was beneficial.

Militarism, Discipline, and Education: *The Waves*

Though Woolf often spoke of *The Waves* as a 'mystical', 'abstract' book, and though for many years critics took her at her word, more recently its social and political concerns have been recognized.[58] One of its concerns is militarism. That Woolf had been concerned with the insidious quality of militarism from the beginning of her career is not in doubt: in *The Voyage Out* the warships of the British Mediterranean Fleet cast 'a curious effect of discipline and sadness on the waters', and even when they have gone, they influence the topic of conversation (*VO*, p. 72). *The Waves* addresses the presence of militarism above all in education. Although the school scenes are a small part of the book, they are significant: they introduce images and ideas that return in later sections; they introduce Percival, and go some way to explaining his charismatic hold on the male characters. As the whole novel is concerned with the relation of the individual to the group, the example of corporate life presented by the school is important. Woolf's personal exclusion from the world of the male public school (and also from that of its female counterpart) may have disadvantaged her in some respects, but it allowed her to take a detached view of its ideals: the games ethic and the ideals of 'character' and 'discipline'. Rather than writing from experience, she drew on literary knowledge and on anecdotal accounts of public school life.

Percival is a martial figure from his very first appearance, on the cricket pitch: 'His magnificence is that of some medieval commander'; Louis imagines he and the other boys 'trooping after him', 'to be shot like sheep, for he will certainly attempt some forlorn enterprise and die in battle' (*W*, p. 28). His future is almost completely predicted in this single vignette, with the qualification that his death is not as heroic as Louis expects. Not only does the passage establish Percival as leader, but it establishes an association between the games ethic and militarism. The association is reiterated in Bernard's summing up: the image of a 'brakeful of boys' going 'cricketing' or 'footballing' is followed immediately by the image of an army marching across Europe (p. 205).

Louis later turns his attention to 'the boasting boys', the group who most fully embody the public school ethos. They are sportsmen, playing cricket and (rugby) football: 'Larpent's brother played football for Oxford; Smith's father made a century at Lords. Archie and Hugh; Parker and Dalton; Larpent and Smith; then again Archie and Hugh; Parker and Dalton; Larpent and Smith—the names repeat themselves; the names are the same always' (*W*, p. 36). The repetition implies that a small number of families have achieved an almost hereditary hold on the school, and on national institutions. A Hogarth Press book of 1932 strongly criticized the public schools for having elevated rugby and cricket to the status of a 'religion'. Sport had become a tyranny, and created an 'athletocracy': the public school authorities 'deify the athlete, hold him up to admiration, [and] load him with honour'.[59] *The Waves* presents Percival in similar terms.

Louis resents the boasting boys not only for being cricketers and for being 'the officers of the Natural History Society', but also for being 'the volunteers'. He may mean that they volunteer for any task or activity, with the implication that they uncritically accept the authority of the school; but he may mean more narrowly that they are volunteers for the Junior Cadet Corps or Officers' Training Corps. If the latter meaning is taken, then their 'forming into fours', 'marching in troops', and saluting their 'general' is not a metaphorical description of sport, but a literal one of the militaristic life of the school. Louis had already enjoyed marching into the chapel, 'two by two' (*W*, p. 25). In *Three Guineas*, Woolf made her analysis of male regimentation more explicit. Ridiculing exclusively male cere-monies, she remarked that, whatever their meaning, men always performed them 'together', 'always in step' (*TG*, p. 178).

The Waves constructs a more complex picture than *Three Guineas*. By presenting the boasting boys through the eyes of Louis, an outsider who wants to be accepted, Woolf presents both their attract-ive and their repellent aspects. Louis admires the 'obedience' of the boys, and admires them in terms which could be aesthetic: he admires the 'simultaneity' of their movements, 'simultaneity' here meaning a mechanical, clockwork coordination; even more abstractly, he admires their 'order'. Yet he is aware of their sadism: 'they also leave butterflies trembling with their wings pinched off; they throw dirty pocket-handkerchiefs clotted with blood screwed up into corners. They make little boys sob in dark passages' (*W*, p. 36).[60] The menace of this description is due to Woolf's suppres-sion of the links between the events. We are left to decide for our-selves how the blood came to be on the handkerchiefs, and how the boasting boys make the little boys sob. In 1912 Woolf herself had heard from Rupert Brooke of a case of rape at Rugby, where 'two fourteen-year-old choirboys' had selected a 10-year-old and had taken turns to rape him in the vestry during a service. The boy, reported Brooke three weeks later, had 'been in bed with a rupture ever since'.[61] Louis's description of school life discordantly juxta-poses the visible world of magnificent, charismatic leaders, and the hidden world of fear and sadism. Woolf may have privately associ-ated the discord with the contrast between Rupert Brooke—a Percival-like figure, much idealized after his death—and the incident he had related. For the majority of her readers, though, the refer-ences to bullying did not relate to particular incidents or individuals, but to leaders and to bullies as types.

Woolf's criticism of militarism and of the public schools is informed by a long radical tradition which can be traced back to the suffrage movement. Anti-suffragists in the period 1908 to 1914 often depended upon the 'argument from force', the argument that women, because they were not physically capable of waging a war, should not be allowed to elect the Parliament which could lead the country into one. Versions of this argument had been in play for some time: an anti-suffrage letter of 1889 had distinguished between those aspects of the state which rested 'upon force', 'the State in its administrative, military and financial aspects', and those such as education and nursing which equally involved men and women; however, this letter did not isolate the military role of men as sharply as the arguments of 1908 to 1914.[62]

Millicent Fawcett advanced several counter-arguments. One drew attention to the existing division of responsibilities: 'the politicians make war, soldiers pay the price and make peace'.[63] The identification of the male electorate with the male army was quite misleading: the electorate included many—those over the age of 60, for example—who would never be called upon to fight.[64] If such an identification were carried to its logical conclusion, then the *only* enfranchised group would be the army: the underlying logic of the argument from force leads to an authoritarian militarist state.

Another form of counter-argument uncovered the hidden suffering that women endured as a consequence of military action. In 1909 Fawcett remarked that a father's premature death would often be attributed to his having lost a son in a recent war (the Boer War was her example); she went on to argue that 'what is true of the father is no less true of the stricken mother. The bullet pierces another heart than that of its immediate victim'.[65] If women were expected to suffer even the indirect effects of war, Fawcett argued, they should be given a share in political responsibility. Recovering this argument gives new significance to the indirect female victims of war in Woolf's post-war fiction. Betty Flanders in *Jacob's Room* is one such victim. In the manuscript, her suffering frames Jacob's life: the final sentence of the manuscript version—'The room waved behind her tears'—recalls her tears in the opening paragraphs.[66] Although Woolf deleted this sentence in the published version, she does not allow Betty to fade from the narrative. In *Mrs Dalloway* two indirect victims of war, Mrs Foxcroft and Lady Bexborough, are mentioned near the beginning (p. 4), preparing the reader for the novel's examination of Rezia's suffering; as noted earlier, the beggar woman's wretched state may also be due to the war.[67] During the First World War, Woolf made similar connections between pacifism and feminism in a letter:

I become steadily more feminist, owing to the Times, which I read at breakfast and wonder how this preposterous masculine fiction keeps going a day longer—without some vigorous young woman pulling us together and marching through it—Do you see any sense in it? I feel as if I were reading about some curious tribe in Central Africa—And now they'll give us votes. (*Letters*, ii. 76)

The change of topic from war to suffrage is not as unmotivated as it might at first appear: Woolf implies that, had women been granted the vote earlier, the war might never have happened, or would not have been conducted as it was. Importantly, she recognizes that the war, or at least *The Times*'s account of it, is filtered through a 'fiction', or what might now be termed an 'ideology'.

Other radical writers criticized militarists for their overt attempts to interfere with education, and identified the more subtle ways in which a militarist ethos influenced the ethos of schools. Florence and Ogden claimed that militarism had ruined education 'with its traditions of discipline and its conception of history'.[68] Between the wars the political values instilled by schools became a contentious issue, and increasingly so in the years following the 1926 General Strike. Conservatives encouraged schools to instil patriotism and an imperialistic viewpoint, while socialists, communists, and liberals attempted to combat injustices in the hiring and firing of teachers, and to redress bias in history textbooks. Mark Starr's *Lies and Hate in Education* (1929) records numerous examples, and although Starr interprets his evidence partially, the Hogarth Press's having published his book makes it a particularly relevant context for *The Waves*. The teaching of history is particularly important. In 1874, J. R. Green's *Short History of the English People* had inaugurated a movement away from a militaristic conception of history and towards social history. Woolf adapted Green's phrase 'drum and trumpet history' in 1907 when she criticized a historical novel for being ' "drum and trumpet" fiction'.[69] In Starr's account, social history had not made a sufficient impact by 1929: 'History, indeed, has been so exclusively a record of wars that when a boy was told in a London class that the League of Nations was going to stop all fighting, he spontaneously remarked, "But then there will be no more history, sir, will there?" '[70] The militarist conception of history encouraged the view, later criticized by Woolf, that a novel should be counted as important if it depicted a battlefield, and trivial if it took place in a drawing room (*ROO*, p. 96). Conflicting conceptions of history also inform responses to Miss La Trobe's village pageant in *Between the Acts*. The pageant form itself allowed divergent representations of the nation's history,[71] and Colonel Mayhew's concern at the exclusion of the army—'What's history without the Army, eh?' (*BTA*, p. 141)—represents the conservative and militarist view.

The 'traditions of discipline' mentioned by Florence and Ogden manifested themselves in with varying degrees of subtlety. At one extreme, conservatives encouraged the formation of Junior Cadet Corps in schools and Officers' Training Corps in universities.[72] 'Field days' and 'mimic battles' were criticized by liberals for persuading schoolboys that it was 'natural and ordinary to hunt down and shoot other people who were our "enemies" '.[73] Reactionaries 'demanded that military drill should be part of every boy's school training', and it appears that their demands have been heeded at the boys' school in *The Waves*.[74] Military drill was criticized both 'because it aims at stiffness and unnatural muscular reactions', and because it represented a Germanization of the educational system. According to its critics, the German ideal of education was of 'a forcing house of industrial and military efficiency'. The terms of the argument echo those of Bergsonian philosophers: the German system aims to produce 'machine-like' servants of the state;[75] by implication, a system that was truly British in spirit would produce imaginative and independent individuals. The troop of army cadets in *Mrs Dalloway* are 'stiff' and have begun to resemble 'statues'. Although Peter Walsh admires their 'very fine training', the terms in which he describes them contradict his admiration: 'life' had been 'drugged into a stiff yet staring corpse by discipline' (*MD*, pp. 43–4). In Bergsonian terms, vitality has submitted to mechanism, psychological time to clock time.

In *The Waves*, the boasting boys are introduced in very similar terms. Although they do not reappear until late in the narrative, the sense of order that they represent for Louis remains important to him. It emerges in his pride as a businessman, 'from chaos making order'. He makes 'commands', albeit courteous ones; he loves to survey an empire on the office map, and he loves punctuality, 'Mr Prentice at four; Mr Eyres sharp at four-thirty' (*W*, p. 139). The militarist implications of his punctuality are illuminated in Bernard's summing up. Echoing Louis with a reference to 'dinner at eight' and 'luncheon at one-thirty', Bernard goes on to reflect that 'it is a mistake, this extreme precision, this orderly and military progress'. Such a mechanical form of time suppresses the undercurrent of 'broken dreams, nursery rhymes, street cries', and other fragmentary sensations (p. 213).

Though by emulating the boasting boys, Louis becomes an authoritarian figure, to describe him as purely authoritarian is to miss the complexity of his personality. He is an insecure figure, an outsider, ashamed of his Australian background, who absorbs the values of the boasting boys in an attempt to quell his insecurity. When the boasting boys reappear, at the end of the Hampton Court reunion, they are seen through the eyes of Bernard. In the immediately preceding paragraphs Bernard has been discussing order: the orderly lives of the lower middle-class shopkeepers, and the narrative order of 'our lives', 'one event following another' like 'the knocking of railway trucks in a siding'. Such an order could be seen as banal and mechanical, but Bernard also recognizes its reassuring aspect: 'Knock, knock, knock. Must, must, must. Must go, must sleep, must wake, must get up—sober, merciful word which we pretend to revile, which we press tight to our hearts, without which we should be undone' (*W*, p. 195). The passage revisits the question posed so directly by Septimus Warren Smith: 'What right has Bradshaw to say "must" to me?' (*MD*, p. 125). Bernard does not concede the right of any individual or authority to compel the individual, but he identifies the compulsion created by everyday routines.

Into this meditation crash the boasting boys. Their appearance complicates the picture, both because they represent the point where orderliness becomes regimentation, and because they all too often break out into disorderly behaviour. Bernard recalls details that Louis has forgotten. Not only does he remember how comical their orderliness could be, 'all turning their heads the same way as the brake rounded the corner', but he remembers them 'getting drunk' and 'breaking the furniture' (*W*, p. 195). Bernard's juxtaposition of shopkeepers with the boasting boys is problematic: in some respects it seems to identify them, yet in others it differentiates them. How far are the values of the upper middle-class boasting boys the same as those of the lower middle-class shopkeepers? The juxtaposition poses a question, but the reader is left to answer it.

The concern that education sought to suppress individuality also informs the puzzling absence of Jacob Flanders from *Jacob's Room*. Although his absence can be interpreted as being due to his death, and the difficulty that his biographer has in fleshing out a biography, it might also be that Jacob as an individual was dead long before he went to war, his individuality crushed by social pressures.[76] Although the young Jacob appears 'obstinate' to his mother (*JR*, p. 8), there is little sign of this obstinacy in the later reports we receive of him. Rather, he becomes the generic figure, 'nice, handsome, interesting, distinguished, well built', seen by Mrs Norman (p. 37), or, 'distinguished-looking', by Mrs Durrant and Sandra Wentworth Williams (pp. 94, 201). Were the epithets more specific, these multiple reports might be mutually confirmatory, but their insipidity suggests that Jacob has become a mass-produced type, possessed of 'character' but lacking individuality. The formation of 'character', in the sense of 'moral strength', was central to the public school ideal. Advocates of character formation saw it as a higher goal than developing 'mere intellectualism' or 'mere culture'.[77] Men with 'character' were able to endure temporary hardships for the sake of a distant goal.[78] Critics of character formation felt that 'character' was created at the expense of individuality. The public schools, wrote one, were 'incapable of understanding, appreciating or directing individuality'; they had 'a passion for "ordinariness" and a horror of the boy who is not "like other people" '.[79] To critics, the discipline imparted by the Officers' Training Corps was a training only in 'passive unreasoning subordination', and was 'quite worthless as moral training'.[80] Defenders of public schools conceded some of these points: 'They [public schools] teach the lesson that the brilliant individualist is often a nuisance in the game of life. They train men to become efficient cogs in the social machinery', wrote Arnold Lunn. Providing that the truly talented were not suppressed, such anti-individualism was socially valuable.[81]

Traditionally minded reviewers criticized Woolf for her failure to convey 'character': Arnold Bennett's remark that the characters in *Jacob's Room* did not 'vitally survive in the mind' particularly stung Woolf, and her essay 'Mr Bennett and Mrs Brown' was part of her reply (*Diary*, ii. 248). 'Character' in the literary sense is not identical to character in the educational sense: a memorable character in a novel may have no 'moral strength', and may be memorable for exactly that reason. However, the literary and the educational concepts are united by metaphors of solidity and permanence. The Greek root of 'character' refers to a thing engraved or inscribed. The critic and poet Herbert Read defined personal 'character' as 'the product of a disciplined education', something which created a 'firm, dependable set of ideas and reactions'. He contrasted it with what he preferred to call 'personality', a self which was open to the immediacy of sensations, and was able to change 'without loss of integrity'. He claimed that, in his experience, 'character' had been inadequate even to the demands of war.[82] In her novels, Woolf was less concerned to create a sense of rigid character than to convey a sense of fluid 'personality', or, as she might have termed it, 'sensibility'. Public school 'character formation' necessarily discouraged attention to the immediate and the sensuous: these were feminine tendencies. If the characters in *Jacob's Room* were 'ghosts' or 'puppets, moved hither & thither by fate', as Leonard Woolf remarked,[83] it may be because Virginia saw England as being peopled by ghosts, even before the First World War. Her failure to create 'character', in the sense that Arnold Bennett expected it, may be due to her desire to expose the hollowness of the public school ideal.[84]

Woolf's approach to social issues is framed by the potentially contradictory ideas of the 'New Liberalism': on the one hand, a passionate belief in the freedom of the individual; on the other, an awareness that the state had a legitimate role in maintaining and developing the physical infrastructure on which all depended. The national efficiency movement in the period 1901 to 1910 had claimed a stronger and more interventionist role for the state, promoting the claims of the scientific expert and proposing the elimination of the 'unfit'. Other imperialists, while preferring to speak of the 'nation' and the 'empire'—they rejected 'the state' as a foreign, continental concept—nevertheless insisted that the interests of the individual should be subordinated to those of the social organism. Woolf's interest in the problem of reconciling the individual and the group was moreover informed by her awareness of the inferior social status accorded to women.

The great strength of Woolf's narrative method is that it allows her to present social issues in their psychological aspects; long before anyone voiced the slogan 'the personal is the political', Woolf identified the connection. In *Night and Day*, she takes the idea that the 'professions' might include 'marriage' and 'living at home', and uses it as the bridge between personal and public. She shows how public norms of behaviour infiltrate the private consciousness of even the most free-thinking individuals. *Jacob's Room* extends this mode of analysis, embodying the public norms in those who provide 'reports' of Jacob, and in the biographer narrator himself.

In *Mrs Dalloway*, Woolf's individualism manifests itself as a largely sympathetic presentation of those individuals who have escaped 'corruption, lies, [and] chatter' (*MD*, p. 156), and an unsympathetic, satirical presentation of those, like the Prime Minister, who embody the power of the state; those, like Hugh Whitbread, who oil its cogs; and those, like William Bradshaw, who enforce its norms. The picture is an essentially tragic one: the escape that Septimus and the female vagrants have achieved is not a sustainable one. Characters like Peter Walsh and Mr Bowley may be less tragic, having achieved an equilibrium between their desires and society's prohibitions, but it is not a happy compromise, leaving them 'sealed with wax over the deeper sources of life' (*MD*, p. 17). The two questions that *Mrs Dalloway* asks may appear to be separate: 'Is the war really over?', and 'What right does he have to say "must" to me?' However, they are linked: in war, the state had exercised compulsion, most obviously in military conscription; five years after the war, it seemed to Woolf, the mechanisms of compulsion remained in place. The 'argument from force' had prevailed. *To the Lighthouse* provides a more optimistic picture. The patriarchal tyranny that Mr Ramsay holds over the household may resemble that of Sir William Bradshaw and the clocks of *Mrs Dalloway*, and Mrs Ramsay's connubial obsession, though more subtle in its workings, may be equally oppressive, but Lily is shown rethinking the norms of the past—Mrs Ramsay's 'old-fashioned ideas' (*TL*, p. 236)—and achieving her vision.

In *The Waves*, Woolf foregrounds the relation of the individual to the group, 'the group' being here both the larger group of the imperial nation, and the private group of friends. She articulates group consciousness using a vocabulary of unanimism. The conflict of the nation's claims on the individual with those of personal friends emerges most clearly in the school scenes, where Woolf uses explicitly martial imagery to expose the militarism that was more usually presented euphemistically in terms of 'discipline' and 'character'. *The Waves*, more than any of her other novels, is the one in which the author's idea of theme is most submerged, but it reveals itself in details of vocabulary and imagery. Woolf's image of the elusive 'fin' in the waste of waters indicates a wish to evade the 'finality' that an authorial consciousness might impose.

CHAPTER 6

SCIENTIFIC AND MEDICAL CONTEXTS

IF one were to take *Mrs Dalloway*'s Dr Holmes and Sir William Bradshaw as typical scientific men, one might assume that Woolf viewed science as authoritarian and inhumane. If one were to take the clocks of Harley Street as representations of the scientific spirit (*MD*, p. 87), one might assume that she saw science as obsessed with quantity at the expense of quality, and believed it was capable of seeing the world only in analysed fragments, never as a whole. One might conclude that the scientific ideas of her time were of little relevance to her writings. The assumption that literature and science are fundamentally opposed has a pedigree stretching back to romanticism: the clocks of Harley Street, '[s]hredding and slicing', might be taken to illustrate Wordsworth's phrase 'we murder to dissect'.[1] As Gillian Beer remarks, for many years, critics saw modernist writing as 'separated from, or even inimical to' the science of the 1920s and 1930s, with the Bloomsbury Group being seen as particularly 'remote' from the discipline.[2] More recently, however, critics have recognized that Woolf was receptive to certain aspects of scientific thinking, and that the popular science writing of the period offered accessible and imaginatively stimulating accounts.

The passages in *Mrs Dalloway* describing an aeroplane may illustrate the contention. To Mr Bentley, who is 'vigorously rolling his strip of turf at Greenwich', the aeroplane becomes a symbol 'of man's soul; of his determination . . . to get outside his body, beyond his house, by means of thought, Einstein, speculation, mathematics, the Mendelian theory' (*MD*, p. 24). For one critic, writing in 1973, not only did Mr Bentley symbolize scientific man, for whom 'Nature is a strip of turf to be vigorously rolled', but the physicist and the geneticist, Einstein and Mendel, were instances of such men.[3] However, to speak of 'science' and 'scientific man' as unchanging archetypes is misleading. As Mr Bentley's own thoughts remind us, science in Woolf''s era was rapidly changing. If Bentley represents the old scientific mentality, the aeroplane might equally represent the liberating possibilities of the new.[4]

Given that scientific ideas are scarcely ever expressed in literary works as coherent theories, but nearly always in fragmentary, allusive form, it is difficult for the reader to determine the extent to which the author was incorporating them consciously. Exceptionally, Woolf's near-contemporary Aldous Huxley included scientists as characters in several of his novels, and allowed them to provide coherent expositions of new theories and their philosophical implications.[5] But Woolf was more reluctant to allow ideas to obtrude. The reader needs to recontextualize her writings to rediscover which scientific ideas might have been taken as common knowledge at the time of writing. Given the range of scientific disciplines that had emerged by the early twentieth century, it is impossible to be comprehensive. Instead, this chapter will examine ideas of mental illness and of physical vitality; theories about the nature of matter; ideas drawn from astronomy and relativity theory; and ideas associated with telecommunications.

Mental Health: *Mrs Dalloway*

What has caused Septimus Warren Smith's breakdown? On a first reading of *Mrs Dalloway*, we may be inclined to agree with Sir William Bradshaw's diagnosis, that he is an example of 'the deferred effects of shell-shock' (*MD*, p. 155). However, there is something awkward about granting diagnostic authority to a man who attracts such suspicion, not only from his patient, but also from Clarissa. Moreover, Bradshaw in June 1923 appears to be out of touch with the latest thinking: in September 1922 a government committee on 'shell shock' had said 'that the term was misleading.[6] More generally still, in this period, there was no universally accepted system for understanding mental illness. Its different causes and different forms, always a matter of disagreement, had been newly thrown into question by Freudian psychoanalysis. *Mrs Dalloway* suggests quite explicitly that Septimus might have been treated more humanely, and suggests more subtly that other diagnoses might have been made.

Sir William Bradshaw recognizes as soon as Septimus walks into his consulting room, that it was 'a case of extreme gravity', and decides within minutes that it was 'a case of complete breakdown—complete physical and nervous breakdown' (*MD*, p. 81). However, his diagnosis does not explain the cause of the illness, but merely groups the symptoms under a convenient label. Bradshaw's repeated reference to Septimus as a 'case' suggests that, unlike psychoanalytic practitioners, he will not be interested in listening to his patient as a person. Bradshaw's distinction between 'physical' and 'nervous' breakdowns betrays the recent separation of the 'nerve specialist' from the more general doctor. The phrase 'nervous breakdown' was a relatively new one: the earliest known examples date from 1904, one of them being in a letter by Woolf (*Letters*, i. 148). It differentiates the specifically nervous illness from a more general 'breakdown' of physical health. As such it reveals the connections between the two conditions, which were still considered important in the 1920s, and indicates the growing specialization of medical treatment: such breakdowns had become the domain of the 'alienist', later the 'nerve specialist', and later still the psychiatrist.

The treatment which Bradshaw prescribes indicates the continued importance of the connection between 'physical' and 'nervous' breakdown. Septimus is required to rest in bed for six months, in solitude, 'without friends, without books, without messages' (*MD*, p. 84). Importantly, he is required to eat well, and to drink milk, to the extent that a man who begins the cure weighing 'seven stone six' comes out 'weighing twelve'. The treatment is the rest cure, devised by the American neurologist Silas Weir Mitchell, and introduced in Britain in the 1880s.[7] Weir Mitchell's description of it as involving 'a combination of entire rest and of excessive feeding' closely matches Bradshaw's prescription. Weir Mitchell's female patients 'were expected to gain as much as fifty pounds on a diet that began with milk and gradually built up to several substantial meals a day';[8] the increases of weight in Bradshaw's system are greater, but comparable.

The rest cure was invented as a treatment for neuraesthenia, one of the two or three accepted categories of mental illness in women in the late nineteenth century. Doctors distinguished between anorexia nervosa, hysteria, and neurasthenia, with some taking anorexia to be a subcategory of hysteria.[9] Hysteria and neurasthenia had many symptoms in common, but while the former condition tended towards disruptiveness and violence, the latter tended to produce temporary disabilities such as the loss of the voice or the paralysis of a limb. A distinction of social class was at work: neurasthenia was the 'more prestigious and attractive form of female nervousness'; neurasthenics 'were thought to be cooperative, ladylike, and well-bred'.[10] When the First World War began to produce cases of mental breakdown, the categories were extended to include men. The social distinction continued: hysterical conditions tended to appear in the ranks, while neurasthenic ones were more prominent among officers.[11] Military neurasthenics tended to suffer from symptoms such as 'nightmares, insomnia, heart palpitations, dizziness, depression, [and] disorientation'.[12] Septimus's symptoms—'headaches, sleeplessness, fears, dreams' (*MD*, p. 77)—place him in this category, and to this extent Bradshaw's rest cure is the appropriate one.

The rest cure imagines the body to have reserves of energy which are easily depleted and difficult to restore. The concept has its roots in physics, specifically in mid-nineteenth-century theories of thermodynamics. According to physicists, energy continually disperses from all bodies: the sun dissipates its energy continuously, like a steam boiler; so too does the human body. The philosopher Herbert Spencer used these concepts to explain differences between the sexes. In his *Principles of Biology* (1867), *Principles of Sociology* (1876), and other works, he argued that each human being had a fixed 'fund' of energy to expend, and that as women needed to preserve their energy 'to meet the cost of reproduction', it was not available for the mental or physical growth of the individual.[13] In Spencer's account, women were simply less completely evolved than men. As Conway notes, Spencer's theory gave 'scientific authority' to the view of women as 'intuitive and irrational'.[14] In 1874, the greatest psychiatrist of his day, Henry Maudsley, argued that adolescent girls expended a great deal of energy in puberty, and had 'little vitality to spare' for other functions.[15] Maudsley's term 'vitality', which might now appear to be part of everyday language, carried the authority of a supposedly scientific theory. Maudsley concluded that girls' education should be sharply differentiated from that of boys; it should be less demanding, physically and mentally. Spencer's theory was taken further in 1889 by the biologists Patrick Geddes and J. Arthur Thomson in *The Evolution of Sex*. They argued that sexual differences could be traced back to basic differences in the metabolisms of male and female cells. Male cells had the tendency to dissipate energy, while female cells stored or built it up. The 'active' qualities of sperm and the 'passive' qualities of ova derived from this distinction. So too did male aggression and female passivity.[16] While Spencer and Darwin saw women's qualities as 'acquired' characteristics of the species, Geddes and Thomson believed them to be so profoundly rooted in metabolic differences that they could never be altered by evolution, still less by legislation. 'What was decided among the prehistoric *Protozoa*', wrote Geddes, 'can not be annulled by act of Parliament'.[17]

Such ideas persisted into the twentieth century. Geddes and Thomson repeated their claims about male and female metabolisms in *Sex* (1914), a non-technical book in the Home University Library series. In 1925 the Hogarth Press published *Woman: An Inquiry* by Willa Muir. Muir claimed to be interested not in purely physical differences between men and women, nor those created by a difference in social power, but in the underlying 'spiritual' differences. Nevertheless, she drew upon Spencer's biological discourse, which had in turn embodied the mid-Victorian relations of men and women. 'Motherhood', wrote Muir, is a 'greater tax on vital energy than fatherhood'. This led her to speculate that there was an 'essential difference' between men and women in 'the distribution of energy'. As all women are 'potential mothers', they need to maintain a 'reserve' of energy. Men therefore have more energy 'at their conscious disposal', while women's energy is 'diverted more into unconscious life'.[18] Though it was refracted through a Freudian terminology of the 'unconscious', the Spencerian idea lived on. In *Mrs Dalloway*, Miss Kilman has told Elizabeth that '[w]hen people are happy, they have a reserve . . . upon which to draw' (*MD*, p. 110). Miss Kilman feels herself to be like a wheel without a tyre: she is not only depleted, but deflated. The rest cure aimed to recharge depleted vitality, but it did not claim to alter the fundamental metabolic differences between men and women.

Sir William Bradshaw's mantra of 'proportion' carries connotations that are rooted in the same patriarchal construction of the female body. 'Sir William said he never spoke of "madness"; he called it not having a sense of proportion' (*MD*, p. 82). Critics have noted that Bradshaw echoes Virginia Woolf's own heart specialist, Harrington Sainsbury, who advised her in August 1922 to 'practise equanimity'.[19] However, this echo was a private matter; 'proportion' was in the public domain. In March 1912, at the height of the militant campaign of the Women's Social and Political Union (WSPU), *The Times* published a long letter from the eminent bacteriologist Sir Almroth Wright (1861–1947). He condemned what he saw as the fatuousness of the aims of the suffragists, and warned of the disastrous consequences if the vote were granted. An editorial on the same day endorsed his account of 'the unchangeable physical basis upon which sex difference rests'.[20] Wright's arguments were a version of the argument from force: 'women are a class of voters who cannot effectively back up their votes by force', he wrote. Though the argument from force need not depend on an energetic conception of the body, Wright's view of physiology clearly derived from Spencer.[21] Wright dismissed the idea that a woman should receive the same wages as a man for doing the same work by stating that 'even if woman succeeds in doing the same work as man, he has behind him a much larger reserve of physical strength'. This 'reserve' was useful to the employer in 'a time of strain', and was worth paying extra for. Moreover, in Wright's view, 'woman' was physiologically unstable. His letter began from the position that for 'man' 'the physiology and psychology of woman is full of difficulties'. Men were mystified when they encountered in women 'periodically recurring phases of hypersensitiveness', 'unreasonableness', and crucially for *Mrs Dalloway*, 'loss of the sense of proportion'. He went on to describe the various 'types' of suffragist, motivated by factors such as adolescent instability, menopausal instability, and lack of sexual fulfilment. In Wright's view there was an 'element of mental disorder' in the suffrage movement; women 'as a class' were 'quite incompetent to adjudicate upon political issues'.

Wright's letter quickly achieved notoriety. It met with unequivocal condemnation in the suffrage and socialist press, as did his later pamphlet *The Unexpurgated Case Against Woman Suffrage*; the only thing that was said in Wright's favour was that he exposed the underlying misogyny and the dubious logic of the anti-suffragists.[22] Given Wright's notoriety, it is very likely that Woolf would have known his letter and his views on 'proportion'. As she had been suffering from mental illness in the early months of 1912, it would have had a particularly personal impact: though not a 'militant' suffragist, she would have been aware that she seemed to prove his argument, and simultaneously aware of that argument's reductiveness and inadequacy. Her feminism and her mental health were certainly connected, but her politics was not pathological. Rather, her experience of the medical profession illuminated the workings of patriarchal authority. By placing 'proportion' at the centre of Bradshaw's idea of normality, Woolf hints at connections between the treatment of soldiers after the war and the treatment of women before it.

Though Bradshaw apparently diagnoses Septimus as a shell-shocked neuraesthenic, both the consultation scene and other scenes hint at other diagnoses. It is clear that ideas of masculinity are significant for Septimus: physically 'weakly' before the war, during it he 'developed manliness'. However, running contrary to his manliness is an element of physical attraction to his officer, Evans. 'It was a case of two dogs playing on a hearth-rug; one worrying a paper screw, snarling, snapping, giving a pinch, now and then, at the old dog's ear . . . They had to be together, share with each other, fight with each other, quarrel with each other' (*MD*, p. 73). The poetry of the First World War often makes reference to such same-sex bonds.[23] However, when Evans is killed, Septimus cannot express his full feelings, and instead congratulates himself 'upon feeling very little' (*MD*, p. 73). Septimus cannot mourn Evans, because to do so would be to reveal a taboo sexuality; but without mourning Evans, he cannot escape from the war. Prevented from feeling for Evans, he becomes unable to feel for anyone. The novel offers enough information about Septimus and Evans for the reader to reach a Freudian diagnosis in terms of 'repression' and 'sublimation'.[24] Some opponents of psychoanalysis had taken the existence of the 'war neuroses' to disprove Freud's theory that neurotic symptoms were due to sexual forces.[25] Freud and his supporters replied that to acknowledge the importance of the traumatic experience of war was not to exclude sexual factors. Woolf knew of Freud's works—the Hogarth Press was publishing them—and would certainly have been aware of his ideas at least in outline, and possibly of the controversy over war neuroses.[26] In a draft version of the novel, even Hugh Whitbread is up-to-date enough to have 'heard of' Freud.[27] Unlike her contemporary Rose Macaulay, whose 1921 novel *Dangerous Ages* is speckled with his terminology, Woolf does not allow Freud to obtrude. However, she hints: immediately after we hear of Septimus congratulating himself on feeling very little, we are told that 'The War had taught him. It was sublime' (*MD*, p. 73). One thing the war may have taught him is to sublimate his sexual desires.

Sir William Bradshaw asks Septimus whether he served in the war, but takes little interest in the details, and apparently never hears about Evans's death. He places the cause of the illness elsewhere, though again, the novel is far from explicit. He is reported as believing that 'unsocial impulses' are 'bred more than anything by the lack of good blood'. 'Blood' here can be read both literally and metaphorically. The 1910–11 *Encyclopedia Britannica*'s discussion of the causes of insanity gave relatively little space to 'mental stress', and none at all to the new Freudian ideas; it gave much more to speculation about toxic agents that poison the nervous system.[28] The authors of its article on insanity drew particular attention to the 'delerium of collapse' which follows infectious diseases such as typhus, pneumonia, and influenza, and which characteristically included hallucinations. Rachel Vinrace's breakdown in *The Voyage Out* can be diagnosed within these terms. It was also recognized that syphilis caused insanity. *The Times*, commenting on the Government report into shell shock, regretted that it had not fully investigated the effects of certain pre-existing 'infections'.[29] Septimus's lack of good blood could be taken to mean that there are poisons in his body. A diagnosis of insanity following an infection would suggest a parallel with Clarissa, the victim of influenza. Influenza was also recognized as causing 'debility and nervous depression': after an influenza epidemic in Paris in 1890, the suicide rate there had increased by 25 per cent.[30] The reader who was aware of this correlation might wonder if Clarissa was going to follow Septimus's example. At one stage in writing the novel, Woolf had indeed intended her to commit suicide, 'or perhaps merely to die at the end of the party'.[31]

It would be more natural to refer to infected blood as 'bad blood', rather than 'the absence of good blood', and it is more likely that Bradshaw attributes Septimus's insanity to 'blood' in the sense of hereditary factors. The *Encyclopedia Britannica* reckoned the 'hereditary transmission of a liability to mental disease' to be 'the most important among all the predisposing causes of insanity'.[32] The foundation for such views was eugenics, a science that aimed to eliminate bad hereditary factors in the human race and to encourage good ones. What counted as good and bad were of course culturally variable. There is a comical side to this: extraordinarily, one writer

believed that ' "strange first names" were symptomatic of latent
family degeneracy'; on this basis, the fantastically named Septimus
was doomed from his christening day.[33] There is also a deadly serious
side: some eugenists advocated the sterilization or killing of
'the unfit', and in Nazi Germany, this proposal became a reality.
Bradshaw does not explicitly advocate eugenic murder or sterilization, but, like some of Woolf's own doctors, he 'forbade childbirth'
(*MD*, p. 84).[34]

Vitality and Women's Writing: *A Room of One's Own*

Throughout *A Room of One's Own*, Woolf remains mindful of science as part of culture, both as a part of culture which has oppressed
women, and as a part to which they have contributed and can continue to contribute. One measure of the poverty of Fernham College
is the very fact that Woolf is lecturing on women and fiction: were it
richer, 'the subject of our talk might have been archaeology, botany,
anthropology, physics, the nature of the atom, mathematics, astronomy, relativity, geography' (*ROO*, p. 27). Because women have been
excluded from science, one cannot 'take an apple and remark, Newton discovered the laws of gravitation and Newton was a woman'
(p. 111). While Woolf's argument is primarily concerned with the
absence of a female literary canon, she is, like the suffrage campaigners, aware of the importance of foremothers in other disciplines. She also suggests that women are gaining access to the
sciences. In *Love's Adventure*, the imaginary novel from which she
quotes, Chloe and Olivia share a laboratory together (p. 108).[35]

Woolf also focuses on specific scientific ideas. Among the mis-
ogynist works that Woolf describes in the British Museum are some
on the small size of women's brains (*ROO*, p. 37). Such works really
existed: in 1887 the biologist George Romanes had stated that wom-
en's brains were, on average, 5 ounces lighter than men's, remarking
that one would consequently expect to find a 'marked inferiority of
intellectual power' in women.[36] The 'sages' who considered women
to be 'shallower in the brain' (*ROO*, p. 38) may have been speaking
metaphorically, but they may also have been speaking neurologically:
Romanes had been informed that the 'grey matter, or cortex' of the
female brain was 'shallower than that of the male'.[37]

The crucial concept for *A Room of One's Own* is vitality. Vitality is the conceptual bridge between the material conditions for literary creation (money and privacy) and the act of creation itself. On the opening page of the manuscript version Woolf had characterized fiction as an art which does not lend itself to examination 'owing to its vast size' and 'its immense vitality', though she deleted 'vitality' and replaced it with 'fertility'.[38] In the third chapter of the published version, she compares the effects of male discouragement on the mind of a female artist to the effects of a diet of 'ordinary' milk on a laboratory rat: the rat fed on ordinary milk was 'furtive, timid and small', while that fed on 'Grade A' milk was 'glossy, big and bold' (*ROO*, p. 68). Woolf explores the idea of vitality more explicitly in the following pages. She considers the effects on a girl in the nineteenth century of being told that women are supported by, and must minister to, men: such opinions 'must have lowered her vitality, and told profoundly upon her work' (p. 70). Woolf repeats the idea in the following paragraph: a woman in the nineteenth century 'was snubbed, slapped, lectured and exhorted', and in consequence her mind 'must have been strained and her vitality lowered' (p. 71). Where writers like Henry Maudsley and Willa Muir had understood vitality in narrowly biological terms, Woolf places it in a broader social context. It was not puberty that lowered the vitality of the adolescent girl, but patriarchy.

In the fourth chapter, Woolf's claim that '[t]he book has somehow to be adapted to the body' seems to grant priority to biology, but again Woolf places her biological terms in a social context. She goes on to say that 'women's books should be shorter' and 'more concentrated' than those of men, 'so that they do not need long hours of steady and uninterrupted work' (*ROO*, p. 101); as her earlier account of Jane Austen has made clear (pp. 86–7), interruptions are a social and not a biological fact. She makes a claim of a more biological character, that 'the nerves that feed the brain would seem to differ in men and women'; she suggests in consequence that the methods of education best suited to one sex might not be suited to the other. The claim is surprising. Woolf's argument about the nerves that feed the brain seems to resemble reductive arguments about brain size. It leaves out the social dimension. However, there is a twist. Such arguments normally invoke the authority of specific scientists, or, at the very least, the authority of 'science'. When Woolf goes to the bookcase, she finds that there is no published evidence to support her case, no 'elaborate study of the psychology of women *by a woman*' (p. 102, emphasis added). Woolf's claim about the nerves forces her reader to think about the reliability of scientific authority. Philosophers of science like Ernst Mach and Karl Pearson had argued that scientific concepts were economical constructs. Woolf takes the argument one stage further by suggesting that they are man-made constructs.

The Atom and Woolf's Idea of Fiction

In two of her later novels, Woolf's characters refer explicitly to the question of what the physical world is made of.[39] In the 1908 episode of *The Years*, Eleanor contemplates the nature of matter. Through-out *The Years*, the Pargiter family frequently contemplate solid domestic objects and wonder at their ability to endure, so there is a significant undercurrent to Eleanor's questions:

But what vast gaps there were, what blank spaces, she thought leaning back in her chair, in her knowledge! Take this cup for instance; she held it out in front of her. What was it made of? Atoms? And what were atoms, and how did they stick together? The smooth hard surface of the china with its red flowers seemed to her for a second a marvellous mystery. (*Y*, p. 148)

Curiously, Eleanor's characterization of her own knowledge provides a characterization of the atom as it had come to be understood since the 1890s: not as a solid sphere, but as a porous space containing 'vast gaps'. The atom was like a miniature solar system, with elec-trons orbiting a core of protons and neutrons. This 'solar' atom could be penetrated by X-rays—Woolf herself had seen X-ray photography demonstrated in 1898 (*PA*, p. 10)—and atoms of one element could disintegrate and mutate into another. For some popu-lar scientific writers, the newly discovered qualities of matter shook the certainty of science, and allowed the reconciliation of science and religion. Such thinking informs the other explicit reference to atoms in Woolf's later novels. In *Between the Acts*, as the crowd disperses after the village pageant, one of the anonymous voices is heard to say that science 'is making things (so to speak) more spiritual . . . The very latest notion, so I'm told is, nothing's solid . . . There, you can get a glimpse of the church through the trees . . .' (*BTA*, p. 179;

Woolf's ellipses). 'Things', it seems, have lost the solidity which defines their 'thingness', and can be 'things' only as a figure of speech. While the concluding remark about the church might appear to represent a change in topic, metaphorically it suggests that matter no longer obscures faith. That Woolf included such sentiments in the novel does not imply that she endorsed them, and she was probably aware of the sceptical attitude that many philosophers took towards such religiose conclusions: as one Cambridge philosopher had said in 1929, 'You cannot turn matter into spirit by making it thin'.[40]

These explicit references to the nature of matter do not exist in isolation. Throughout her career Woolf used a contrast between 'solidity' and 'transparency' to characterize both the nature of the self, and the nature of her experiments in fiction. Most famously, in 'Modern Novels' (1919), and its successors, she termed Bennett, Galsworthy, and Wells as 'materialists'.[41] The designation 'materialist' can be understood in philosophical terms, in contrast to 'idealist' or 'spiritualist' (see the section 'Perception and Reality' in Chapter 4, above), but it is also suggestive when considered from a scientific point of view. Woolf ironically praises Bennett for the solidity of his craftsmanship. She says explicitly that, for those who continue to write traditional novels, the labour of proving the 'solidity' of the story, its 'likeness to life', is labour wasted, because the solidity obscures what is important in fiction. Implicitly, that labour is misdirected because scientific materialism has been overthrown, and science has shown that even the most solid things in the world are not what they seem. In characterizing the future of fiction, as represented by James Joyce, Woolf draws upon the vocabularies of psychologists and physicists: Joyce reveals 'the flickerings of that innermost flame which flashes its myriad messages through the brain'; in the sixth chapter of *Ulysses* he presents us with 'restless scintillations', 'flashes of deep significance succeeded by incoherent inanities'. While talk of 'messages passing through the brain' derives from psychology, 'flickerings', 'flashes', and 'scintillations' are all terms that could be associated with the vacuum tube of the X-ray machine. 'Scintillation' had long been used to refer to sparks and flashes of light, but from 1903 onwards was used specifically to refer to the flashes of visible or ultraviolet light emitted by fluorescent substances when struck by high-energy particles. Nor was this a word used only in laboratories: it can be found in at least one popular science review that Woolf might have read.[42] The modern novelist, Woolf implies, should see through the world of appearances, the world of solid matter, and should show us the truly restless and unstable nature of reality. The 'innumerable atoms' that shower our senses are not solid: they form a 'semi-transparent envelope' or 'luminous halo'. Woolf's often-quoted phrases might be used to describe the appearance of flesh in an X-ray photograph: she implies that the realism of the modern novelist should be the realism of the X-ray photograph or of physicists' observations of disintegrating atoms; it is a realism adequate to a world where nothing is stable.

Waves in *The Waves*

Among the many things suggested by the title of *The Waves* is the language of science. Several different aspects of science may be involved: to some the title has suggested wave theories of matter,[43] but the waves may also refer to scientific accounts of the creation of the earth. The undulations in *The Waves* are not exclusively sea-borne: Jinny, at home in the country, notes how the hay 'waves over the meadows' (*W*, p. 31). Louis, leaving school for a life in business, has a more extended reflection: 'a poignant shadow, a keen accent, falls on these golden bristles, on these poppy-red fields, this flowing corn that never overflows its boundaries, but runs rippling to the edge' (pp. 51–2). Both descriptions clarify the nature of wave motion: the wave is an immaterial form that moves through material particles without permanently changing them. Stalks of wheat sway backwards and forwards, but remain rooted to the same spot; particles of water rise and fall, but do not move in the direction of the wave.

Such theories have a long philosophical and religious history, beginning before modern science. When W. B. Yeats explained to Woolf that *The Waves* expressed in fiction 'the idea of pulsations of energy throughout the universe', he added that the theory was common to modern physicists and psychic researchers.[44] Ideas of reincarnation could be described as wave theories: an immaterial form, the soul, flows through a portion of matter, temporarily giving it shape; when at death the soul leaves the body, the matter reverts to being a heap of formless atoms. There is no evidence that Woolf believed in reincarnation, but the theory was artistically convenient to her. In *The Waves* Louis certainly claims to have had previous lives in ancient Egypt, classical Greece, Elizabethan England, and in France at the court of Louis XIV; he alludes to one of these lives immediately after the passage about the flowing corn fields. The narrator of *Jacob's Room* advances a wave theory concerning 'the beauty of women': 'They all have it; they all lose it', he says, and goes on to explain that 'if you talk of a beautiful woman you mean only something flying fast which for a second uses the eyes, lips, or cheeks of Fanny Elmer, for example, to glow through' (*JR*, pp. 157–8).

The physicists were dealing with more abstract waves. In the mid-1920s, the 'solar' theory became incompatible with the quantum theory of energy, and was rejected. Though the 'solar' atom had been porous, it consisted of solid particles possessing definite positions and velocities. The new theories of the atom recognized that when science dealt with structures as small as the atom, the act of observation altered the thing being observed. The very waves of light that one might use to see into an atom would disrupt the position or momentum of its electrons.[45] Indeterminacy and uncertainty became part of physics. In one of the new theories, Erwin Schrödinger's, the universe consisted of another kind of waves, theoretical entities with no real physical existence.[46] Schrödinger's waves are waves of probability. In certain places, where the waves converge and coalesce to form a stormy region, they form something recognizable as an electron. A small concentrated storm indicates an electron with very definite position, while a larger storm indicates an electron about which the observer can be less certain.[47]

The characters in *The Waves* are conscious that the world does not exist independently of the means that we use to observe and describe it. In their case, the main tool is language. As noted in Chapter 4, Neville proposes that mental 'discrimination' alters the world: '[n]othing should be named lest by so doing we change it' (*W*, p. 65). His words are waves that 'fall and rise' to a rhythm: ideally their rhythm is sympathetic to the world they describe, but there is a constant danger that they will become 'artificial' and 'insincere' (p. 66). Similarly, as the friends meet to bid Percival farewell, Bernard asks what emotion has brought them together 'at a particular time, to this particular spot': 'Shall we call it, conveniently, "love"?' He considers that 'love' is 'too small, too particular a name' to attach to 'the width and spread of our feelings' (pp. 103–4). His use of 'particular' is suggestive. Bernard recognizes that the universe can be understood as a collection of finite particles, be they particular places and times, or particular words, but he recognizes that to describe it thus leaves out something wider and broader, the waves that flow through the particles. Not only the interaction of language with the world, but the interaction of one person with another is described in these terms. In one scene, Neville's presence affects Bernard like 'a long wave': it is 'devastating', 'dragging me open, laying bare the pebbles on the shore of my soul' (p. 71). Just as the observation of a particle reduces all its possible positions and momentums down to one single measurement, Neville has reduced the many Bernards 'into a single being' (p. 72). Although plural, the pebbles also symbolize the finite world of distinct, countable objects.

As Yeats recognized in the 1930s, and as others have recognized since, the language and imagery of *The Waves* are suggestive of the ideas of modern physics. However, physics itself did not exist in isolation from other disciplines. As we have seen (Chapter 4), the characteristic contrast between something spread out and something 'particular' can also be interpreted in terms established by Henri Bergson in the 1880s and 1890s. Woolf borrows eclectically from various disciplines, sometimes synthesizing, sometimes allowing quite contradictory vocabularies to work within the same novel.

Astronomy and Human Isolation: From *Night and Day* to *The Waves*

Many of Woolf's novels concern the conflicting forces of isolation and communication. Under the guise of privacy and a room of one's own, isolation can be a positive thing, but it also implies solitude. Hearing of the young man's death, Clarissa Dalloway reflects that 'one was alone' (*MD*, p. 156). More melodramatically, Mr Ramsay recites from a poem, 'The Castaway', which includes the line 'we perished, each alone' (*TL*, pp. 224–5). In the context of such questions, Woolf often alludes to ideas from astronomy. As a young woman she had been struck by the way that, in *Two on a Tower*, Thomas Hardy contrasted the stars with 'minute human loves' (*PA*, pp. 386–7). In *Night and Day* she does something similar. Spending

Christmas with her cousins in Lincolnshire, Katharine Hilbery steps into the garden of their country house one December evening to consider her relationship with William Rodney, whom, with little enthusiasm, she expects to marry. Woolf introduces the stars partly to remind the reader of Katharine's intellectual ambitions (*ND*, p. 201). Moreover, Katharine's initial absent-minded attitude towards them recalls the scene in chapter 11 where she browsed through William's books (pp. 199, 144). However, as she focuses more distinctly on them, they flash back 'a ripple of light'.

Without knowing or caring more for Church practices than most people of her age, Katharine could not look into the sky at Christmas time without feeling that, at this one season, the Heavens bend over the earth with sympathy, and signal with immortal radiance that they, too, take part in her festival. Somehow, it seemed to her that they were even now beholding the procession of kings and wise men upon some road on a distant part of the earth. And yet, after gazing for another second, the stars did their usual work upon the mind, froze to cinders the whole of our short human history, and reduced the human body to an ape-like, furry form, crouching amid the brushwood of a barbarous clod of mud. (*ND*, pp. 202–3)

Why, one might ask, does Katharine imagine the stars seeing 'now' events which had taken place centuries previously? And why does she turn from thinking of Jesus to thinking of an 'ape-like, furry form'?

Katharine's ideas are informed not only by the vast scale of the universe, but by popular scientific expositions of the finite velocity of light. It had been known for over two centuries that light has a finite velocity, but the fact was becoming newly topical as Woolf wrote *Night and Day*. In everyday human life, we ignore the phenomenon: reading a book, one does not think of the light reflected from its pages as 'travelling' towards the retina; the time taken is so infinitesimal that we may disregard it. However, over long distances, it becomes significant: if the sun were to be extinguished instantaneously, eight minutes would pass before anyone on earth became aware of its demise. Popular accounts of astronomy used even more dramatic examples: if one were situated on a suitably distant planet, and possessed an extraordinarily powerful telescope, a pivotal historical event such as the Battle of Waterloo would appear to be taking place 'now', in the present.[48] Woolf saw that 'the telescope is a time machine of sorts, in that looking out into space always marks a looking back in cosmological time'.[49] Within these terms, Katharine's belief that the stars 'now' behold the Nativity carries a grain of truth, as does the idea that they can see earlier states of human evolution. The elevated diction of the passage echoes at least one of the popular accounts: the stars are not 'seeing' the Nativity, but 'beholding' it. In the English translation of Camille Flammarion's *Astronomie populaire*, images from the earth 'escape' in the form of light, and go on to reveal themselves 'to the eyes of distant beholders'.[50] Regardless of whether her choice of phrase specifically recalls Flammarion, Woolf attributes to Katharine the slightly pompous diction of popular astronomy, a genre which often encouraged its readers to wonder at the vast distances involved, but which less commonly encouraged them to think scientifically.[51]

Woolf's reference to the finite velocity of light was strangely, and perhaps unintentionally, topical. It was central to Einstein's special and general theories of relativity that the velocity of light is finite, and that nothing can exceed that velocity. Einstein had published his special theory in 1905, and his general theory in 1916, but non-specialist accounts did not begin to appear until 1918, and they appeared in large numbers only in November 1919, when the experimental proof of the general theory was announced.[52] Woolf had drafted the passage in January 1917, and had submitted the manuscript to Gerald Duckworth in March or April 1919, just as popular accounts began to appear in the *Athenaeum*.[53] The passage poses an irresolvable problem of contextualization. In later years, there are clear signs that Woolf knew of Einstein's theory, at least in outline: in 1926 and 1927, Vita Sackville-West referred to the delay of news in the post as an 'Einsteinian' effect; in 1930, and again in 1937, Woolf read James Jeans's popular account of the new physics, *The Mysterious Universe*.[54]

Woolf returned to the imagery of starlight in *To the Lighthouse* and *The Waves*.[55] Walking with William Bankes, looking 'at the dunes far away', Lily feels a sense of sadness: 'partly because distant views seem to outlast by a million years . . . the gazer and to be communing already with a sky which beholds an earth entirely at rest' (*TL*, p. 30). The image introduces the themes of memory, posterity, and haunting. Mr Ramsay, imagining his intellectual pursuits as a doomed mountain expedition, pictures himself on a peak where he can see 'the waste of the years and the perishing of stars', and imagines his fame as a 'little light': 'His own little light would shine, not very brightly, for a year or two, and would then be merged in some bigger light, and that in a bigger still' (p. 50). While the image does not require a knowledge of astronomy to be intelligible, the cosmic perspective of 'the perishing of stars' suggests the relevance of such a context. Mrs Ramsay does not invoke astronomy so explicitly, but nevertheless recognizes the relative smallness of 'her fifty years', and thinks of it in visual terms: it is 'a little strip of time' which 'presented itself to her eyes' (p. 81). In the background of all these images of light is the image of the lighthouse.

The imagery of light achieves its full relevance after Mrs Ramsay's death. Popular science writers sometimes used the idea of haunting in discussing astronomical phenomena: one had suggested that some of the stars we see might in fact be the ghosts of stars long extinguished, their light having travelled around the universe and returned to its starting point; the idea caught the imagination of Vita Sackville-West.[56] Mrs Ramsay's light comes back to haunt Mrs McNab, and later the family. Mrs McNab's memories are so vivid that the past appears to be in the present: 'She could see her now, stooping over her flowers'. Moreover, memory is figured as telescopic vision: the image of Mrs Ramsay is 'faint and flickering, like a yellow beam or the circle at the end of a telescope' (*TL*, p. 186); Mr Ramsay similarly appears seen as if through a telescope, 'in a ring of light' (p. 190). The novel's astronomical vocabulary overlaps with its central image. The 'little airs' that erode the house are directed by a light that may come from a ship, or from 'an uncovered star', or from the lighthouse itself (p. 172). The phrase equates all three sources. That Mrs Ramsay can appear like 'a yellow beam' further identifies her with the lighthouse. Her light and her husband's light travel outwards into space, perhaps to be recovered by some distant telescope, perhaps to be lost. Communication becomes something fragile and miraculous. Astronomical ideas allow Woolf not only to present an exaggerated image of human isolation, but also to suggest the possibility of communication across barriers of space and time.

The Waves forces us to view the lives of its characters at several widely different scales. The italicized passages describing the progress of the sun imply that, from one perspective, a whole human life might appear to last for only a single day. The use of astronomical imagery creates an even more distant perspective. The 'loop of light' which Bernard describes in his opening sentences recalls Mrs McNab's metaphorical telescope in *To the Lighthouse*, and suggests that every speech in the novel is a description of life viewed through a telescope. At least one critic has used such a metaphor to describe the simultaneous impression of intimacy and detachment which characterizes the novel's narrative method.[57] The more explicit astronomical references appear later. In his summing up, Bernard refers explicitly to the 'light of the stars' falling on his hand 'after travelling for millions upon millions of years' (*W*, p. 223). More tangential allusions occur during the reunion at Hampton Court. The historical associations of the palace prompt both Bernard and Louis to consider their places in history. Their invocation of a cosmic scale indicates at first how insignificant they feel; like Katharine Hilbery, they are spectators of history, not participants in it. Louis is the first to refer to 'the world moving through abysses of infinite space' and, in a phrase that echoes Mrs Ramsay's 'little strip of time', he speaks of 'the lighted strip of history' (*W*, p. 188). The relation of 'the lighted strip' to scientific ideas becomes clearer when Bernard refers to 'Our English past' as 'one inch of light', and to history in general as a stream or flood of light. He underestimates the length of English history by many orders of magnitude: given the speed of light, every second of history would occupy a 'lighted strip' 186,000 miles long. The underestimate diminishes the imperial grandeur of English history, as does its transformation into something as fragile as light. However, the diminution of English history does not empower Bernard: he and his friends, with 'the random flicker of light in us that we call brain and feeling', can do little to oppose the 'flood' of history; '[o]ur lives too stream away, down the unlighted avenues, past the strip of time, unidentified' (p. 189).

Selves as Planets: *The Waves*

There are many different explanations for the title of *The Waves*. Some invoke politics—Britannia ruling the waves—but others invoke science. Flammarion's description of light travelling through space is particularly intriguing. Every day the appearance of distant worlds changes, and images of those worlds travel through space until they reach the earth: 'it is as if a series of waves bearing from afar the past of worlds should become present to observers ranged along its passage!'[58] Considered this way, the reader becomes the astronomer, and each short speech is a breaking wave of information.

The certain knowledge that Woolf read Jeans's *The Mysterious Universe* gives the title another kind of significance. As several critics have noted, Bernard's reflections on the origin of the earth echo contemporary thinking: he sees it as 'a pebble flicked off accidentally from the face of the sun' (*W*, p. 187).[59] His reflection does more than place the characters in a framework of immense distances and times. *The Waves* is centrally concerned with the relation of the individual to the group. Writing it, Woolf sought to find a language for the processes whereby individuals are detached from a group, and whereby they merge with it again. The vocabulary of unanimism offered one solution; ideas from cosmology offered another. Jeans begins his book by describing stars in anthropomorphic terms that would have interested Woolf: most are 'solitary travellers', voyaging in 'splendid isolation'.[60] Nevertheless, some two thousand million years ago, a star passed what is now our own sun. Its gravitational pull raised a wave on the surface of the sun, 'a mountain of prodigious height'.

And, before the second star began to recede, its tidal pull had become so powerful that this mountain was torn to pieces and threw off small fragments of itself, much as the crest of a wave throws off spray. These small fragments have been circulating around their parent sun ever since. They are the planets, great and small, of which our earth is one.[61]

Cosmology often speaks in anthropomorphic terms of parents and children, of 'sister' planets and stars. One of the oddities of *The Waves* is that on two separate occasions characters refer to 'our mother', in the singular, although the six speakers are not siblings. Bernard, recalling their departure for school, speaks of it as a 'second severance from the body of our mother' (*W*, p. 102). At Hampton Court, when Rhoda and Louis are rejoined by the other four, Neville says that they are in an 'exhausted' state of mind, and wish 'only to rejoin the body of our mother from whom we have been severed' (p. 194). The 'mother' in both cases is metaphorical: she is a primal state in which individual identity does not exist. Characters think of themselves as 'separate drops' (p. 188), and they struggle, on reuniting, to merge. The barrier is primarily imagined as a shell of individuality that forms over the soul, like a snail's shell (p. 213), but such a model is not incompatible with the idea of the self as a ball of stellar gas or liquid which gradually solidifies into a planet. In this interpretation, the waves are individuals torn from a larger fluid mass: from the sea, or from the sun.

Telecommunications as Reality and as Metaphor

Woolf's individuals are not as isolated as might at first appear. Not only can they commune, figuratively speaking, with the past, but new technologies allow other real but almost miraculous forms of communication. In *Night and Day*, the telephone makes several distinctive appearances. Katharine Hilbery receives three calls in succession, from Mary Datchet, William Rodney, and Ralph Denham (*ND*, pp. 322–6). Woolf describes in what may seem excessive detail the alcove on the stairs in which the Hilbery family keep their apparatus. It is a 'pocket for superfluous possessions', harbouring 'the wreckage of three generations': 'Prints of great-uncles, famed for their prowess in the East' hang above 'Chinese teapots' and the works of outmoded authors (pp. 324–5). The surroundings are important, says the narrator, because it seems to Katharine that 'the thread of sound, issuing from the telephone, was always coloured by the surroundings which received it' (p. 325).

As this extended description suggests, the telephone was a relative novelty. Telecommunications had developed throughout the nineteenth century. From its experimental beginnings in 1837, the telegraph network had grown to cover the entire globe. Information which had previously been conveyed by hand or by carrier pigeon could be transmitted almost instantaneously. However, at the point of departure and receipt, it was still a written medium. The telephone, patented in the United Kingdom in 1876 by Alexander Graham Bell, made the new combination of proximity and distance something that could be experienced directly by individuals. The human voice, associated with presence, could now be heard over immense distances. The telephone was, however, relatively expensive, and available to only a minority of the population. In 1907, although Britain had the second highest level of telephone ownership in Europe, there were about ten telephones for each thousand of population.[62]

Such technological changes do not affect Woolf''s novels as they might more popular genres. For genres such as the detective novel, where the transmission of information can be crucial to the plot, telegraphy and telephony transform the possibilities of storytelling. For Woolf, the effect of the telephone is more oblique. In *Night and Day* it has practical uses, as Katharine tries to find Ralph (*ND*, p. 467), but Woolf is more often interested in its associations. In an essay of 1923, 'How It Strikes a Contemporary', Woolf comments briefly on the telephone in a way that apparently interprets the scene from *Night and Day*. She defends the modern age against the charge that it is 'barren and exhausted' by saying that it does not altogether lack 'colour': 'The telephone, which interrupts the most serious conversations, has a romance of its own'. She does not explain what this romance consists of, but the next sentence depicts an analogous phenomenon: 'the random talk of people who have no chance of immortality' often has a setting 'of lights, streets, houses, human beings, beautiful or grotesque, which will weave itself into the moment for ever' (*EVW* iii. 356). The 'romance' of the telephone consists, it seems, of a kind of modern dramatic irony, the kind created by incongruous juxtapositions. The telephone line threads together Katharine and Ralph, but at the same time, and without his realizing it, Ralph's words are woven together with china teapots and Katharine's uncles. Katharine realizes that such ironies occur not only in space, but also in time. The print of the great-uncle pre-dates 1857: he gazes out 'with an air of amiable authority' into a world which 'beheld no symptoms of the Indian mutiny' (*ND*, p. 325). This sort of dramatic irony is exactly the same as that created by the finite velocity of light: light too is a messenger, a line of communication. It is notable that Woolf again uses the verb 'to behold'. The telephone in the cluttered alcove suggests the approach that Woolf and other modernists would take to writing fiction and poetry, one in which meanings were generated by incongruous juxtapositions.

The contents of the alcove require further explanation: while the novel has emphasized the Hilbery family's past, its colonial connections have been neglected. By bringing in India and China, Woolf associates telecommunications with the interconnectedness of the entire globe. When the telephone bell rings in the suffrage campaign office, Sally Seal feels that 'it was at this exact spot on the surface of the globe that all the subterranean wires of thought and progress came together' (*ND*, p. 277). The call that she answers is not international, but the telephone created such associations. In 1928, Woolf described in a letter how Clive Bell, 'quarrelsome drunk', and a friend, 'merry drunk', had telephoned her at midnight, while she and her friends were sober. She was fascinated by such 'instant communication' between two rooms. Part of her fascination apparently lies in the incongruous mixture of drunkenness and sobriety, but she also describes how at one moment she was 'so near' it was as if she could see into 'the lights of the billiard room'; then, with the receiver down, 'the whole Atlantic', 'very dark', separated the two parties (*Letters*, iv. 474). Bell was apparently in London, as was Woolf, so the Atlantic separating them was purely metaphorical.

Telecommunications also provide a context for Woolf's idea of invisible interconnections between people, and for the unanimist vocabulary of 'fibres' and 'waves'. The telegraph system was frequently understood, in an extended metaphor, as the nervous system of the imperial body politic, and a vocabulary of 'nerves', 'fibres', and 'filaments' was often found in discussions of telecommunications.[63] Radio transmission, first achieved experimentally in 1902, was soon seized upon as a source for metaphors of communication and invisible sympathies: D. H. Lawrence used it extensively in his unorthodox book of psychology, *Fantasia of the Unconscious* (1923); the metaphor of being 'on someone's wavelength' came into the language in 1927. In Romains's *Death of a Nobody*, the porter who delivers the telegram containing the news of Godard's death is said to envy 'business men, agents, journalists, directors whose thoughts and words spread themselves like a sensitive web over the world'.[64] In *The Waves* we find one such businessman, Louis, who with 'letters and cables' and 'commands on the telephone' has 'laced together' the 'different parts of the world' (*W*, pp. 138–9). However, the literal representation of telecommunications is less important for *The Waves* than the underlying metaphor of telecommunication. The six characters in *The Waves* appear to be communicating not directly through the words they utter, but telepathically. The language in which Woolf articulates this process is rooted in the world of telecommunications: the waves of the title might refer to radio waves; Neville's understanding of himself as 'a net whose fibres pass imperceptibly beneath the world' (p. 178) invokes metaphors more commonly seen in discussions of telegraphy.

Many of the most interesting ideas in Woolf's novels cannot be accounted for by reference to a single context. She may have derived 'filaments' from unanimist fiction, or from thinking about telecommunications; furthermore, in one account of the birth of the earth, 'filament' was the term that Jeans used for the wave of solar matter which created the solar system.[65] Wrenched from its scientific contexts, Woolf's scientific language loses in accuracy, but gains in resonance.

CHAPTER 7

RECONTEXTUALIZING AND RECONSTRUCTING WOOLF

Nobody sees any one as he is, let alone an elderly lady sitting opposite a strange young man in a railway carriage. They see a whole—they see all sorts of things—they see themselves. (*JR*, p. 36)

THE truth is a construct, and—as Woolf herself recognized—not only strange young men but also literary fictions find themselves reconstructed according to the viewer's perspective. Present-day interpretations of Woolf's works are different from those that prevailed forty years ago. Moreover, the interpretations made as adaptations for a commercial cinema audience are very different from those made for the readers of academic criticism: interpretation varies not only with historical period and with geographical region, but also with culture and subculture.

As a matter of principle, one might wish that biographical reconstructions of Virginia Woolf the person would have no bearing on how we interpret her texts, but biographical practices of interpretation are deeply embedded in English-speaking cultures. Such practices value elements in the texts only if they express the essence of the writer's character or life story. Readers of Michael Cunningham's *The Hours*, and viewers of Stephen Daldry's film-adaptation of it, are confronted with a Woolf who was, above all, a suicide.[1] The final act of her life is allowed to dominate all that went before it. Having read or seen this account, it is difficult to remove her death from one's interpretations of the works. Septimus's suicide becomes valuable because it prefigures Woolf's. However, by recognizing that biographies are stories, and that biographers face choices in their telling, one can partly free oneself from this outlook.

The ideas that would shape Woolf's work after her death were developing during her lifetime. The idea of 'The Bloomsbury Group' entered public discourse in the late 1920s in Roy Campbell's hostile satirical poetry, and appeared in a favourable critical study as early as 1935.[2] Woolf was fully aware that the idea had become public currency, and warned one critic against it (*Letters*, v. 91). Many critics saw Bloomsbury as being restricted in its view of the world by its aestheticism and its socially privileged position; they saw it as a clique in which friends were able to publish each other's books and to review them favourably in Bloomsbury-dominated periodicals: the atmosphere of 'mutual admiration', wrote one, amounted to 'narcissism'.[3] Given the common association of narcissism with homosexuality, the reference also encourages the reader to construct Bloomsbury in terms of the sexuality of several of its members, and to see its sexuality as deviant and untrustworthy. Of course, even 'Bloomsbury' is open to different constructions: some emphasized the influence of Lytton Strachey, others G. E. Moore. But in any case, the qualities attributed to Bloomsbury were then attributed to Woolf's work.

The dominance of F. R. Leavis in British post-war literary criticism has also shaped attitudes towards Woolf. In the light of Leavis's demand for 'moral seriousness' in literature, 'Bloomsbury' attitudes often appeared 'frivolous'.[4] As the novelist Angus Wilson argued in 1958, Bloomsbury was believed to have ignored man 'as a social being' and to have treated 'personal relationships and subjective sensations in a social void'.[5] Leavis's 'Great Tradition' of novelists excluded Woolf: for him, D. H. Lawrence was the pre-eminent writer of the early twentieth century. Nevertheless, it is easy to exaggerate the extent of Leavis's influence. Woolf was not completely ignored. Even Boris Ford's 1961 Leavisite survey of English literature gave space to her, and though its account is often apologetic, it takes *To the Lighthouse* seriously, and ranks it with the works of Jane Austen and George Eliot.[6] Even university syllabuses that made use of the 'Great Tradition' found space for novels and novelists beyond Leavis's canon.

The construction of Bloomsbury as 'limited' has often gone hand in hand with a construction of Virginia Woolf as sheltered, sickly, and spinsterish. Again, this caricature developed in Woolf's lifetime. In *Men Without Art* (1934), Wyndham Lewis took as the key to Woolf's work Clarissa Dalloway's belief that 'it was very, very dangerous to live even one day' (*MD*, p. 7): he found a similar 'peeping', 'tittering', 'old-maidish' quality in the work of Woolf, Marcel Proust, and Lytton Strachey.[7] Critics writing after Woolf's death connected Woolf's illnesses more explicitly with the attitudes they saw in her writing.[8] Michael Holroyd, in his biography of Lytton Strachey, depicted Woolf much as Lewis had done. He made little distinction between Woolf's appearance and her intellect, describing both in the same vocabulary. He describes her in early photographs as looking 'less robust' than Vanessa, 'rather anaemic and ethereal'. This leads him to conclude that she is 'gaz[ing] out fearfully at the cold, slow terrors of the universe'. Even when Holroyd allows Woolf to be adventurous, he qualifies his remarks: her 'curiosity' about human activity, though 'often passionate', remained 'bloodless and trivial'.[9] In spite of its dismissive account of Woolf, Holroyd's biography, by reviving serious interest in Bloomsbury, did something to revive scholarly interest in her work.

The late 1960s and early 1970s mark a crucial turning point in Woolf's reputation. In the United States, the title of Edward Albee's play, *Who's Afraid of Virginia Woolf?* (1962), made her name a household word. It rekindled interest in her works, though it also established an enduring association of her name with fear.[10] In Britain the Labour Government's 'civilized society' legislation of the late 1960s was seen by both its supporters and its detractors as being inspired by Bloomsbury liberalism.[11] Many accounts of Bloomsbury in the late 1960s and early 1970s compare it to the counter-culture of that period: as one critic wrote in 1972, Bloomsbury had 'claim[ed] freedom from rules and conventions in the name of good sense, honesty, candour and generosity', much like the 'young people' of her own day.[12] Some aspects of this identification were short-lived, but it had a significant and enduring legacy in the feminist movement's rehabilitation of Woolf as an important ancestor.

The 1972 biography by Woolf's nephew, Quentin Bell, was the first biographical account to draw upon the full range of her letters and diaries. It has been widely criticized for perpetuating the family image of her as an apolitical invalid, but, for that very reason, marked a turning point in the recontextualization of Woolf.[13] The appearance of the six volumes of Woolf's letters from 1975 onwards, of *Moments of Being* in 1976, and of the five volumes of her diaries from 1977 onwards, allowed critics to construct many different biographical stories for Woolf, and opened up many different kinds of interpretation. 'Sketch of the Past' enabled a reappraisal of the causes of her nervous breakdowns and stimulated psychoanalytic approaches to her texts.[14] The publication of Vita Sackville-West's letters to Woolf further enabled an understanding of Woolf's sexuality, and a recognition of the coded lesbianism in her texts.[15]

Though her family continued to insist on a Woolf who 'wasn't a feminist' and 'wasn't political',[16] the demolition of the myth of the 'invalid of Bloomsbury' allowed a fuller recognition of Woolf's engagement with political issues. Marxist and feminist approaches to politics and literature allowed the recognition that a writer can be political without being propagandist. The recognition that she possessed an intellect as well as a sensibility has allowed the exploration of her affiliations with scientific and philosophical thinking. Biographical sources allowed a fuller recognition of Woolf's anger, and of her strategies for dealing with an emotion considered unladylike in her time.[17] Alex Zwerdling's *Virginia Woolf and the Real World* (1986) marked a bold shift away from a subjective, private Woolf, towards a public and political figure: perhaps too bold a shift, in that the title discounts Woolf's very political questioning of 'reality' and of the authority figures who construct it. Later accounts have recognized the extent to which the 'real' is mediated through language and representation, while developing the interpretation of Woolf as a politically engaged writer.

Film and Stage Adaptations

To date there have been only three film adaptations of Woolf's novels: Colin Gregg's *To the Lighthouse* (1983), Sally Potter's *Orlando* (1992), and Marleen Gorris's *Mrs Dalloway* (1998). The interpretations they make of Woolf's novels often diverge from those of contemporaneous literary criticism, reflecting the distinctive conventions of film as a medium, and the distinctive expectations of its audiences. Each film has its own social and historical context, which shapes the artefact just as much as the individual decisions of actors, scriptwriters, and directors. The stage has proved a medium more resistant to Woolf's works: given her concentration on interior life, and lack of interest in conventional action, they are difficult to adapt for the popular theatre. However, there have been three stage adaptations of *Orlando* and one of *The Waves*, as well as an adaptation of *A Room of One's Own* (1989) to which we shall return shortly.[18]

Any adaptation of an existing artistic work has a peculiar status, being both an independent work in its own right, yet also merely a supplement or annex to the original. Reviewers and literary critics all too often approach adaptations with a strong idea of the original in mind, and treat the adaptations as deviations from it. They judge the adaptation a success only to the extent that it is 'faithful' to the original, or rather, to the critic's idea of the original, which is itself already an interpretation. By these criteria, television and film adaptations must inevitably fail: being in a different medium, they cannot hope to match the originals. A more productive approach is suggested by Gene Moore, writing about adaptations of Joseph Conrad's novels. We must understand adaptation as 'a two-way process'. By processes of omission and emphasis, the film can highlight features of the original work which more conventional forms of criticism tend to neglect: 'the study of films can help us to understand Conrad's literary works precisely because the former are "unfaithful" to the latter. A truly "faithful" film, were such a thing possible, would have nothing to teach us'.[19] The adaptation, then, has much in common with a work of criticism, and particularly with the kind of evaluative criticism in which the critic's moral or political position plays an active part.

However, unlike most critical works, films are collaborative productions. While the scriptwriter may take responsibility for the structure of the narrative and for the details of dialogue, other important choices rest with other individuals: above all with the director, but also with those responsible for casting, for costume and set design, for filming, for editing, and for the score, as well as with the actors themselves. These elements are particularly important in adaptations of Woolf's novels. Her novels reward the reader not through traditional narrative, but through the subtle presentation of consciousness. Alterations to small details of imagery can be as significant as the loss of whole scenes.

COLIN GREGG'S *TO THE LIGHTHOUSE* (1983)

Unlike the two later adaptations, Colin Gregg's *To the Lighthouse* was a film made for television, first broadcast on BBC2 on 23 March 1983. It was based on a script by Hugh Stoddart, and was filmed on location in Cornwall over five weeks in the summer of 1982.[20] It was produced towards the end of the economic recession of the early 1980s, in the early years of Margaret Thatcher's Conservative Government. Following the Broadcasting Act of 1980, and the establishment of Channel Four, the economic, legal, and political context for television was changing; so too were the cultural and economic motives for producing costume dramas and literary adaptations, and the dominant style of television drama.[21] Within television and without there was an apparent rise in 'heritage culture'.

It seemed to many commentators in the mid-1980s that mass culture was increasingly marked by nostalgia. In television drama, the ideals of the BBC's 'Play for Today' series were being supplanted by a glossier and more escapist style.[22] Beginning in the mid-1960s, 'Play for Today' had presented single-episode, self-contained dramas, dealing with 'provocative and controversial' contemporary issues; in their early years they had been studio-based; most were essentially filmed plays within the tradition of stage realism.[23] The newer form was epitomized by Granada Television's 1981 adaptation of Evelyn Waugh's *Brideshead Revisited*. It consisted of historical drama running to several episodes, usually shot on location rather than in the studio. In this, and in the quality of the camera work and the use of music, the new drama more closely resembled film.

It seemed to many that the avoidance of contemporary issues was connected to the rise of the Conservative party, or the recession, or both. As historian David Cannadine wrote, shortly before *To the Lighthouse* was broadcast: 'Not since the 1890s or the 1930s has the worship of wistfulness been so widespread. And there, in part, lies the explanation: then, as now, depression is the begetter of nostalgia, disenchantment the handmaid of escapism'.[24] Many of the nostalgic dramas of the early 1980s were set in the early twentieth century, though there is little consensus about why, or how, the Edwardian era relates to the era of Thatcher: to one critic the Edwardian era was one in which 'social status [was] known and kept'; to another, one in which power was passing from the landed aristocracy to the urban middle classes.[25] If we accept Raphael Samuel's explanation that heritage culture encourages identification with a social elite, we might find a different form of explanation: the complex pleasure of nostalgic drama derives from identifying simultaneously with a social class which one knows to be doomed, and with the class that was to displace them.[26]

The qualities of the new drama could also be attributed to an increasingly international market for English-language television drama. As one critic noted in February 1983, where once television companies had produced literary adaptations to gain 'cultural respectability', they had now discovered that 'period adaptations' were among 'their biggest export earners'. Cultural capital had given way to financial capital. By involving overseas companies, they could attract 'huge amounts of "co-production" finance'. This was not always to the benefit of the film itself: the same critic contrasted a relatively low-budget adaptation of Lawrence's *Sons and Lovers*, which had emphasized the realism of Lawrence's work, with a more recent adaptation of his novella *The Captain's Doll*: 'one can't help but feel that the lush settings are part and parcel of an ersatz co-production "look" that has far more to do with the international market for television programmes than anything Lawrence himself wrote'.[27] The prospective international market motivated not only the high production values, but also the preference for literary adaptation and for nostalgia. For an international audience, the topical and local references of contemporary drama are less readily comprehensible than those found in literary adaptations and in nostalgic drama. The international market favours interpretations in terms of a universal 'human condition'.

The dominance of the nostalgic mode is important for all three adaptations, but particularly for *To the Lighthouse*: Woolf's novel was already a historical novel, though it dealt with very recent history; it was already concerned with the relation of the present to the past, and with a barrier between the two which could be surmounted only in memory. The novel may evoke responses of nostalgia, but it also critiques those responses: Lily revisits the past not to escape from the present, but to escape from the weight of tradition, to 'improve away' Mrs Ramsay's old-fashioned ideas (*TL*, p. 236). The question to ask of Colin Gregg's adaptation is whether the dominance of nostalgia within costume drama obscures the more critical stance taken by Woolf.

The adaptation received mixed reviews, and a comparison of them suggests further questions to ask.[28] Several reviewers praised its production values: Philip Purser noted the similarities with 'the languid, visually-sumptuous style established by "Brideshead" '; Julian Barnes felt that it seemed 'like a grown-up feature film', and suggested that the 'shimmeringly attentive camera-work' created a 'visual counterpart' to Woolf's prose. Barnes's remark is particularly interesting, in that it subscribes to the ideal of fidelity, but recognizes that fidelity to Woolf's style is as important as fidelity to dialogue or event. Barnes also noted with apparent pleasure the period detail of 'Norfolk jackets' and 'lace blouses'. For him, the adaptation was enjoyable in the same way as a family saga: 'the rolling maul of an extended family, pottering, bickering, being smug and principled together'. Whatever his intentions, the terms of Barnes's praise might be taken to support Phil Hardy's more critical view: that Gregg and Stoddart had reduced a powerful 'novel of ideas' to 'a simple celebration of the trials and tribulations of family life before the Great War'.

Stoddart's script is bold and inventive, and, crucially, it is relatively spare: it allows room for moods, feelings, and ideas to be conveyed not only by dialogue, but by sound and image; it allows the film to escape its original. At times the film's own techniques echo those of Woolf. Woolf achieves great compression and suggestiveness by combining a character's thoughts with a record of some apparently incidental detail: for example, Mrs Ramsay asking 'But what have I done with my life?' while 'taking her place at the head of the table, and looking at all the plates making white circles on it' (*TL*, p. 112). At one point the film shows Mrs Ramsay quietly looking at her children asleep in their bedroom, but gives on the soundtrack the voice of Mr Ramsay talking to her about her philanthropical work.[29] The juxtaposition raises questions about the relationship of her public and her private roles, and whether she treats those she visits as if they were children. We may assume that Mrs Ramsay is remembering his words, and making the connection for herself, but the point is made subtly.

However, for all its resourcefulness, Stoddart's script cannot find an equivalent for Woolf's internal monologues which is as fluid and as subtle as the original. In a novel, everything is presented through the medium of language: there is a continuity between a visual description of a scene, and a character's thoughts about that scene; this is particularly so in *To the Lighthouse*, where description and thought are both presented through individual characters. In film, there is a sharp discontinuity between the visual and the aural. To have an actor speak words which Woolf wrote as internal monologue is to make the character appear unambiguously conscious of them. In the film Lily's description of her technical problem—'There must be a structure in a painting so that I can pour in everything'[30]—echoes remarks found in the novel, but the film medium requires that she voice them explicitly, and so her thinking seems less subtle. Her soliloquy on landscape—'Landscape is a record of men's labour to transform nature'[31]—is even less successful: it seems to derive from a post-1970 art-history textbook. The overall effect is mixed: Lily appears less intuitive and more programmatic in her artistic method, but because her reflections are no longer embedded in the rest of her mental life, she can appear priggish.

An analogous problem, peculiar to this novel, is how to present Lily's painting: the novel gives only broad hints about the extent to which the painting is figurative or abstract, and leaves the reader imaginatively to complete it. To present the painting on-screen is to reduce that range of possible images to one particular image. The paintings used in Gregg's adaptation were in an Impressionist style, more conservative than the work of 'Bloomsbury' artists around 1912; other painters who have since attempted to actualize Lily's work have employed a more surrealistic idiom, with hints of Chagall and De Chirico.[32] However, the particular form taken by the paintings is less significant than the fact of including them. The very impossibility of including a painting within a verbal medium works to Woolf's advantage: the reader can focus on the creative *process* rather than the *product*; Gregg's decision to depict the paintings changes the centre of gravity.

A long scene in which Lily and Mrs Ramsay discuss marriage and independence exhibits some of the worst faults of the adaptation, and in particular its tendency to frame Woolf's novel as a 'classic'.[33] Given the intimacy of the scene, the script and its delivery are very formal. For example, when Mrs Ramsay consoles her as 'poor Lily', Lily responds: 'I'm not poor Lily: you must not say that. Why must you always insist that the likes of me stand shivering outside the gates to bliss just because we do not have a man to pamper and serve?'[34] The dialogue is stagy, and Suzanne Bertish's delivery of the line does nothing to counteract this effect. These are the 'stilted tones which scriptwriters seem to regard as "period" '.[35] The immediate effect is to make Lily seem self-conscious: the speech appears rehearsed, and her insistence on independence seems inauthentic. However, there is a more general effect: many viewers will recognize in these lines a generic marker of costume drama, its use of distinctively 'literary' language in dialogue. The stiltedness of the lines serves less as a marker of Lily's personal qualities than as a marker of the film's literariness.

I have considered the genre and form of Gregg's *To the Lighthouse* at length because the form of Woolf's novels is crucial to the way that they communicate ideas and emotions; the recontextualizing effect created by the change in medium is as significant as those created by narrative alterations. Nevertheless, there are many narrative alterations in Stoddart's script, of varying degrees of subtlety. The most immediately obvious is the transplantation of the action from the Hebrides to Cornwall, and the concomitant alteration of the Scottish surname 'McAllister' to the Cornish 'Trevorrow'. The transplantation makes the film a biographical reading: fidelity to the author's life compensates for infidelity to the text. Drastic as it might appear, it has no narrative consequences: in the novel, 'the Hebrides' merely signifies a place by the sea, far from London and Cambridge, without any history or culture of its own; 'Cornwall' is an acceptable substitute.

More significantly, the film reduces the number of characters and changes some of their personal qualities. Mr Bankes is removed altogether, and his functions are divided between Paul Rayley and Charles Tansley: it is with Rayley that Lily discusses painting, but Tansley whom Mrs Ramsey would like to see her marry.[36] As the Tansley in the film is no more likeable than the Tansley of the novel, Mrs Ramsay's matchmaking seems all the more perverse. Augustus Carmichael becomes a more active and vocal character, and less of an enigma, acting as a sounding board for Mr Ramsay's self-doubts. The revision makes Mr Ramsay a less isolated figure, allowing material contained in the novel's interior monologue to become plausible dialogue. The film christens Mr and Mrs Ramsay as 'Michael' and 'Caroline': the revision personalizes them, and reduces the extent to which they appear types of 'masculine' and 'feminine' or of 'husband' and 'wife'. The casting of Michael Gough as Mr Ramsay created some subtle complications. As Philip Purser recalled, Gough had often played 'forbidding figures' in television drama; the casting might in consequence seem to establish Mr Ramsay as 'forbidding' from his first appearance. However, the casting also means that the ideal audience is more surprised by the behaviour of Ramsay/Gough during the cricket game on the beach: though he is characteristically unforgiving to James, he is also playful, carrying his son down to the sea saying 'I don't want this little fish in my net'.[37] Critics were divided: Purser was surprised to find 'warmth and fun' in Mr Ramsay, while Julian Barnes queried whether he was not 'more dislikeable' than in the novel.

There are several significant narrative alterations in 'The Window'. The most interesting and controversial is the 'tournament' scene, in which Mr Ramsay presides over a village festival and wrestling competition. Julian Barnes felt that Stoddart's invention would offend only severe Woolfians who were 'looking for offence'; Denis Hackett, however, considered the scenes foolhardy, and Peter Kemp found Mr Ramsay's enthusiasm for 'rural pugilism' implausible. One might dismiss the tournament scenes as a generic feature of costume drama, invoking nostalgia for lost customs and quaint costumes. However, they make a serious contribution to Gregg's adaptation. The tournament scenes are interleaved with the scenes of Mrs Ramsay visiting the poor in the village: in each, the adaptation situates the Ramsay family within a social structure. The costumes in the tournament scenes are not merely decorative: the hats in particular mark a social structure, glossy top hats marking the upper middle classes, brown bowlers the lower middle classes, and cloth caps the working classes. The tournament scenes can be read as criticizing Woolf's novel for having studied the family in isolation from the class system. If so, they judge her by a standard derived from Victorian classic realism, with its concern for the 'condition of England', and more immediately from the social realist tradition of television drama. Mr Ramsay himself acknowledges that his family are only visitors, not fully integrated with the local community. The film's inclusion of other social classes makes it less easy to mistake the Ramsays' tribulations as universal. However, this eruption of class into the film is incidental: the fundamental narrative is not altered. Moreover, the criticism is less radical than at first appears: Stoddart reinserts the Ramsays in a social structure, but by removing the character of Mrs McNab from the 'Time Passes' section, he diminishes our awareness of the family's comfort being dependent on the labour of others.

The wrestling competition also allows Stoddart to emphasize questions about gender and physical force. This becomes explicit when Nancy asks why men endanger themselves, and Prue replies 'that's just the way they are'.[38] Mr Ramsay, meanwhile, rebukes Andrew for not taking an interest in the wrestling: it is Andrew, of course, who is later endangered and killed by the war. The scene allows Stoddart to expose tensions within the family: Mr Ramsay ignores Prue's question about whether he has prepared his speech; Andrew and Prue ridicule him for knowing everything. At the end of the scene, after Mr Ramsay's prize-giving speech, Prue says in close-up 'He's won again'. That her words could refer to the winner of the wrestling competition, or to her father, creates a connection between the two. The wrestling is a literalization of the wrestling that goes on within the Ramsay family. For viewers who also know the novel, Prue's phrase echoes Mrs Ramsay's concluding thought in 'The Window': 'she had triumphed again'.

At the present moment, we may still be too close to the assumptions of the early 1980s fully to recognize how they inform Gregg's adaptation. It still appears natural and inevitable that the novel should be adapted in the form of classic costume drama, but to do so alters its treatment of historical fact and historical process. Moreover, because classic costume drama is essentially realist in its narrative mode, Woolf's subtle presentation of consciousness is lost, and with it the more philosophical aspects of her writing.

GARLAND AND ATKINS'S *A ROOM OF ONE'S OWN*

The earliest recontextualization of *A Room of One's Own* is Vita Sackville-West's *All Passion Spent* (1931), a novel which makes frequent allusion to Woolf's essay.[39] However, the first proper adaptation appeared in 1989, as a staged performance adapted and directed by Patrick Garland, starring Eileen Atkins.[40] The adaptation has for the most part been praised for returning Woolf's text to its origins as lectures, and thereby bringing it to life. However, there have been some criticisms. Even if Atkins had delivered the full text her performance would still constitute an interpretation. Given that Woolf writes the book in the hazy-edged persona of Mary Seton, Beton, or Carmichael, the decision to deliver the play in the persona of Virginia Woolf is itself an interpretation, though one that has apparently gone unquestioned. Rosemary Dinnage questioned whether Atkins's delivery was authentic, speculating that Woolf 'probably dropped and murmured more' and that 'her body language may have been languid rather than incisive'.[41] For her, Atkins's mannerisms recalled Maggie Smith's performance in *The Prime of Miss Jean Brodie* (1969). Jane Marcus has made a similar criticism, though one less concerned with 'authenticity' and more with the ideological effects of Atkins's performance: by playing Woolf as a 'scolding spinster', Atkins has missed '[t]he whole point of the book', which is to 'mock the authority of the lecture itself'.[42] Though Rosemary Say felt the first performance to be 'sharp and witty', it would seem that some of the playful and ironic quality of the book was lost.

As Brenda Silver has noted, the adaptation also edits and rearranges the text. The arguments of Woolf's text are complex and potentially contradictory. The argument that the writer should be androgynous, and that it is 'fatal for any one who writes to think of their sex' (*ROO*, p. 136), potentially contradicts both Woolf's argument that women writers should think back through their mothers (p. 99), and her opinion that 'it would be thousand pities if women wrote like men' (p. 114).[43] Garland's adaptation emphasizes androgyny at the expense of difference; in Silver's words, it emphasizes 'the transcendent universality of art'.[44] It smooths away the spikier historical allusions, such as Woolf's reference to Sir Chartres Biron, the judge who had banned Radcliffe Hall's lesbian novel *The Well of Loneliness*.[45] While Garland's motivation may have been to produce a text that was accessible, such access comes at a cost.

SALLY POTTER'S *ORLANDO* (1992)

Orlando: A Biography has been reworked in many media, beginning with a play for young teenagers in 1960.[46] There have followed an abandoned opera, with a libretto by Angela Carter;[47] an avant-garde film adaptation, Ulrike Ottinger's *Freak Orlando*, 'a history of society's "deformed", its "freaks", over five epochs, framed by the androgynous wanderer Orlando';[48] two plays, one of which is a monologue delivered by a single actress, the other of which frames Orlando's life in a biographical narrative of Woolf, Vita Sackville-West, and others; and, most recently, a ballet.[49] More distantly related is Jacqueline Harpman's novel *Orlanda* in which a 35-year-old college lecturer finds herself suddenly doubled in masculine form.[50]

The best-known and most readily accessible adaptation is Sally Potter's film. Filmed between February and April 1992, and first shown at the Venice Film Festival that September,[51] it went on

Rosemary Harris as
Mrs Ramsay in
To the Lighthouse,
1983, dir. Colin
Gregg

Tilda Swinton in *Orlando*,
1992, dir. Sally Potter

commercial release in Britain on 12 March 1993. Potter and her team created a visual style that is as distinctive in its medium as Woolf"s novel was in hers. Though Gregg's *To the Lighthouse* was inventive, it was nevertheless working within the bounds of television costume drama. Potter's film works within a British tradition of 'European-influenced art cinema': the score is more modern in its musical idioms than those usually found in costume drama; the production design was stylized rather than naturalistic.[52] In order to find a 'live, cinematic form', Potter realized that she had at times to be 'ruthless' with the novel.[53] She was also prompted—not least by the film's financial backers—to ask why *Orlando* was relevant to the present day, and how a modern audience would connect with the story. She believed that audiences would connect with the tone of the book: 'melancholy at its heart', it is nevertheless 'witty in its delivery'.[54]

Potter's focus on tone and her predominantly visual interpretation of the text rendered the film incomprehensible to critics who understand Woolf in terms of thematic issues. The remarks of the American critic Jane Marcus are worth considering in detail. They occur in the context of a comparison of American attitudes towards Woolf with those found in English culture, and follow Marcus's praise for the 1992 and 1993 editions of Woolf published by Penguin, Oxford University Press, and Vintage.

It doesn't seem fair. We send them Sandra Gilbert's sparkling introduction to the Penguin *Orlando*, and they send us Tilda Swinton in a black velvet straitjacket. Sally Potter's blancmange *Orlando* turns a masterpiece of comic satire for grown-ups into milk pudding from the nursery. . . . Potter takes a scathing critique of English imperialism and racism and the repression of sexual identity and reduces it to a tapioca pudding. . . . This ridiculously bad film illustrates—perhaps most vividly as the camera follows Tilda Swinton's clumsy attempts to avoid the furniture—the great gaps that separate cultures. I can't believe anyone who helped with the making of this mockery of genius has ever read the book. The director and the film-makers use Woolf and a certain upper-class romanticized white feminism to reinforce a Yuppie Englishness entranced by Great Houses and Elizabethan extravagance. They were not familiar with the contested meanings critics have seen in *Orlando*, because it is not even a minor 'classic' in England, or they would not have dared to desecrate it. They did not envision viewers so familiar with the book that they might say lines over to themselves as favorite scenes approach—and be rudely disappointed at their absence.[55]

While Marcus touches on questions—such as nostalgia—which have also exercised film critics, her quasi-religious commitment to the sacred text, and her prioritization of thematic content over form and tone, make her criticisms valuable primarily as a symptomatic misreading.

Much of the humour of Woolf's *Orlando* derives from its status as a parodic biography and parodic history, and from the narrator's difficulties in making Orlando's extraordinary life fit a conventional framework. Potter's interpretation, however, does not include a distinct narrator figure, nor does it use the camera narratorially. Instead, more subtly, it gives the narratorial role to Orlando him-and-herself. In the opening scene, an off-screen Orlando provides the narratorial voice-over; this, however, is interrupted by the on-screen Orlando, who turns and looks at the camera, replacing the narrator's 'he' with 'I'.[56] This look to the camera, the first of many, is one of the distinctive and most immediately comical qualities of the film. Orlando's 'looks' break the realist convention whereby characters are unaware that they are being filmed. Moreover, many of the direct addresses introduce a conspicuously modern idiom: for example, Orlando's remark that his engagement to Sasha 'would never have worked', or his praise for *Othello* as a 'terrific play'.[57] Potter intended Orlando's 'looks' as 'an instrument of subversion', subverting the 'historical pageant' by creating a 'complicity' with the audience. Not only were they meant to be funny, they were meant to make the audience feel 'that although Orlando's journey lasted 400 years and was set in the past, this was essentially a story about the present'.[58] By parodying biography the novel broaches the theme of mediation: a life story cannot be told as it 'really' is, but must always be mediated through language and literary form, and therefore through a particular set of values. The film broaches the theme of mediation more subtly, and there is a danger that Orlando's 'looks' do not achieve everything that was intended for them.

The casting of the film also disrupts its realism. Several members of the cast are better known for work outside theatre and film: Quentin Crisp had achieved notoriety for his book *The Naked Civil Servant* (1968), an autobiographical account of growing up effeminate and homosexual; Jimmy Somerville had come to prominence as pop singer who took sexual identity as a serious political issue; Ned Sherrin was best known as a raconteur and as the presenter of a radio

chat show; and Heathcote Williams was in 1993 best known for
Whale Nation (1988), an illustrated volume of eco-conscious poems.
Ideally, the audience recognizes these actors as contemporary public
figures, and so the relation of actor to character is not transparent.[59]

The film also develops the theme of mediation by parodying the
role of costume within heritage drama. Heritage drama often dwells
on the shape and texture of costume, using it not only to establish
character or advance the narrative, but as an index of authenticity.[60]
Orlando exaggerates this trait. This is apparent from the outset, in
the scene where Orlando has to be helped into his clothes by 'three
extremely anxious valets' before meeting the Queen.[61] It is apparent
from the excessive size of Queen Elizabeth's skirts and later of
Orlando's: excessive, that is, if we judge them against costumes in
comparable costume dramas.[62] It becomes most apparent in the
scene where Orlando, having returned to England, walks through
the long gallery of her home in an 'enormously wide' white crinoline,
and struggles to negotiate the furniture.[63] We are aware that the
costumes are actively restricting the protagonist; indeed, they have
become his/her antagonists. Through the visual rhyme of Orlando's
crinolines with the draped furniture, the scene asks whether women
at that period in history differ from 'furniture'. The parodic use of
costumes creates a visual equivalent for one of the novel's major
themes. As Bergson had recognized, life cannot be contained by the
artificial conventions of intellect and civilization; as Woolf recognizes, a life cannot be contained by the conventions of 'life-writing'.

Woolf's novel explores the theme of mediation by parodying
the division of history into distinct periods, eras, or ages. Thus, in
chapter 4, Orlando inhabits a simplified version of the literary
'Augustan' age, in which, improbably, Addison, Dryden, and Pope
all converse in the same coffee house; as the century changes at the
end of the chapter, the weather changes with it to become stereo-
typically nineteenth century. The reader is made aware of the arbitrariness of historical periodization. For the film, the production
designers Van Os and Roelfs distinguished each period with a 'colour
coding' scheme: 'The England of Elizabeth is gold and red, that of
James grey and silver, the eighteenth century is dominated by a
powdery blue, and so on'.[64] Although the scheme provides a visual
equivalent for the sharp distinctions of period found in Woolf's
novel, the film does not alert its viewers to the arbitrariness of those

distinctions; consequently, there is a danger that the viewer will interpret the visual qualities of the film not as parody, but as pageantry. As Francke recognized, Potter's *Orlando* is a self-contradictory text: 'the overladen visual style perversely turns the film into a celebration of the cultural heritage that Orlando in her liberated female state must reject'.[65] Similar feelings also emerge in Jane Marcus's remarks. It is not altogether clear why Tilda Swinton in a 'black velvet straitjacket' is an insult to the United States of America, nor why the scene in the Long Gallery illustrates the failings of British (or English) culture, but it appears that Marcus reads both as signs of a heritage culture 'entranced by Great Houses and Elizabethan extravagance', and neglects the more subtle uses to which costume is being put. Her reference to 'Yuppie Englishness' suggests that she has placed the film in the same cultural category as *Brideshead Revisited* and *Chariots of Fire*. I would argue that it is better to understand the film as belonging to a different and more critical cultural formation, one that, through books such as Patrick Wright's *On Living in an Old Country* (1985), had reached a more critical understanding of heritage culture, and that, through films like Peter Greenaway's *The Draughtsman's Contract* (1982), had seen how the conventions of costume drama might be parodied.[66] Moreover, as Francke recognizes, it is better to understand the film as one that has only imperfectly realized its critique. For some critics—Pidduck, for example—Orlando's looks to camera are enough to deflate the 'potential claustrophobia and preciousness' of the production;[67] for others, the pageantry dominates.

If the film does not provide a 'scathing critique' of imperialism, as Marcus would wish, that may be simply because the novel itself is never so direct as to be 'scathing'. The novel announces the theme in its opening scene, in the image of Orlando 'slicing at the head of a Moor' (*O*, p. 13), and its account of how Orlando's father or grandfather had brought it home, while the film presents an altogether more reflective Orlando beneath an oak tree. Nevertheless, the film's scenes of 'The East' are more sharply critical of Western imperialism than is the novel. The Khan directly accuses the English of 'collecting' countries.[68] The hypocrisy of Western imperialism is brought out very economically in the scene in which the Archduke advises Orlando that, in putting on a party for his investiture, he should respect the 'local customs' and '[p]rotocol'.[69] So saying, the elaborately bewigged archduke pushes aside a group of women dressed in burkas.

Though Orlando's 'looks' provide a partial substitute for the narrator, Potter does not translate the full narratorial commentary on the nature of the self and on gender difference. She provides some economical equivalents. When Orlando changes sex, Woolf's narrator tells us that although he had become a woman, 'in every other respect, Orlando remained precisely as he had been' (*O*, p. 133). In the film, Orlando turns to camera and remarks 'Same person. No difference at all. Just a different sex'.[70] Woolf's narrator is at this point expressing a liberal humanist philosophy, which treats socially constructed differences, such as gender difference, as less significant components of the self than individual idiosyncrasies. Potter's Orlando espouses the same view. However, the more complex position proposed later in the novel by Woolf's narrator proves more resistant to the film medium. After Orlando's rejection of Archduke Harry's advances, the narrator reflects on whether gender differences are socially produced, by clothes for example, or whether social conventions reflect more profoundly rooted differences. The narrator momentarily endorses the latter position and, contradicting his earlier account, says that there had been 'a change in Orlando herself that dictated her choice of a woman's dress and of a woman's sex' (*O*, pp. 180–1). He then goes on to qualify his view of gender difference, arguing that the sexes, although different, intermix, and the individual vacillates between male and female; the role of clothes is to stabilize this vacillating self (p. 181). While, through its excessively lavish costumes, Potter's film illustrates the idea that 'clothes wear us' (p. 132) and not we them, it does not provide any equivalent for the novel's psychological speculations. The film reinterprets the novel as being primarily about the relation of sex to property, and downplays its concerns with subjectivity. While the novel gives no explanation for Orlando's change of sex, the film provides a clear causal sequence: during the uprising, Orlando is dismayed by masculine attitudes to violence, specifically Archduke Harry's remark that a dying man 'is not a man, he is the enemy'.[71] Immediately afterwards, he falls into a swoon. While the pacifist theme is entirely consistent with Woolf's personal views, it reinterprets the theme of sex and gender, subordinating it to more public questions.

Like Woolf's novel, Potter's film extends to its own present day. While this is fundamentally an act of fidelity to the text, it necessitates a revisionary attitude. Potter was least comfortable with Orlando's privileges of class and property.[72] Woolf, addressing Sackville-West personally, had little room in which to be critical. Potter announces the theme in the opening voice-over. Having heard the expected lines ('there can be no doubt about his sex'), we hear something unusual: 'And there can be no doubt about his upbringing. Good food, education, a nanny, loneliness and isolation'. There is an element of anachronism about this, and 'nanny' in particular connects Orlando's privileges (and pains) with those of the children of contemporary professional classes. Potter's *Orlando*, rather like Woolf's Jacob Flanders, is destined for great things: 'destined to have his portrait on the wall and his name in the history books'.[73] Towards the end, there is another significant narrative alteration. Whereas Woolf's Orlando gains 'undisturbed possession of her titles' (*O*, p. 243), Potter's loses everything unless she has a son. Woolf's *Orlando* contains an element of wish-fulfilment: it restores to Sackville-West the estates which in reality she had lost, and so in the final scene, Woolf's Orlando returns to the great house as its mistress. Potter's Orlando returns as a tourist. The concluding voice-over explicitly interprets this conclusion as a positive one: 'She's no longer trapped by destiny. And ever since she let go of the past, she found her life was beginning'.[74] However, although framed by voice-overs about class, the film does not fully integrate the theme. If Woolf's novel offers a simple wish-fulfilment, Potter's film offers more complex pleasures: as with costume drama set in the Edwardian period, we can identify with both the declining aristocratic class and the rising middle class; and we can be reassured that, as the aristocrats (the 'good' ones, at least) do not become utterly destitute, we have nothing to fear ourselves. Potter's contemporary Orlando sports an expensive leather jacket and rides a vintage motorcycle. Marcus's remark about 'Yuppie Englishness' and 'Great Houses' contains an element of truth: we can identify both with the aristocratic Orlando and with her yuppie successor. The freedom from destiny which Potter grants Orlando is the 'freedom' of the young urban professional in a free-market economy.

MARLEEN GORRIS'S *MRS DALLOWAY* (1998)

Marleen Gorris's film version of *Mrs Dalloway*, based on a script by Eileen Atkins, is superficially more 'faithful' to its text than either Gregg's or Potter's films. The extent to which Atkins has invented new scenes or incidents is minimal; much of the dialogue and of Clarissa's voice-over comes verbatim from the text. Everything is done on authority. However, this fidelity is superficial, as Gorris does not find a filmic equivalent for the novel's use of free indirect discourse nor its use of symbolism and parallelism. It is important to consider the ways in which the form of the film reinterprets the novel.

Gorris's *Mrs Dalloway* follows the rules laid down by generations of classic literary adaptations. Throughout the film the camera work is steady, and most scenes are constructed from relatively long continuous shots. Classical music is used to enhance the mood, and generally speaking the music does not emanate from within the depicted location, but is a 'narratorial' addition. The exceptions are the singing during the boating party at Bourton, the music at Clarissa's party, and possibly the music in the scene of Elizabeth and Miss Kilman at the café, but even in these cases, the music is appropriate to the mood, and creates a proxy 'narrator' within the text.

The choice of this mode means that the film cannot capture the sense of abundance and energy which characterizes Woolf's London. The novel establishes a different mood:

In people's eyes, in the swing, tramp, and trudge; in the bellow and the uproar; the carriages, motor cars, omnibuses, vans, sandwich men shuffling and swinging; brass bands; barrel organs; in the triumph and the jingle and the strange high singing of some aeroplane overhead was what she loved; life; London; this moment of June. (*MD*, p. 4)

The mode of the film cannot capture the energy of the alliteration in this passage, nor of its present participles. Woolf uses the verbal equivalent of a hand-held camera, shaky, and 'imperfect' by the canons of classical cinema, but able to move rapidly from object to object; and she uses the verbal equivalent of the fast editing we would associate with an action movie rather than a literary adaptation. The choice of mode has important consequences for the way that the film treats Septimus's insanity, and I will return to these shortly.

The other distinctive feature of the film is the dominance of

Clarissa's voice-over and the uses to which it is put. It is not the nostalgic, retrospective voice-over of *Brideshead*. Clarissa's voice-over provides access to her private thoughts as they occur: the voice-over comments and evaluates, but it does not tell a story. In this respect, the voice-over is the film's equivalent of the novel's free indirect discourse, but there are several significant differences. Above all, while the novel allows access to the minds of its three central characters (Clarissa, Septimus, and Peter), and to a host of minor characters, the film privileges Clarissa's perspective. Gorris invited Atkins to give voice-overs to all the characters, but Atkins felt that the film would become too much of a 'mishmash';[75] however, the richness of Woolf's novel derives from exactly that complexity. In the novel we are invited to understand each character by a process of comparison and contrast with other characters; in spite of its title, the novel gives considerable time to Septimus and Peter. The form of the novel could be said to embody Clarissa's unanimist theory that she does not exist in one particular place, but is 'everywhere', and that to know anyone, 'one must seek out the people who completed them' (*MD*, p. 129). In the film, we are invited to understand Clarissa by listening to her commentary on herself; the analogies with Septimus and Peter are still there, but are considerably weakened. The privileged position given to Clarissa's perspective in the film is one factor that makes Gorris's treatment of her appear more sympathetic than Woolf's: Woolf's Clarissa can appear self-satisfied, most notably in her belief that her love of her roses could help the victims of genocide (p. 102); there is nothing in Vanessa Redgrave's portrayal of the mature Clarissa, and almost nothing in the script, to suggest that the audience are invited to judge her.

At several points the voice-over is used, along with the dialogue, to emphasize points which could have been made visually. For example, in the film as in the novel, two characters note Peter's habit of playing with his pocket knife: Clarissa, twice during their meeting in the morning (*MD*, pp. 37, 39), and Sally during the party (p. 159). Rather than conveying their thoughts by giving a close-up of Peter's hands playing with the knife, Gorris draws it to our attention by voice-over and by characters admonishing Peter for his habit.[76] A similar instance occurs in the scene where Clarissa retires to her attic room in the late morning:

Like a nun withdrawing, or a child exploring a tower, she went upstairs, paused at the window, came to the bathroom. . . . There was an emptiness about the heart of life; an attic room. Women must put off their rich apparel. At midday they must disrobe. . . . The sheets were clean, tight stretched in a broad white band from side to side. Narrower and narrower would her bed be. (*MD*, p. 26)

The film briefly shows Clarissa's narrow bed with its tight-stretched sheets, but relies on the voice-over to draw our attention to its existence: 'It's all over for me: the sheet stretched and the bed narrow'.[77] Had the film drawn attention to the bed visually, by allowing the camera to linger on it, and had it drawn attention to the emptiness of the room aurally, by allowing the sound of foot-steps on bare floorboards to be heard, it would have left the audience less certain of Clarissa's degree of self-consciousness about her situation. Woolf's use of free indirect discourse is subtle: reading *Mrs Dalloway*, we cannot tell whether the comparison of Clarissa to a nun derives from a narratorial voice, or from Clarissa's own mind. If we take it to come from Clarissa, we cannot be sure how conscious of it she is. Similarly, though the imperative that women 'must' disrobe may be in Clarissa's voice, we are uncertain how far she is endorsing it. It seems to derive from some external figure of authority, that of her husband, perhaps, though he in turn echoes the authority of the doctors (*MD*, p. 102). The film camera can reproduce some of this ambiguity—we can never be sure how far its point of view is also that of a character—but the voice-over cannot. The decision to have Clarissa voicing her awareness of the 'narrowness' of her life is an interpretative deci-sion. Although in the novel Clarissa thinks almost exactly the same thing—'It was all over for her' (*MD*, p. 40)—the thought comes somewhat later, in response to seeing Peter Walsh, while in the film it arises in response either to the attic room or to her recollection of Septimus.

The choice of a dominantly realist mode, and the privileging of Clarissa's perspective, have important consequences for Septimus's position in the film. In the novel, the presentation of the world from Septimus's point of view necessarily places us in sympathy with him. His thoughts become meaningful by a process of association, much as the thoughts of the other characters do. In considering his belief that men must not cut down trees because they are alive (*MD*, p. 21), we might note, for instance, Clarissa's belief that she was 'part . . . of the trees at home' (p. 8). We can also consider extra-textual sources: the skeletal trees of the European battlefields, for instance. In the novel, there is a continuum of representational modes: the depiction of Septimus employs the same 'language' as that of the other characters. In the film it is different. Septimus's mental condition is depicted primarily from the outside. Occasionally we are shown the world from his perspective: subtly, in the scene where he listens to the pigeons,[78] and less so when the sounds of war replace the realistic sounds of the park, and when he hallucinates Evans advancing in battle gear.[79] However, this representational mode is exceptional. There are two distinct visual languages in the film, and the one used to represent insanity is marked as anomalous. With the exception of Clarissa's brief recollection of Septimus,[80] this language is associated exclusively with Septimus. The adaptation removes both Peter Walsh's dream (the 'solitary traveller' section, *MD*, pp. 48–50), and his mythological reworking of the beggar woman (pp. 68–70), presumably because they are unrepresentable within its dominant language; had it included them, the distinction between 'normal' and 'abnormal' might have been eroded. Thus, in terms of the form of the film, Septimus is marked as different. What sympathy the audience feels for him depends largely on the strength of Rupert Graves's performance.

The formal differences have several interpretative consequences. While the novel encourages us to read insanity as a protest against authoritarian rationality, the film presents it simply as a puzzling and distressing illness. Prevented from seeing much of Septimus's mind, the audience is placed in the perspective of those responsible for looking after him: Rezia and Sir William Bradshaw. The novel is not unsympathetic to Rezia, but the nature of the film allows more space to her feelings. Denied the parallelisms and symbolic connections that link Sir William with the clocks of Harley Street, with 'Proportion' and 'Conversion', with Big Ben, and with the militarist ideals of regularity and uniformity, the audience is less able to interpret him as a symbol of authoritarian rationality, and is encouraged instead to see him as an individual.

The film's portrayal of Septimus and of his insanity reinterprets the novel in a number of ways. It gives little indication of Septimus's affection for his Evans, nothing of their being 'like two dogs playing on a hearth-rug' (*MD*, p. 73), and so we also lose the suggestion that Septimus's illness might be related to repressed sexual desire. Septimus becomes more purely a victim of the war, and less a victim of a repressive ideology. We should also note that the film, in focusing on the war, dilutes the novel's focus on the continuing power of militarism. Thus, the film depicts the war-wounded in its opening scenes, but it does not include the troop of uniformed boys which Peter follows (p. 43), nor does it dwell on the statues of great leaders which he admires (p. 44). The film can depict events, such as the war, but finds it more difficult to depict the workings of ideologies.

The scene of Septimus in Bradshaw's consulting room is particularly interesting, incorporating much of Woolf's text (*MD*, pp. 81–4), but changing its significance. Broadly speaking, Gorris's Bradshaw is a more sympathetic figure. While the novel connects Bradshaw to clock time, Big Ben, and the political and ideological machine, the film cannot bring out the significance of such connections. Bradshaw checks his pocket watch towards the end of the interview, but the film cannot readily depict the clocks of Harley Street shredding and slicing. Bradshaw emerges as an individual, not the representative of a system. For viewers familiar with Robert Hardy, the casting of him as Bradshaw will be the most significant change. Hardy has frequently played pompous father figures, men who are sometimes self-absorbed and infuriating, but who are essentially well intentioned, and his portrayal of Bradshaw follows this lineage. The film makes one major structural change: in the novel, Septimus and Rezia enter the consulting room together, before Bradshaw sends out Septimus momentarily; in the film, Bradshaw speaks to Rezia privately before inviting Septimus in. The change in itself makes Bradshaw seem less dismissive of Septimus. Moreover, Rezia is filmed mostly from Bradshaw's perspective, in close-up throughout. The novel gives the impression that Bradshaw pays little personal attention to his patients, but the camera's position softens this aspect. In the film, as in the novel, Bradshaw uses the term 'proportion', but the effect is very different:

BRADSHAW: Mrs Warren Smith, your husband is very seriously ill. From everything you've told me and from Dr Holmes's report I believe he is suffering from delayed shell shock.

REZIA: He's not mad is he?

BRADSHAW: Oh, I never use that word. I prefer to say 'lacking a sense of proportion'.

REZIA: But Dr Holmes said there was nothing the matter.

In the novel, Bradshaw's idea of 'proportion' forms part of a system of oppressive normalization, and for some of its original readers would have recalled Sir Almroth Wright. In the film his use of the word appears merely euphemistic. His sheltering Rezia from the truth is certainly patronizing, but is well intentioned. Similarly, in the scene with Septimus, Bradshaw uses a phrase that appears in the novel, 'We all have our moments of depression'. While in the novel the phrase suggests that Bradshaw does not recognize the serious-ness of Septimus's condition, in the film, following a long speech from Septimus, it looks like an attempt to defuse a potentially con-frontational situation. If one grants that Bradshaw in this scene is a more humane figure than in the novel, Clarissa's later reflection that he had always seemed obscurely evil seems less reasonable than in Woolf's text; in the novel it confirms what we already knew, but in the film it might force us to revise our opinions of the doctor.

Gorris's *Mrs Dalloway* is highly faithful to the text of Woolf's novel, taking whole passages verbatim and incorporating them as dialogue or voice-over. Nevertheless, it alters the kind of knowledge we have of the characters, alters the balance of our sympathies, and reinterprets the novel's politics. While some of these reinterpreta-tions may have been deliberate decisions on the part of Atkins or Gorris, it seems likely that many occur primarily because of the change of medium. The transposition into the realist medium of costume drama alters the meaning of the text whether the adapter likes it or not.

Michael Cunningham's *The Hours* (1998) and Robin Lippincott's *Mr Dalloway* (1999)

Although we have no league table to refer to, it would appear that by the late 1990s *Mrs Dalloway* had displaced *To the Lighthouse* as the most significant work in Woolf's *oeuvre*; and if not that, certainly as the work most attractive to creative interpreters. Within two years of Gorris's film being released, two novels were published that recon-textualized *Mrs Dalloway*, both of them emphasizing the question

Vanessa Redgrave as
Clarissa Dalloway in
Mrs Dalloway, 1998,
dir. Marleen Gorris

Meryl Streep
as a modern
Mrs Dalloway in
The Hours, 2002,
dir. Stephen Daldry

of sexuality: Michael Cunningham's *The Hours* (1998), and Robin Lippincott's *Mr Dalloway* (1999).[81]

Cunningham's novel reinterprets *Mrs Dalloway* very differently from Gorris's film, and from a greater variety of angles. It employs a form of postmodern historical narrative similar to those seen in Peter Ackroyd's *Hawksmoor* (1985) or Jeanette Winterson's *Sexing the Cherry* (1989); it interweaves historically distinct narratives, and implies non-causal connections between one period and the other. In the 'Prologue', Cunningham presents the day of Woolf's suicide in 1941, but in the body of the novel he presents Woolf on an imaginary day in 1923, during which she is thinking about and writing *Mrs Dalloway*. In the second period, he presents a day in the life of Laura Brown, a housewife in Los Angeles in 1949, constrained and depressed by the conservatism of post-war America; Laura is organizing a modest birthday party for her husband, and is reading *Mrs Dalloway*; during the course of the day, she contemplates suicide. In the third he presents Clarissa Vaughan, a well-off 52-year-old New Yorker planning to throw a party for her friend Richard, a respected poet who is dying of AIDS. Not only does Richard's nickname for Clarissa, 'Mrs Dalloway', connect her to Woolf's novel, but her friends and the minor characters in this strand echo Woolf's creations.

The first section recontextualizes *Mrs Dalloway* within a biographical frame. That frame itself interprets Woolf's life in the light of her death: by beginning the novel with Woolf's death, Cunningham makes her a suicide first, and a writer second. All biographies must necessarily reduce lives to themes and to coherent narratives, but the structure that Cunningham creates is potentially very reductive: it encourages the reader to see every detail of Woolf's life as prefiguring her death. In fact, the multi-stranded nature of the narrative attenuates this reductiveness: the anticipatory force of the opening scene refers as much to Laura in 1949 and Richard in the late nineties as it does to Virginia Woolf, and so the effect is less drastic than it may appear to be in summary. Nevertheless, Cunningham's account of Woolf emphasizes the private, the familial, and the tragic, at the expense of the public and political sides of her life. For readers of *The Hours* well versed in Woolf's life story, other allusions create a more specific interpretation of her suicide. For example, in one scene Woolf looks into a bathroom mirror, and feels that behind her is a 'dark manifestation of air', with 'porcine eyes'.[82] Although as a depiction of fragile mental health this scene works independently of its sources, it refers unmistakably to Woolf's description of Gerald Duckworth 'explor[ing]' her private parts in front of a mirror at Talland House; the 'porcine' eyes suggest her characterization of the Duckworth brothers as pigs.[83] Through these allusions, Cunningham endorses interpretations of Woolf's mental health and her suicide as being due primarily to the effects of child abuse.

Like Tom Stoppard's script for *Shakespeare in Love*, the biographical strand of Cunningham's novel works by a circular process: it takes elements from the writer's published works, and inserts them in fictitious scenes from the writer's life; it then encourages the reader to see the works as echoes of the life. Thus, when her niece and nephew, in a fictitious scene, find a dying bird in the garden at Hogarth House, we are presented with an anticipation of *Mrs Dalloway*: 'Oh, thinks Virginia, just before tea, here's death.'[84] The reader is invited to believe that this scene inspires Clarissa Dalloway's reaction to the discussion of Septimus's death: 'Oh! thought Clarissa, in the middle of my party, here's death, she thought' (*MD*, p. 156).

Similarly, Cunningham presents Virginia and Vanessa's fictitious kiss[85] as the 'inspiration' for Clarissa kissing Sally in *Mrs Dalloway*. At the climax of the 'Mrs Woolf' chapters, Cunningham makes this quite explicit: 'Yes, Clarissa will have loved a woman. Clarissa will have kissed a woman, only once'.[86] By taking the kiss as the crucial catalyst to Woolf's creation of the novel, Cunningham foregrounds its treatment of sexuality, while making its treatment of the war less significant. There are biographical precedents for Clarissa Dalloway other than her author—for example, Kitty Maxse[87]—but the explicit narrative of the novel erases them in favour of a biographical reading. Cunningham's Woolf goes on to give another aspect of her personality to another character, unnamed but recognizably Septimus Warren Smith: 'someone strong of body but frail-minded; someone with a touch of genius, of poetry, ground under by the wheels of the world, by war and government, by doctors'.[88] Again, Cunningham reinterprets the novel within a narrow biographical framework.

Laura Brown's own reading of *Mrs Dalloway* implicitly endorses Cunningham's biographical reading. On reading two paragraphs from the opening pages of the novel, Laura does not ask questions about London, or about Clarissa, but asks how someone who could write such sentences could come to kill herself.[89] The Laura Brown chapters propose a mysterious connection between authors and readers: Laura and Kitty's kiss echoes that of Virginia and Vanessa; her car journey to downtown Los Angeles parallels Virginia's abortive attempt to escape to central London on the train; above all, Laura's contemplation of suicide echoes Woolf's actual death. Like Ackroyd's *Hawksmoor*, the novel implies a provisional belief in metempsychosis, the transmigration of souls; in this case, the literary text is the medium through which the soul is transmitted. Like Clarissa Dalloway, Laura Brown has '[o]dd affinities with people she had never spoken to' (*MD*, p. 129; also p. 8).

Although in this respect the Laura Brown chapters appear to endorse a reductive reading of *Mrs Dalloway*, in other regards they create a space for a more critical and historical questioning of their parent text. The question they ask, implicitly, is whether the years from 1923 to 1949 had increased or reduced the choices available to women. Is the post-war reaction endured by Laura Brown better or worse than that endured by Virginia Woolf or Clarissa Dalloway? The suburban confinement imposed on Virginia Woolf had at least the justification of preserving her health, however misguided that treatment might have been; Laura Brown is restricted simply by virtue of her sex. In asking these questions, *The Hours* also invokes other texts by Woolf. Most obviously, Laura's journey to the Normandy Hotel is an attempt to find a room of her own, though in her case it is a room in which to read, rather than to write. Given that checking into a hotel becomes her recurrent simile for suicide, her finding a room may seem an ambivalent success, but it seems possible that Cunningham is also distantly evoking Woolf's injunction to kill 'The Angel in the House': the self that Laura has temporarily killed is the compliant housewife. The scene of the birthday party resembles *To the Lighthouse* more closely than *Mrs Dalloway*:

As Laura sets the plates and forks on the table—as they ring softly on the starched white cloth—it seems she has succeeded suddenly, at the last minute, the way a painter might brush a final line of color onto a painting and save it from incoherence; the way a writer might set down a line that brings to light the submerged patterns and symmetry in the drama. It has to do, somehow, with setting plates and forks on a white cloth.[90]

The scene echoes both Mrs Ramsay at the start of the dinner, look-ing at the plates on the table (*TL*, p. 112), and Lily Briscoe at the very end of the novel, placing the final line on her canvas (p. 281). The allusions remind us of the continuities between Woolf's novels of 1925 and 1927, both being concerned with a hostess attempting to make order out of chaos. The allusion suggests that Laura Brown is, like Mrs Ramsay, a frustrated artist; however, the absence of an obvious equivalent for Lily Briscoe might suggest that, by 1949, women's scope for creative expression had become more restricted.

The third strand of the novel, 'Mrs Dalloway', presents the rich-est and most complex rereading and rewriting of Woolf's original. The question I have so far evaded, of whether one needs to know *Mrs Dalloway* to understand *The Hours*, becomes unavoidable. In their publicity for the novel Cunningham's publishers reportedly claimed that a knowledge of Woolf's text was not prerequisite,[91] but no doubt they wished it to find as wide a market as possible. Mark Bostridge's characterization of the novel is more pertinent: 'The book is like an echo-chamber in which the references from the ori-ginal *Mrs Dalloway* connect with the latter-day stories and then seem to take on a life of their own'.[92]

By relocating *Mrs Dalloway* to New York in the late twentieth century, and by creating equivalents for some but not all of the original novel's scenes, Cunningham reinterprets it, implicitly mak-ing critical judgements about what is essential to it and what acci-dental. The primarily gay social milieu of the 'Mrs Dalloway' strand of *The Hours* emphasizes the importance of same-sex relationships in the original. The thoroughly conservative Hugh Whitbread is transformed into the youthfully gay 40-year-old Walter Hardy, while Evelyn Whitbread is transformed into his partner Evan. Peter Walsh, whose 'Uranian' side was only hinted at in Woolf's novel, is transformed into the openly gay Louis Waters. Woolf's Mrs Dalloway becomes Clarissa Vaughan, a publisher; while Sally Seton emerges as Sally, Clarissa's partner of eighteen years. Elements of Woolf's Richard Dalloway enter into Sally (her meeting with the gay film star Oliver St Ives parallels Mr Dalloway's meeting with Lady Bruton), but the name Richard is given to Clarissa's close friend, the poet.

As the pattern of the 'Mrs Dalloway' strand becomes clear, the reader might expect to find a modern-day embodiment of Septimus

Warren Smith: a traumatized survivor of the Vietnam War, for example, or a former soldier with Gulf War Syndrome. What becomes slowly apparent is that HIV has been as devastating as any war: few have been untouched by it. Richard is dying from AIDS, and his mind has been affected; Walter Hardy's partner has HIV but is surviving on a cocktail of drugs; another unnamed character is unable to come to Clarissa's party because his partner's AIDS has developed into leukaemia. Richard and Clarissa think of themselves as Woolf's Mr and Mrs Dalloway, but tragically and unwittingly they have become Septimus and Rezia.

While Cunningham's novel is all the more powerful for not creating one-for-one equivalents for Septimus and Rezia, the decision highlights some distinctive qualities of Woolf's novel. *Mrs Dalloway*, with its concern for the 'social system', has something in common with the 'condition of England' novels of the mid-Victorian era such as Elizabeth Gaskell's *North and South* or Charles Dickens's *Bleak House*. Though largely set in London, it is concerned with the geographically wider effects of British imperialism. *The Hours* does not claim to be a novel about 'America' or about America's quasi-imperial tendencies. Peter Walsh returns to London from India, but his equivalent Louis Waters has travelled from within the USA. The Prime Minister's car is rewritten as a trailer containing an unidentified film star. With the latter rewriting of Woolf, Cunningham provocatively asks whether film stars are now as important as political leaders, but to recognize that they are as prominent is not to say that they are as powerful. Cunningham's recontextualizing implies that Woolf is a novelist concerned primarily with sexuality and personal relations, and that her interest in national and international politics is unimportant. Thus, although Cunningham's recontextualization of Woolf is in tune with recent critical interest in Woolf's sexuality, in other respects it returns to an older interpretation of her work as apolitical.

Stephen Daldry's film adaptation of *The Hours* (2002) has undoubtedly brought both Cunningham's novel and Woolf's work to the attention of a wider audience. Daldry's adaptation necessarily changes the emphasis of the novel, and a critical study of Michael Cunningham's works would have to consider it in great detail. However, as a recontextualization of *Mrs Dalloway*, Daldry's film does little that has not already been discussed in connection with

Cunningham's novel: the film, like the novel, begins with Woolf's suicide, and includes the scene of her kissing her sister, thus placing a biographical frame around key incidents in *Mrs Dalloway*. Like most films, Daldry's finds it difficult to represent thought processes. In consequence Woolf's process of creativity is inadequately represented by Nicole Kidman smoking and frowning. For the same reasons, Laura Brown's biographical interpretations of Woolf are less prominent than in the novel; consequently the importance of Woolf to her thoughts of suicide is diminished, and the importance of her oppressive social milieu is reciprocally increased. The film alters the 'Mrs Dalloway' strand in many small ways: for example, whereas the novel gives a sense of Richard being part of a gay community, the film treats him as an isolated individual; whereas in the novel AIDS is omnipresent, in the film Richard appears to be an isolated case. However, these alterations are not likely directly to alter the way that anyone reads Woolf's novel. Indeed, while a reader of *The Hours* who knows Mrs Dalloway cannot help but think back to the original text, the same person watching the film could be forgiven for forgetting that Clarissa, Richard, Sally, and Louis have textual precedents: the film gives them an independent existence.

Robin Lippincott's *Mr Dalloway*, like Cunningham's novel, teases out the strand of Woolf's novel concerned with sexuality, and weaves a new narrative from it. However, while Cunningham's late twentieth-century strand places Woolf's narrative outline in a new social context, quite literally recontextualizing it, Lippincott's novel takes the form of a sequel, coming back to Clarissa and Richard on 28–9 June 1927. As such it forms part of a late twentieth-century trend of prequelling and sequelling, of which the best-known instance is *Wide Sargasso Sea* (1966), Jean Rhys's prequel to Charlotte Brontë's *Jane Eyre*. However, like Cunningham in his 'Mrs Dalloway' strand, Lippincott broadly follows the structure of Woolf's narrative: again there is a party, in this case thrown by Richard Dalloway for Clarissa to celebrate their thirtieth wedding anniversary, and again there is a ghost at the feast. Other smaller incidents are repeated from Woolf's novel: Richard begins by offering to buy the flowers himself, and Richard looks in the window of Hatchard's bookshop much as Clarissa had done.[93] The first surprise of the novel is that it presents the world from Richard Dalloway's perspective. It does so through the medium of a free indirect discourse which unostentatiously resembles Woolf's, though it is occasionally flawed by implausibly American idioms.[94] The second surprise is that Richard Dalloway, far from being an insensitive patriarch along the lines of Mr Ramsay, has a susceptibility to sense impressions as delicate as that of Peter Walsh or Clarissa. The third surprise is that since the middle of June 1923, Richard Dalloway has had a sexual relationship with another man. Subsequently he has had a nervous breakdown, and has left the House of Commons.

Many readers will find the developments in Richard's sexuality surprising. The degree of its plausibility will differ from reader to reader, according to life experience as much as to literary taste. The difficulty that Lippincott faces is that there is very little evidence in either *The Voyage Out* or *Mrs Dalloway* to suggest a repressed homosexual side to Richard Dalloway. The incident with Rachel Vinrace in the earlier novel might suggest a repressed impulsiveness, an aggressive sexuality concealed beneath a tepid, asexual exterior; but his instability need not make his homosexuality more plausible. To make Richard's sexuality more plausible Lippincott creates a more detailed background for him. He gives Richard a brother, Duncan, of whom he was very fond, and, through the course of the day, Richard recalls how as adolescent boys he and Duncan had had an exploratory sexual relationship, and how, soon afterwards, Duncan had killed himself. He also supplies other testimonies about Richard. For example, Sally Rosseter reflects on his buying flowers for Clarissa: 'For there had always been something—was "feminine" the right word? There had always been that something, whatever it was, about him, in spite of his love of the outdoors: it was something soft; something pliant and unmanly'.[95] While the prose is plausibly Woolfian, it is not clear that Richard's buying flowers in Woolf's novel necessarily denoted femininity, still less latent homosexuality. Lippincott's evidence is fabricated skilfully, but it lacks plausibility. It attempts not so much to reread the earlier novels as to rewrite them.

Though *Mr Dalloway* is set in 1927, its concerns are identifiably more modern. It reinterprets *Mrs Dalloway* as a narrative concerned primarily with sexuality. The narrative concerning Septimus and Rezia is not brought up to date, nor does Lippincott attempt to parallel *Mrs Dalloway*'s concern with political power. Unlike its original, *Mr Dalloway* is less deeply rooted in the social and political culture of its moment. The backdrop that Lippincott provides for his characters, the total eclipse of the sun on 28 June 1927, was a momentous natural event, but it did not change the course of history.

Woolf's novels are complex, multi-stranded, and multi-levelled. If, like Mrs Norman anxiously regarding Jacob Flanders, their interpreters have not seen them exactly as they are, that is because the novels do not have a single, essential identity; they have been filtered through various meshes, such as those marked 'Bloomsbury', 'biography', 'sexuality', or 'nostalgic drama'. One could, like *Jacob's Room*, make a pessimistic comedy from this scenario, one in which the original essence always escapes the blundering interpreter. Certainly film-makers have found it difficult to reproduce the delicately balanced portrayal of consciousness that characterizes Woolf's novels. However, reinterpretations of Woolf have themselves been complex and multi-stranded, bearing different meanings for different reading communities, and occasioning fierce debate between those who believe themselves truly to understand her work. Their richness and even their apparent misinterpretations suggest a more optimistic, and more nuanced narrative. The creative interpreter may find him- or herself in Lily Briscoe's position towards Mrs Ramsay, wanting to remain faithful to the much-loved, much-admired forebear, while retaining his or her own personal and artistic independence; wanting to pay tribute to the power of Woolf's work, but also acknowledging her historical limitations, and, where necessary, overriding her wishes.

NOTES

CHAPTER 1 . The Life of Virginia Woolf

1. Louie Mayer, in J. Russell Noble (ed.), *Recollections of Virginia Woolf* (1972; Harmondsworth: Penguin, 1975), 189.
2. At that time called 13 Hyde Park Gate South: see F. W. Maitland, *The Life and Letters of Leslie Stephen* (1906; London: Duckworth, 1910), 322.
3. Ibid.; Q. Bell, *Virginia Woolf*, 2 vols. (London: Hogarth, 1972), i. 22.
4. L. Stephen, *Some Early Impressions* (1903; London: Hogarth, 1924), 98.
5. Ibid. 124, 151.
6. Maitland, *Leslie Stephen*, 254; H. Lee, *Virginia Woolf* (London: Chatto and Windus, 1996), 74.
7. Lee, *Virginia Woolf*, 101.
8. Ibid. 103–4.
9. Maitland, *Leslie Stephen*, 370.
10. Ibid. 387, 383.
11. Ibid. 387.
12. Ibid. 395.
13. Ibid. 365.
14. L. Stephen, letter to Mrs W. K. Clifford, 25 July 1884, quoted ibid. 384.
15. Ibid. 474.
16. For her age, see letter to Ethel Smyth, 12 Jan. 1941: *Letters*, vi. 460.
17. Lee summarizes them and discusses the incident further: *Virginia Woolf*, 125–8.
18. Maitland, *Leslie Stephen*, 431.
19. Q. Bell, *Virginia Woolf*, i. 37–9.
20. Quoted in Lee, *Virginia Woolf*, 178.
21. L. Stephen, *Some Early Impressions*, 103; V. Bell, 'Life at Hyde Park Gate after 1897', in *Sketches in Pen and Ink*, ed. L. Giachero (London: Hogarth, 1997), 67. Virginia's account confirms this: he was 'deaf, eccentric, and absorbed in his work, and entirely shut off from the world': *MB*, p. 35.
22. Lee, *Virginia Woolf*, 139; V. Curtis, *Stella and Virginia: An Unfinished Sisterhood* (Bloomsbury Heritage, 30; London: Cecil Woolf, 2001), 38.
23. Lee, *Virginia Woolf*, 139.
24. V. Bell, *Sketches*, 70–1.
25. Ibid. 71.
26. Ibid. 72.
27. Maitland, *Leslie Stephen*, 400.
28. Ibid. 481.
29. V. Bell, *Sketches*, 75.
30. Ibid. 73.
31. Ibid.; *MB*, pp. 36–42.

32. Interpretations summarized in Lee, *Virginia Woolf*, 196; S. Trombley, *All that Summer She was Mad* (New York: Continuum, 1981), 7.

33. *MB*, p. 46; V. Bell, *Sketches*, 98–9.

34. Lee, *Virginia Woolf*, 220.

35. In 'Notes on Bloomsbury', Vanessa dates the end of 'Bloomsbury' to 1916 (*Sketches*, 113); for Leonard Woolf, it only really began in 1918: *Downhill all the Way: An Autobiography of the Years 1919 to 1939* (London: Hogarth, 1967), 114.

36. V. Bell, *Sketches*, 60; Lee, *Virginia Woolf*, 115.

37. Lee, *Virginia Woolf*, 143, 223.

38. Woolf, 'Report on Teaching at Morley College', in Q. Bell, *Virginia Woolf*, i. 203.

39. Lee, *Virginia Woolf*, 117–18.

40. *MB*, p. 59; L. Woolf, *Downhill*, 99–103.

41. Lee, *Virginia Woolf*, 275, 282–6.

42. A. Stephen, *The 'Dreadnought' Hoax* (London: Hogarth, 1936), 32.

43. Ibid. 39–42.

44. Ibid. 21–2.

45. A. Gruetzner Robins, *Modern Art in Britain 1910–1914* (London: Merrell Holberton, 1997), 15–16.

46. Q. Bell, *Virginia Woolf*, i. 175.

47. Lee, *Virginia Woolf*, 259–60; V. Woolf, *Letters*, i. 424 n. 2.

48. Q. Bell, *Virginia Woolf*, i. 170–2; V. Woolf, *Letters*, i. 469–70, 485–6.

49. H. Lee, *Virginia Woolf*, 329–30.

50. L. Woolf, *Downhill*, 49.

51. Ibid. 11.

52. Q. Bell, *Virginia Woolf*, ii. 35.

53. V. Woolf, *Letters*, ii. 95. He was called up again in October 1917, and similarly exempted: see *Diary*, i. 59.

54. L. Woolf, letter to L. Strachey, 10 Feb. 1915, *Letters of Leonard Woolf*, ed. Frederic Spotts (London: Weidenfeld and Nicolson, 1989), 210; L. Woolf, *Beginning Again: An Autobiography of the Years 1911 to 1918* (London: Hogarth, 1964), 233.

55. *Letters of Leonard Woolf*, 279.

56. Lee, *Virginia Woolf*, 599, 704–5.

57. R. Lehmann, 'For Virginia Woolf', *Penguin New Writing*, 7 (1941), 53–8, at 53–4.

58. Q. Bell, *Virginia Woolf*, ii. 65–7.

59. Lee, *Virginia Woolf*, 423.

60. N. Nicolson in Noble (ed.), *Recollections*, 157.

61. L. Mayer, ibid. 189.

62. L. Mayer, ibid.

63. L. Woolf, *Downhill*, 52–3.

64. *Diary*, ii. 250; L. Woolf, *Downhill*, 117–18.

65. *Diary*, ii. 187 n. 1; S. Raitt, *Vita and Virginia* (Oxford: Clarendon, 1993), 170–1.

66. Vita Sackville-West to H. Nicolson, 17 Aug. 1926, quoted in Raitt, *Vita and Virginia*, 2; V. Woolf, *Letters*, iii. 306–7.
67. *Diary*, ii. 236; iii. 124–5; H. Lee, *Virginia Woolf*, 506.
68. L. Woolf, *Downhill*, 64, 141–5.
69. Ibid. 190; *Diary*, iv. 311.
70. Lee, *Virginia Woolf*, 586.
71. Ibid. 589–90.
72. P. Stansky and W. Abrahams, *Journey to the Frontier* (London: Constable, 1966), esp. 397–401.
73. Extracts from the memoir are printed in Q. Bell, *Virginia Woolf*, ii. 255–9; Lee, *Virginia Woolf*, 703.
74. L. Woolf, *The Journey and Not the Arrival that Matters: An Autobiography of the Years 1939 to 1969* (London: Hogarth, 1969), 90–1.
75. V. Woolf, *Letters*, vi. 486; *Letters of Leonard Woolf*, 250.

CHAPTER 2. The Fabric of Society: Nation and Identity

1. P. J. Cain and A. G. Hopkins, *British Imperialism: Innovation and Expansion* (London: Longman, 1993), 7.
2. E. J. Hobsbawm, *Industry and Empire* (1968; London: Penguin, 1990), 172–94.
3. R. C. K. Ensor, *England 1870–1914* (Oxford: Clarendon, 1936), 347.
4. J. Stevenson, *British Society 1914–45* (1984; London: Penguin, 1990), 43.
5. G. R. Searle, *The Quest for National Efficiency* (Oxford: Blackwell, 1971), chs. 1–3.
6. Ibid., p. 16.
7. L. Woolf, Memorandum to the Parliamentary Labour Party, 8 Nov. 1918, in *Letters of Leonard Woolf*, ed. F. Spotts (London: Weidenfeld and Nicolson, 1989), 388–9.
8. *PA*, p. 179; 'Thunder at Wembley', in *EVW* iii. 410–14. See also J. M. MacKenzie, *Propaganda and Empire: The Manipulation of British Public Opinion 1880–1960* (Manchester: Manchester UP, 1984), 96–120.
9. J. Davis, *A History of Britain, 1885–1939* (Basingstoke: Macmillan, 1999), 61–2.
10. F. Bealey and H. Pelling, *Labour and Politics, 1900–1906* (London: Macmillan, 1958), 71. J. Davis (*History of Britain*, 77) puts the figure as high as £42,000.
11. A. J. P. Taylor, *English History, 1914–1945* (Oxford: Clarendon, 1965), 114.
12. Davis, *History of Britain*, 119–20.
13. H. Lee, *Virginia Woolf* (London: Chatto and Windus, 1996), 207.
14. V. Woolf, *Letters*, i. 217; Ensor, *England*, 376–8.
15. V. Woolf, *'The Hours': The British Museum Manuscript of Mrs. Dalloway*, transcribed and ed. H. M. Wussow (New York: Pace University Press, 1996), 260; Davis, *History of Britain*, 199.

16. Hansard, HC (series 5) vol. 4, col. 474 (29 Apr. 1909).

17. Ibid. 480–2.

18. Ibid. 532.

19. J. A. Hobson, *Problems of Poverty* (London: Methuen, 1891), 189.

20. S. Webb, 'The Difficulties of Individualism', *Economic Journal*, 1 (1891), 368.

21. Hobson, *Problems of Poverty*, 195.

22. Ibid. 198.

23. Davis, *History of Britain*, 91.

24. Ensor, *England*, 424.

25. Davis, *History of Britain*, 94.

26. W. S. Churchill, letter of 4 Jan. 1908, in Randolph S. Churchill, *Winston S. Churchill, Companion*, pt. 2 (London: Heinemann, 1969), 759.

27. Hansard, HC (series 5) vol. 21, cols. 83 (6 Feb. 1911) and 1071 (15 Feb. 1911).

28. Ensor, *England*, 453.

29. Ibid. 477–8.

30. Davis, *History of Britain*, 108–9.

31. M. Fawcett, *Men are Men and Women are Women* (London: NUWSS, 1909), 10; anon., *Physical Force* (London: NUWSS, 1909).

32. [V. Stephen], 'Lysistrata', *Englishwoman*, 8/22 (Nov. 1910), 91–3; L. Housman, *Lysistrata: A Modern Paraphrase from the Greek of Aristophanes* (London: Woman's Press, 1911), 41, 47.

33. Anon., *Is Woman's Only Sphere the Home* (London: NUWSS, 1909).

34. C. Hamilton, *Life Errant* (London: J. M. Dent, 1935), 68.

35. The NUWSS summarized the history in *Unfulfilled Pledges: Our Case Against Mr Asquith* (London: NUWSS, 1914).

36. M. M. Childers, 'Virginia Woolf on the Outside Looking Down: Reflections on the Class of Women', *Modern Fiction Studies*, 38/1 (1992), 61–79, at 65–6.

37. Hobsbawm, *Industry and Empire*, 126–8, 151–3; J. Harris, *Private Lives, Public Spirit: Britain 1870–1914* (1993; London: Penguin, 1994), 19–20.

38. S. D. Pennybacker, *A Vision for London, 1889–1914: Labour, Everyday Life and the London County Council Experiment* (London: Routledge, 1995), 16.

39. J. Davis, 'The Progressive Council, 1889–1907', in A. Saint (ed.), *Politics and the People of London* (London: Hambledon, 1989), 27–48, at 27.

40. S. Webb, quoted in Harris, *Private Lives, Public Spirit*, 200.

41. S. Webb, quoted in Pennybacker, *Vision for London*, 4.

42. Woolf, letter dated 12 May 1918: *Letters*, ii. 238; diary for 6 Mar. 1923: *Diary*, ii. 238.

43. Ensor, *England*, 127–8.

44. Parl. Debs. (series 4) vol. 188, cols. 957–8 (12 May 1908).

45. Ibid. 949.

46. Hansard HC (series 5) vol. 35, col. 1414 (15 Mar. 1912).

47. Harris, *Private Lives, Public Spirit*, 52.

48. Stevenson, *British Society 1914–45*, 224–5.

49. Ibid. 221–2.

50. C. V. Butler, *Domestic Service: An Enquiry by the Women's Industrial Council* (London: G. Bell and Sons, 1916), 9; Harris, *Private Lives, Public Spirit*, 42.

51. J. Duckworth Stephen, 'The Servant Problem' [editorial title] (1893), in D. F. Gillespie and E. Steele (eds.), *Stories for Children, Essays for Adults* (Syracuse, NY: Syracuse UP, 1987), 248–52.

52. T. M. McBride, *The Domestic Revolution: The Modernisation of Household Service in England and France 1820–1920* (New York: Holmes and Meier, 1976), 114.

53. P. Horn, *The Rise and Fall of the Victorian Servant* (1975; Gloucester: Alan Sutton, 1986), 152.

54. E. Mills, *The Domestic Problem* (London: John Castle, 1925), 74.

55. Anon., *The Servant Problem* (Leyton [London]: E. R. Alexander & Sons, 1922), 7.

56. Horn, *Rise and Fall of the Victorian Servant*, 167.

57. Harris, *Private Lives, Public Spirit*, 62.

58. Ibid. 45–6; M. C. Braby, *Modern Marriage and How to Bear it* (London: T. Werner Laurie, [1908]), 188–9.

59. S. Webb, *The Decline in the Birth-Rate* (London: Fabian Society, 1907), 6.

60. Ibid. 17.

61. Ibid. 19.

62. Stevenson, *British Society 1914–45*, 303–6; S. K. Kent, *Making Peace: The Reconstruction of Gender in Interwar Britain* (Princeton: Princeton University Press, 1993), 120.

63. G. Dangerfield, *The Strange Death of Liberal England* (1935; London: Serif, 1997), 13–14.

64. P. Stansky, *On or About December 1910: Early Bloomsbury and its Intimate World* (Cambridge, Mass.: Harvard University Press, 1996), 4; J. Briggs, *'This Moment I Stand On': Woolf and the Spaces in Time* (London: Virginia Woolf Society of Great Britain, 2001), 7–12.

65. Taylor, *English History*, 120–1.

66. Davis, *History of Britain*, 125.

67. H. Read, *Naked Warriors* (London: Art and Letters, 1919), 14; see also Read, *Annals of Innocence and Experience*, 2nd edn. (London: Faber, 1946), 142–3.

68. P. Fussell, *The Great War and Modern Memory* (New York: Oxford University Press, 1975), 21–2.

69. C. Bell, *Peace at Once* (London and Manchester: National Labour Press, 1915), 18–20.

70. Taylor, *English History*, 120.

71. R. Strachey, 'Changes in Employment', in Strachey (ed.), *Our Freedom, and its Results* (London: Hogarth, 1936), 128.

72. Taylor, *English History*, 38.

73. C. Hamilton, 'The Backwash of Feminism', *Time and Tide*, 3/36 (8 Sept. 1922), 853.

74. G. Orwell, *The Road to Wigan Pier*, in *Collected Works*, ed. P. Davison (London: Secker and Warburg, 1986), 113.

75. G. Crossick, 'The Emergence of the Lower Middle Class in Britain', in Crossick (ed.), *The Lower Middle Class in Britain 1870–1914* (London: Croom Helm, 1977), 12.

76. The phrases derive from the Labour party's Clause Four, instituted in 1918: see H. Pelling and A. J. Reid, *A Short History of the Labour Party*, 11th edn. (Basingstoke: Macmillan, 1996), 39.

77. D. H. Lawrence, *Sons and Lovers* (1913), ed. H. Baron and C. Baron (1992; London: Penguin, 1994), 70.

78. [J. F. Stephen], 'Gentleman', *Cornhill Magazine*, 5 (1865), 336–7.

79. Crossick, 'Emergence', 29.

80. M. Arnold, *Culture and Anarchy* (1869; Cambridge: Cambridge UP, 1931), 52, 100–1.

81. Ibid. 57.

82. J. Bright, quoted in J. Harris, 'Between Civic Virtue and Social Darwinism: The Concept of the Residuum', in D. Englander and R. O'Day (eds.), *Retrieved Riches: Social Investigation in Britain 1840–1914* (Aldershot: Scolar Press, 1995), 74.

83. Harris, 'Between Civic Virtue and Social Darwinism', 72.

84. Bright and Bosanquet, quoted ibid. 71.

85. For Nietzsche, and much else on this topic, see J. Carey, *The Intellectuals and the Masses: Pride and Prejudice among the Literary Intelligentsia, 1880–1939* (London: Faber, 1992).

86. T. Carlyle, *Past and Present* (London: Chapman and Hall, 1843), 286.

87. J. K. Stephen, *The Living Languages: A Defence of the Compulsory Study of Greek at Cambridge* (Cambridge: Macmillan and Bowes, 1891), 47–8; N. G. Annan, 'The Intellectual Aristocracy', in J. Plumb (ed.), *Studies in Social History* (London: Longmans, 1955), 241–87.

88. Woolf, *The Pargiters* ed. M. Leaska (New York: New York Public Library, 1977), 151; the scene itself survives in *Y*, pp. 65–71.

89. Webb, *Decline in the Birth-Rate*, 5–8.

90. Denise Riley, *'Am I that Name?': Feminism and the Category of 'Woman' in History* (Basingstoke: Macmillan, 1988).

91. Woolf, *Pargiters*, 151–2.

92. Harris, *Private Lives, Public Spirit*, 70.

93. L. Davidoff, *The Best Circles: Society Etiquette and the Season* (London: Croom Helm, 1973), 41–4.

94. J. Conrad, 'Heart of Darkness', in *Youth, Heart of Darkness, The End of the Tether*, ed. R. Kimbrough (Oxford: Oxford University Press, 1984), 115.

95. Davidoff, *Best Circles*, 99.

96. Harris, *Private Lives, Public Spirit*, 10.

97. For 'young' races, see H. Fielding Hall, *A People at School* (London: Macmillan, 1906), 29.

98. W. Holtby, 'Feminism Divided' (1926), in V. Brittain and W. Holtby, *Testament of a Generation*, ed. P. Berry and A. Bishop (London: Virago, 1985), 48.

99. C. Hamilton, quoted in Kent, *Making Peace*, 124.

100. L. Strachey, *Queen Victoria* (London: Chatto and Windus, 1921), 31.

101. Davidoff, *Best Circles*, 51–2.

102. Mrs A. Colquhoun, *The Vocation of Woman* (London: Macmillan, 1913), 314.

103. F. M. Mayor, *The Rector's Daughter* (1924; London: Penguin, 1992), 170.

104. J. Purvis, *A History of Women's Education in England* (Milton Keynes: Open University Press, 1991), 107; C. Dyhouse, *No Distinction of Sex? Women in British Universities, 1870–1939* (London: UCL Press, 1995), 12.

105. F. J. C. Hearnshaw, *The Centenary History of King's College London 1828–1928* (London: Harrap, 1929), 312–18, 438–42, and Oakeley, 'King's College for Women', in *Centenary History*, 496.

106. Q. D. Leavis, review of *Three Guineas*, repr. in R. Majumdar and A. McLaurin (eds.), *Virginia Woolf: The Critical Heritage* (London: RKP, 1975), 418.

107. M. Vicinus, *Independent Women: Working and Community for Single Women, 1850–1920* (London: Virago, 1985), 125.

108. Dyhouse, *No Distinction of Sex?*, 2.

109. R. Strachey, *The Cause* (1928; London: Virago, 1978), 260.

110. Oakeley, 'King's College for Women', 502–5; Dyhouse, *No Distinction of Sex?*, 45.

111. 'A University Degree for Housewives', by 'Educationist', *Freewoman*, 1/1 (23 Nov. 1911), 16–18; Mills, *Domestic Problem*, 84.

112. These views are attributed to 'Imperialists and Eugenists' by anon., 'Freewomen and the Birth-Rate', *Freewoman*, 1/2 (30 Nov. 1911), 35–7.

113. Mrs A. Colquhoun, *Vocation of Woman*, 4, 7.

114. L. Strachey, *Eminent Victorians* (1918; London: Chatto and Windus, 1948), 196.

115. R. Wake and P. Denton, *Bedales School: The First Hundred Years* (London: Haggerston, 1993).

116. R. Fieldhouse, 'The Nineteenth Century', in Fieldhouse (ed.), *A History of Modern British Adult Education* (Leicester: NIACE, 1996), 23–4, 30–2.

117. Ibid. 32.

118. Ibid. 37.

119. B. Groombridge, 'Broadcasting', in Fieldhouse (ed.), *History of Modern British Adult Education*, 355–61.

120. Woolf, '*The Hours*', 298.

121. W. J. Perry, 'The Distribution of Man', *Nation and Athenaeum*, 36 (27 Dec. 1924), 474–5.

122. Anon., 'The Racial Factor', *Time and Tide*, 5/23 (6 June 1924), 541. The tripartite schema was promoted by Lothrop Stoddard in *Racial Realities*

in Europe (1924): see anon., 'The Newest of Sciences', *Nation and Athenaeum*, 36 (27 Dec. 1924), 476.

123. M. Higgs, *The Evolution of the Child Mind* (London: Froebel Society, 1910), 8.

124. G. Eliot, *Adam Bede* (1858; Harmondsworth: Penguin, 1980), 50.

125. D. H. Lawrence, 'John Galsworthy' (1928), in *Phoenix* (London: Heinemann, 1936), 546.

126. L. Woolf, 'The World of Books: Racial Fantasies', *Nation and Athenaeum*, 39 (29 May 1926), 209.

127. For fuller accounts, see: D. J. Childs, *Modernism and Eugenics: Woolf, Eliot, Yeats, and the Culture of Degeneration* (Cambridge: Cambridge University Press, 2001); D. Bradshaw, 'Eugenics', in Bradshaw (ed.), *A Concise Companion to Modernism* (Oxford: Blackwell, 2003), 35–55.

128. C. Holmes, *Anti-Semitism in British Society, 1876–1939* (London: Arnold, 1979), 3.

129. Ibid. 5.

130. L. Woolf, 'Anti-Semitism', in *Encyclopedia Britannica*, 11th edn. (1910–11), ii. 134–46, at 136.

131. W. Evans-Gordon, Parl. Debs. (series 4) vol. 145, col. 718 (2 May 1905).

132. G. C. Lebzelter, *Political Anti-Semitism in England, 1918–1939* (London: Macmillan, 1978), 9; Holmes, *Anti-Semitism*, 27–8.

133. Sir C. Dilke, Parl. Debs. (series 4) vol. 145, cols. 695, 698 (2 May 1905). See also E. Barker, *National Character and the Factors in its Formation* (London: Methuen, 1927), 10–12.

134. Woolf, *Carlyle's House and Other Sketches*, ed. D. Bradshaw (London: Hesperus Press, 2003), 14–15. The sketch derives from a 1909 notebook which was rediscovered only in 2002.

135. H. Lee, *Virginia Woolf*, 314.

136. D. Bradshaw, 'Hyams Place: *The Years*, the Jews and the British Union of Fascists', in M. Joannou (ed.), *Women Writers of the 1930s: Gender, Politics and History* (Edinburgh: Edinburgh University Press, 1999), 179–91, at 189.

CHAPTER 3. The Literary Scene

1. W. B. Yeats, 'Man and the Echo' (1938), in *Yeats's Poems*, ed. A. N. Jeffares (Basingstoke: Macmillan, 1989), 469.

2. W. H. Auden, 'In Memory of W. B. Yeats' (Feb. 1939), in *Collected Poems*, ed. E. Mendelson (London: Faber, 1991), 248.

3. P. Keating, *The Haunted Study: A Social History of the English Novel 1875–1914* (London: Secker and Warburg, 1989), 405.

4. Ibid. 407–11.

5. A. Snaith, *Virginia Woolf: Public and Private Negotiations* (Basingstoke: Macmillan, 2000), 125–6.

6. B. J. Kirkpatrick and S. N. Clarke, *A Bibliography of Virginia Woolf*, 4th edn. (Oxford: Clarendon, 1997).

7. 'Circulating Libraries Association', *The Times*, 2 Dec. 1909, p. 12.

8. Keating, *Haunted Study*, 23; M. Sadleir, 'Ambiguities of the Book Trade', in *Books and the Public*, by the Editor of the *Nation* et al. (London: Hogarth, 1927), 43.

9. Keating, *Haunted Study*, 25–6.

10. W. Heinemann, 'Circulating Libraries and Novels' [letter], *The Times*, 2 Dec. 1909, p. 12; M. Sadleir, 'Why only Dickens?', *Nation and Athenaeum*, 34 (9 Feb. 1924), 667–8.

11. 'Circulating Libraries Association', *The Times*, 2 Dec. 1909, p. 12.

12. J. Stevenson, 'Banned Books' [letter], *New Statesman*, 32 (20 Oct. 1928), 47.

13. J. Carey, *The Intellectuals and the Masses* (London: Faber, 1992).

14. Keating, *Haunted Study*, 58; 'Copyright', *Encyclopedia Britannica*, 11th edn. (Cambridge: Cambridge University Press, 1910–11), vii. 124–5.

15. Keating, *Haunted Study*, 58.

16. J. Conrad, *The Collected Letters*, ed. F. R. Karl and L. Davies, 6 vols. to date (Cambridge: Cambridge University Press, 1983 onwards), v. 249, 434, 620.

17. E. Gosse, 'The Influence of Democracy on Literature', *Contemporary Review*, 59 (1891), 523–36, at 528.

18. R. Graves, *Poetic Unreason* (London: C. Palmer, 1925), 21.

19. Sadleir, 'Ambiguities', 35–6.

20. H. G. Wells, *Kipps* (London: Macmillan, 1905), 405–6.

21. H. G. Wells, *Ann Veronica* (1909; Harmondsworth: Penguin, 1968), 16, 18, 257. The first two are imaginary; the last three were actual novels.

22. Sadleir, 'Ambiguities', 40.

23. e.g. Wilkie Collins's *Basil* (1852), quoted in L. Hartley, *Physiognomy and the Meaning of Expression in Nineteenth-Century Culture* (Cambridge: Cambridge University Press, 2001), 135.

24. *Punch*, 169 (23 Dec. 1925), 673.

25. *Diary*, iv. 129.

26. For a fuller account, see M. H. Whitworth, 'Logan Pearsall Smith and *Orlando*', *Review of English Studies*, 55 (2004), 598–604.

27. L. P. Smith, *The Prospects of Literature* (London: Hogarth, 1927), 14.

28. Ibid. 27.

29. Ibid. 30.

30. Most influentially J. Benda's *La Trahison des clercs* (1927), translated both as *The Great Betrayal* and *The Betrayal of the Intellectuals*.

31. E. Pound, 'A Retrospect' (1918), in *Literary Essays*, ed. T. S. Eliot (London: Faber, 1954), 6.

32. T. S. Eliot, 'Contemporanea', *Egoist*, 5/6 (June–July 1918), 84.

33. Cf. A. Bennett, *Literary Taste: How to Form It* (London: New Age Press, 1909), 89.

34. D. J. Palmer, *The Rise of English Studies* (Oxford: Oxford University Press, 1965), 56–65, 116, 151.

35. E. Muir (writing as 'Edward Moore'), *We Moderns* (London: George Allen and Unwin, 1918), 128.

36. T. S. Eliot, 'Tradition and the Individual Talent', in *Selected Prose of T. S. Eliot*, ed. F. Kermode (London: Faber, 1975), 38.

37. R. Strachey, *The Cause* (1928; London: Virago, 1978), 384–5.

38. L. Tickner, *The Spectacle of Women: Imagery of the Suffrage Campaign, 1907–14* (London: Chatto and Windus, 1987), 18, 254–60.

39. Strachey, *Cause*, 316.

40. C. Hamilton, *Life Errant* (London: J. M. Dent, 1935), 82.

41. C. Hamilton, *Marriage as a Trade* (London: Chapman and Hall, 1909), 193–4.

42. J. King, *The Last Modern: A Life of Herbert Read* (London: Weidenfeld and Nicolson, 1990), 71.

43. P. Faulkner, *Modernism* (London: Methuen, 1977), 19–20; M. Bradbury and J. McFarlane, 'Movements, Magazines and Manifestoes', in Bradbury and McFarlane (eds.), *Modernism 1890–1930* (London: Penguin, 1990), 192–205; J. Symons, *Makers of the New: The Revolution in Literature, 1912–1939* (London: André Deutsch, 1987), 155; L. Rainey, *Institutions of Modernism* (New Haven: Yale University Press, 1998), 39, 91–9.

44. V. Woolf, *Letters*, iii. 356; *Diary*, iii. 40; *Letters*, iii. 297; *Congenial Spirits*, ed. J. T. Banks (London: Hogarth, 1989), 169.

45. D. May, *Critical Times: The History of the 'Times Literary Supplement'* (London: HarperCollins, 2001), 414–21.

46. Keating, *Haunted Study*, 268–71.

47. Quoted ibid. 243.

48. P. N. Furbank, *E. M. Forster: A Life*, 2 vols. (London: Secker and Warburg, 1978), ii. 153–5; Woolf, 'The Censorship of Books', *Nineteenth Century and After* (Apr. 1929), 446–7.

49. R. Ellmann, *James Joyce* (New York: Oxford University Press, 1959), 517–19.

50. V. Sackville-West, *The Letters of Vita Sackville-West to Virginia Woolf*, ed. L. DeSalvo and M. Leaska (1985; San Francisco: Cleis Press, 2001), 118; V. Woolf, *Letters*, iii. 298.

51. M. Kinkead-Weekes, *D. H. Lawrence: Triumph to Exile 1912–1922* (Cambridge: Cambridge University Press, 1996), 277–8.

52. Keating, *Haunted Study*, 244–51, 271–6.

53. P. Miles (ed.), *A Child of the Jago* by A. Morrison (London: Dent, 1996), 216–52, esp. 230–1; R. H. Deming (ed.), *James Joyce: The Critical Heritage* (London: Routledge and Kegan Paul, 1970), 62–3.

54. R. P. C. Corfe, *The Times* (13 Dec. 1909), 12.

55. R. P. Draper (ed.), *D. H. Lawrence: The Critical Heritage* (London: Routledge and Kegan Paul, 1970), 93–5.

56. *Letters of Leonard Woolf*, ed. F. Spotts (London: Weidenfeld and Nicolson, 1989), 199–200.

57. R. Graves and L. Riding, *A Survey of Modernist Poetry* (London: Heinemann, 1927).

58. R. P. Blackmur, Introduction to *The Art of the Novel* by Henry James (New York: Charles Scribner's Sons, 1934), p. xvi.

59. T. S. Eliot, '*Ulysses*, Order, and Myth' (1923), in *Selected Prose*, 177.

60. W. James, *Psychology* (New York: Henry Holt, 1910), 151–75.

61. M. Sinclair, 'The Novels of Dorothy Richardson', *Egoist*, 5 (Apr. 1918), 57–9.

62. Snaith, *Virginia Woolf*, 63–71.

63. J. Joyce, *Ulysses*, ed. J. Johnson (Oxford: Oxford University Press, 1993), 89.

64. Ibid. 240–2.

65. M. Sinclair, *Mary Olivier: A Life* (London: Cassell, 1919), 3.

66. Ibid. 5.

67. Ibid. 9.

68. W. Lewis, *Tarr* (1928; London: Penguin, 1984), 312.

69. Sinclair, *Mary Olivier*, 112.

70. Ibid. 234.

71. Ibid. 296.

72. R. Macaulay, *Potterism* (London: Collins, 1920), 33.

73. J. H. Buckley, *Season of Youth: The Bildungsroman from Dickens to Gissing* (Cambridge, Mass.: Harvard University Press, 1974), 17–18.

74. J. Little, '*Jacob's Room* as Comedy: Woolf's Parodic Bildungsroman', in J. Marcus (ed.), *New Feminist Essays on Virginia Woolf* (London: Macmillan, 1981), 105–24.

75. e.g. Lionel Portman's *Hugh Rendal* ([1905]), cited in [M. S. Florence and C. K. Ogden], *Militarism versus Feminism* (London: G. Allen and Unwin, 1915), 52.

76. A. Lunn, *The Harrovians* (1913; London: Methuen, 1926), 291.

77. E. M. Forster, 'Pessimism in Literature' (1906), quoted in J. E. Miller, *Rebel Women* (London: Virago, 1994), 39.

78. Miller, *Rebel Women*, 73.

79. Keating, *Haunted Study*, 208–16; Miller, *Rebel Women*, 40–84.

80. Miller, *Rebel Women*, 72–3.

81. E. Mordaunt, *The Park Wall* (London: Cassell, 1916), 107.

82. Miller, *Rebel Women*, 82–3.

83. J. A. Boone, 'Modernist Maneuvrings of the Marriage Plot', *PMLA* 101 (1986), 374–88.

84. It has been suggested that the 'condition of England' genre was revived by C. F. G. Masterman's non-fictional text of that name (1909), the best-known example being E. M. Forster's *Howards End* (1910): see L. Pykett, *Engendering Fictions: The English Novel in the Early Twentieth Century* (London: Edward Arnold, 1995), 34, 119–23.

85. Portman, *Hugh Rendel*, ch. 18.

86. L. Strachey, *Eminent Victorians* (1918; London: Chatto and Windus, 1948), 7.

87. E. Muir, 'Lytton Strachey', *Nation and Athenaeum*, 37 (25 Apr. 1925), 102–4.

CHAPTER 4. Philosophical Questions

1. S. P. Rosenbaum, 'The Philosophical Realism of Virginia Woolf', in Rosenbaum (ed.), *English Literature and British Philosophy* (Chicago: University of Chicago Press, 1971), 316–56, at 316; J. Hintikka, 'Virginia Woolf and Our Knowledge of the External World', *Journal of Aesthetics and Art Criticism*, 38 (1979–80), 5–14, at 5–6.

2. R. Fry, 'An Essay in Aesthetics', in *Vision and Design* (1920; Harmondsworth: Pelican, 1937), 22.

3. Ibid. 23.

4. J. Harrison, *Ancient Art and Ritual* (London: Williams and Norgate, 1913), 230.

5. A. Gruetzner Robins, *Modern Art in Britain 1910–1914* (London: Merrell Holberton, 1997), 21–4; Fry, *Cézanne: A Study of his Development* (New York: Macmillan, 1927); Fry, 'Chinese Art', *Chinese Art*, by Fry et al. (London: B. T. Batsford for the *Burlington Magazine*, 1925), 5–12.

6. D. Grant, *Still Life* (*c.*1915), and *Interior* (1915), reproduced in Robins, *Modern Art in Britain*, 154, 155.

7. V. Bell, *Composition* (1914), reproduced ibid. 157.

8. Fry, 'Essay in Aesthetics', 25.

9. Harrison, *Ancient Art and Ritual*, 133.

10. Fry, 'Essay in Aesthetics', 24–5; see also Harrison, *Ancient Art and Ritual*, 210, 212, 216.

11. Fry, 'Essay in Aesthetics', 36.

12. e.g. B. Russell, *The Problems of Philosophy* (1912; Oxford: Oxford University Press, 1967), 2–3.

13. E. Mach, *Popular Scientific Lectures*, trans. T. J. McCormack, 4th edn. (Chicago: Open Court, 1910), 192.

14. K. Pearson, *The Grammar of Science* (London: Walter Scott, 1892), 128.

15. L. Stephen, 'What is Materialism?', in *An Agnostic's Apology and Other Essays* (London: Smith, Elder, and Co., 1893), 127–67, at 129–31.

16. M. H. Whitworth, *Einstein's Wake: Relativity, Metaphor, and Modernist Literature* (Oxford: Oxford University Press, 2001), 97.

17. L. Stephen, 'What is Materialism?', 129.

18. e.g. H. Elliot, 'The Principle of Relativity', *Edinburgh Review*, 232/474 (Oct. 1920), 316–31, at 321; H. Wildon Carr, *The General Principle of Relativity in its Philosophical and Historical Aspect* (London: Macmillan, 1920), 158.

19. M. Sinclair, *Mary Olivier: A Life* (London: Cassell and Co., 1919), 45; Sinclair's philosophical work, *A Defence of Idealism* (London: Macmillan, 1917), engages with Bergson.

20. The critical debate is summarized by Mary Anne Gillies, *Henri Bergson and British Modernism* (Montreal and Kingston: McGill-Queen's University Press, 1996), 107–8.

21. *Letters of Leonard Woolf*, ed. F. Spotts (London: Weidenfeld and Nicolson, 1989), 485–6, 571.

22. J. Harrison, *Reminiscences of a Student's Life* (London: Hogarth Press, 1925), 81.

23. e.g. C. Brereton, 'The Prussianization of Germany', *Common Cause*, 6/304 (5 Feb. 1915), 697–8.

24. A. Banfield, *The Phantom Table: Woolf, Fry, Russell and the Epistemology of Modernism* (Cambridge: Cambridge University Press, 2000), 34–5; K. Costelloe's paper, 'What Bergson Means by "Interpenetration" ', was read on 13 Feb. 1913, and printed in *Proceedings of the Aristotelian Society*, 13 (1912–13), 131–55.

25. Gillies, *Henri Bergson and British Modernism*, 109.

26. S. Waterlow, 'The Philosophy of Henri Bergson', *Quarterly Review*, 430 (Jan. 1912), 152–76.

27. Ibid. 166.

28. Ibid. 164.

29. Hintikka, 'Virginia Woolf and Our Knowledge of the External World', 6.

30. F. R. Leavis, *The Great Tradition* (1948; London: Penguin, 1993), 20, 127, 129, 131.

31. G. E. Moore, *Principia Ethica* (Cambridge: Cambridge University Press, 1903), 1–2, 36.

32. Ibid. 2–3.

33. Ibid. 22.

34. J. M. Keynes, 'My Early Beliefs', in *The Collected Writings of John Maynard Keynes* (London: Macmillan, for the Royal Economic Society, 1972), x. 433–50, at 446. As Paul Levy notes, however, Lytton Strachey and Leonard Woolf paid at least some attention to the fifth chapter: *Moore: G. E. Moore and the Cambridge Apostles* (London: Weidenfeld and Nicolson, 1979), 239.

35. Levy, *Moore*, 124–7.

36. *PA*, p. 249; *Letters*, i. 340, 347, 352–3, 357, 364.

37. Woolf took the passage from Moore, *Principia*, 17 (ch. 1, sect. 14).

38. Ibid. 188.

39. Ibid. 28.

40. Ibid. 203.

41. Keynes, *Collected Writings*, x. 436.

42. Moore, *Principia*, p. vii.

43. Keynes, *Collected Writings*, x. 440.

44. L. Woolf, quoted in Rosenbaum, 'Philosophical Realism of Virginia Woolf', 318.

CHAPTER 5. Society, Individuals, and Choices

1. F. W. Bradbrook, 'Virginia Woolf: The Theory and Practice of Fiction', in B. Ford (ed.), *The Modern Age*, vol. vii of the *Pelican Guide to English Literature* (1961; Harmondsworth: Penguin, 1964), 257–69.

2. Linden Peach has termed this process 'cryptographic reading': *Virginia Woolf* (Basingstoke: Macmillan, 2000), 33–9.

3. *Letters*, ii. 521; *Diary*, ii. 205.

4. *Diary*, ii. 189; V. Woolf, *'The Hours': The British Museum Manuscript of Mrs. Dalloway*, transcribed and ed. H. M. Wussow (New York: Pace University Press, 1996), 411.

5. *Diary*, ii. 316; iii. 4; *Letters*, iii. 154.

6. H. Lee, *Virginia Woolf* (London: Chatto and Windus, 1996), 456.

7. Woolf appears to have recognized the homoerotic element in male military companionship, long before it became a topic of critical discussion: P. Fussell, *The Great War and Modern Memory* (New York: Oxford University Press, 1975), 279–309; A. Caesar, *Taking It Like a Man: Suffering, Sexuality and the War Poets* (Manchester: Manchester University Press, 1993).

8. Mrs A. Colquhoun, *The Vocation of Woman* (London: Macmillan, 1913), 62; her source was W. C. Roscoe, 'Woman', *National Review*, 7 (1858), 333–61. Similarly, A. E. Wright, *The Unexpurgated Case Against Woman Suffrage* (London: Constable, 1913), 35.

9. K. J. Phillips, *Virginia Woolf Against Empire* (Knoxville: University of Tennessee Press, 1994), 15–16.

10. 'Uranian' translated *Urning*, a German term introduced by K. H. Ulrichs in the 1860s, deriving from *Uranos*, 'heaven': N. Greig, 'Introduction', in E. Carpenter, *Selected Writing, i. Sex* (London: GMP, 1984), 59.

11. E. Carpenter, *The Intermediate Sex* (London: Swan Sonneschein, 1908), 18.

12. Ibid. 27, 33.

13. Ibid. 23.

14. Ibid. 13.

15. The homosexual proselytizer George Ives lived there, and Oscar Wilde made The Albany the address for 'Ernest Worthing' in *The Importance of Being Earnest*. See Wilde, *The Importance of Being Earnest and Other Plays*, ed. P. Raby (Oxford: Clarendon, 1995), 358–9; R. Ellmann, *Oscar Wilde* (London: Hamish Hamilton, 1987), 403–4.

16. G. R. Searle, *The Quest for National Efficiency* (Oxford: Blackwell, 1971), 22; see also 24–7, 80–3.

17. L. T. Hobhouse, *Democracy and Reaction* (London: T. Fisher Unwin, 1904), 121.

18. Greig, 'Introduction', 59; A. Sinfield, *The Wilde Century: Effeminacy, Oscar Wilde and the Queer Movement* (London: Cassell, 1994), 124–5.

19. Mrs C. Chesterton, *In Darkest London* (London: Stanley Paul and Co., 1926), 156, 230, 232.

20. M. Fulton, *Blight* (London: Duckworth, 1919), 66.

21. S. Graham, 'Human Derelicts', *Nation and Athenaeum*, 37 (4 Apr. 1925), 7–8. See also Chesterton, *In Darkest London*, 22.

22. C. E. Stephen, *Light Arising: Thoughts on the Central Radiance* (Cambridge: Heffer and Sons, 1908). Jane Marcus hypothesizes many connections between Caroline Emelia and Virginia in 'The Niece of a

Nun', in J. Marcus (ed.), *Virginia Woolf: A Feminist Slant* (Lincoln, Nebr.: Nebraska University Press, 1984), 7–36.

23. A. McLaurin, 'Virginia Woolf and Unanimism', *Journal of Modern Literature*, 9/1 (1981–2), 115–22; McLaurin, 'Consciousness and Group Consciousness in Virginia Woolf', in E. Warner (ed.), *Virginia Woolf: A Centenary Perspective* (Basingstoke: Macmillan, 1984), 28–40.

24. C. E. Stephen, *Light Arising*, 112.

25. Ibid. 113.

26. The principal exceptions are the exchanges between Rhoda and Louis (*W*, pp. 114–15, 188–9, 191–4), and what J. W. Graham refers to interchangeably as 'antiphonal exchanges' and 'choruses' in the farewell dinner scene (*W*, pp. 100–3, 110–14, 118–19), and the Hampton Court scene (*W*, pp. 187–8, 189–91): see *The Waves: The Two Holograph Drafts*, ed. J. W. Graham (London: Hogarth Press, 1976), 217, 538, 554; 159, 161.

27. F. S. Flint, 'Contemporary French Poetry', *Poetry Review*, 1/8 (Aug. 1912), 355–414; J. Harrison, 'Unanimism and Conversion', *Alpha and Omega* (London: Sidgwick and Jackson, 1915), 42–79; [Leonard Woolf], ' "Les Copains" ', in *EVW* ii. 16–18; J. Romains (Louis Farigoule), *The Death of a Nobody* trans. D. MacCarthy and S. Waterlow (London: Howard Latimer, 1914). The review of *Les Copains* was first attributed to Virginia Woolf in the 3rd edn. of B. J. Kirkpatrick's *Bibliography of Virginia Woolf* (Oxford: Clarendon Press, 1980), hence its appearance in *EVW* ii (1987); the 4th edn. of the *Bibliography*, co-authored with Stuart N. Clarke (Oxford: Clarendon Press, 1997), 304, attributes it to Leonard. The 'band' around *The Death of a Nobody* is preserved in the copy in the Bodleian Library, Oxford.

28. M. S. Florence and C. K. Ogden, 'Women and War: Hopes and Fears for the Future', *Jus Suffragii*, 9/5 (1 Feb. 1915), 234–5.

29. Romains, *Death*, 27, 52.

30. Ibid. 110.

31. Ibid. 56.

32. Ibid. 10, 32, 74, 115, 140.

33. Ibid. 56.

34. Ibid. 37.

35. G. Le Bon, quoted in S. Freud, *Group Psychology and the Analysis of the Ego, Standard Edition of the Complete Psychological Works* (London: Hogarth, 1955–74), xviii. 75, 81.

36. J. W. Graham, *Evolution and Empire* (London: Headley Bros., [1912]), 194.

37. R. Strachey, *The Cause* (1928; London: Virago, 1978), 364–5.

38. M. MacCarthy, *A Nineteenth-Century Childhood* (London: Heinemann, 1924), 83–4.

39. Anon., 'The Glorified Spinster', *Macmillan's Magazine*, 58 (1888), 371–6, at 373.

40. Anon., 'Where Women Work', *Freewoman*, 1/11 (1 Feb. 1912), 205–8; ibid. 1/13 (15 Feb. 1912), 245–7; ibid. 1/16 (7 Mar. 1912), 315–16.

41. J. Lewis, *Women in England 1870–1950: Sexual Divisions and Social Change* (Brighton: Wheatsheaf, 1984), 156.

42. R. McKibbin, *Classes and Cultures: England 1918–1951* (Oxford: Oxford University Press, 1998), 48, 133–4.

43. Anon., 'Glorified Spinster', 374.

44. The manuscript is held in the Berg Collection, New York Public Library, and is reproduced on *Virginia Woolf: Major Authors CD ROM*, ed. M. Hussey (Woodbridge, Conn.: Primary Source Media, 1997). The first page begins with the passage 'She could not entirely forget William's presence . . .' (*ND*, p. 141).

45. *Letters*, ii. 232; see *ND*, pp. 362–3.

46. K. Mansfield, repr. in R. Majumdar and A. McLaurin (eds.), *Virginia Woolf: The Critical Heritage* (London: Routledge and Kegan Paul, 1975), 79–82.

47. C. Hamilton, *Marriage as a Trade* (London: Chapman and Hall, 1909), pp. v, 265, 241.

48. Ibid. 155, 162.

49. Ibid. 228; see also Lewis, *Women in England*, 75–6.

50. S. Webb, *The Decline in the Birth-Rate* (London: Fabian Society, 1907), 19.

51. [M. S. Florence and C. K. Ogden], *Militarism versus Feminism: An Enquiry and a Policy, Demonstrating that Militarism involves the Subjection of Women* (London: George Allen and Unwin, 1915), 57. The text first appeared as a special supplement to *Jus Suffragii*, the monthly newspaper of the International Woman Suffrage Alliance; it was described as 'the joint production of several collaborators', under the direction of Florence and Ogden: *Jus Suffragii*, 9/6 (1 Mar. 1915), p. i.

52. S. K. Kent, *Making Peace: The Reconstruction of Gender in Interwar Britain* (Princeton: Princeton University Press, 1993), 119–20.

53. These phrases are also discussed by D. L. Parsons, *Streetwalking the Metropolis: Women, the City, and Modernity* (Oxford: Oxford University Press, 2000), 118.

54. Hamilton, *Marriage*, 22.

55. J. Conrad, 'Heart of Darkness', in *Youth, Heart of Darkness, The End of the Tether*, ed. Robert Kimbrough (Oxford: Oxford University Press, 1984), 115.

56. Anon., 'Glorified Spinster', 374–5.

57. B. Brecht, *Brecht on Theatre*, ed. and trans. J. Willett (London: Methuen, 1964), 137.

58. J. Marcus, 'Britannia Rules *The Waves*', in K. Lawrence (ed.), *Decolonising Tradition: New Views of Twentieth-Century 'British' Literary Canons* (Urbana: University of Illinois Press, 1988), 136–62; G. Beer, Introduction to *The Waves* (Oxford: Oxford University Press, 1992); J. Goldman, *Virginia Woolf: To the Lighthouse; The Waves* (Cambridge: Icon, 1997), 148–9.

59. L. B. Pekin, *Public Schools: Their Failure and Reform* (London: Hogarth, 1932), 80–5.
60. K. Phillips, in her arraignment of Louis as a 'fascist', edits out his ambivalence, and misleadingly implies that he watches their sadistic acts 'with envy': *Virginia Woolf Against Empire*, 161.
61. R. Brooke, letter of 9 Mar. 1912, quoted in Lee, *Virginia Woolf*, 296.
62. Mrs H. Ward, 'An Appeal Against Female Suffrage' (June 1889), in J. Lewis (ed.), *Before the Vote was Won* (London: Routledge and Kegan Paul, 1987), 409–17; among the co-signatories was 'Mrs Leslie Stephen'.
63. M. Fawcett, '*Men are Men and Women are Women*', NUWSS pamphlet A69 (London: NUWSS, 1909), 10.
64. An argument by Arthur Balfour included in the anthology *Physical Force*, NUWSS pamphlet A70 (London: NUWSS, 1909).
65. Fawcett, '*Men are Men*', 10.
66. Woolf, *Jacob's Room: The Holograph Draft*, transcribed and ed. E. Bishop (New York: Pace University Press, 1998), 275.
67. M. Usui concentrates on Rezia and Doris Kilman in their own right, rather than as adjuncts of men: 'The Female Victims of the War in *Mrs. Dalloway*', in M. Hussey (ed.), *Virginia Woolf and War: Fiction, Reality, and Myth* (Syracuse, NY: Syracuse UP, 1991), 151–63.
68. [Florence and Ogden], *Militarism versus Feminism*, 4.
69. Woolf [unsigned review of *The Northern Iron* by G. A. Birmingham], *TLS*, 19 Dec. 1907, p. 390.
70. M. Starr, *Lies and Hate in Education* (London: Hogarth, 1929), 14.
71. J. D. Esty, 'Amnesia in the Fields: Late Modernism, Late Imperialism, and the English Pageant-Play', *ELH* 69 (2002), 245–76.
72. Starr, *Lies and Hate*, 78.
73. Pekin, *Public Schools*, 112–13.
74. J. Langdon-Davies, *Militarism in Education: A Contribution to Educational Reconstruction* (London: Headley Bros., [1919]), 40.
75. Ibid. 16.
76. Aspects of this reading are suggested by E. L. Bishop, 'The Subject in *Jacob's Room*', *Modern Fiction Studies*, 38/1 (1992), 147–75; Bishop, however, does not specify Jacob's education as the particular mechanism of his subjection.
77. A. Lunn, *The Harrovians* (1913; London: Methuen, 1926), 67. In Lunn's novel the quoted phrases come from an imaginary essay on 'The Public School Spirit'.
78. P. E. Matheson, 'Education To-day and To-morrow', *Fortnightly Review*, NS 100 (Oct. 1916), 614–21, at 616.
79. Pekin, *Public Schools*, 15.
80. Ibid. 116.
81. Lunn, *Harrovians*, 45.
82. H. Read, *Annals of Innocence and Experience* (London: Faber, 1940), 90.
83. Woolf, *Diary*, ii. 186.

84. For Bennett's criticism, see Majumdar and McLaurin (eds.), *Virginia Woolf: The Critical Heritage*, 112.

CHAPTER 6. Scientific and Medical Contexts

 1. W. Wordsworth, 'The Tables Turned' (1798), in Duncan Wu (ed.), *Romanticism: An Anthology*, 2nd edn. (Oxford: Blackwell, 1998), 260.
 2. G. Beer, *Wave, Atom, Dinosaur: Woolf's Science* (London: Virginia Woolf Society of Great Britain, 2000), 3.
 3. A. McLaurin, *Virginia Woolf: The Echoes Enslaved* (Cambridge: Cambridge University Press, 1973), 154.
 4. G. Beer, *Virginia Woolf: The Common Ground* (Edinburgh: Edinburgh University Press, 1996), 162.
 5. e.g. Calamy in A. Huxley's *Those Barren Leaves* (London: Chatto and Windus, 1925).
 6. Lord Southborough, ' "Shell Shock": A Misleading Designation', *The Times*, 2 Sept. 1922, p. 13. For a fuller account, see S. Thomas, 'Virginia Woolf's Septimus Smith and Contemporary Perceptions of Shell Shock', *English Language Notes*, 25/2 (Dec. 1987), 49–57.
 7. E. Showalter, *The Female Malady: Women, Madness, and English Culture, 1830–1980* (1985; London: Virago, 1987), 138–40.
 8. Ibid. 138–9.
 9. Ibid. 129.
10. Ibid. 134.
11. Ibid. 174.
12. Ibid.
13. J. Conway, 'Stereotypes of Femininity in a Theory of Sexual Evolution', *Victorian Studies*, 14 (1970), 47–62, at 48. See also J. Lewis, *Women in England, 1870–1950: Sexual Divisions and Social Change* (Brighton: Wheatsheaf, 1984), 83–5; Showalter, *Female Malady*, 121–5.
14. Conway, 'Stereotypes', 49.
15. H. Maudsley, 'Sex in Mind and in Education' (1874), summarized in Showalter, *Female Malady*, 124–5.
16. Conway, 'Stereotypes', 50–1.
17. P. Geddes, quoted ibid. 53.
18. W. Muir, *Woman: An Inquiry* (London: Hogarth Press, 1925), 13–14.
19. H. Lee, *Virginia Woolf* (London: Chatto and Windus, 1996), 454; D. Bradshaw, in his edition of *Mrs Dalloway* (Oxford: Oxford University Press, 2000), 179–80.
20. A. E. Wright, 'Suffrage Fallacies', *The Times*, 28 Mar. 1912, pp. 7–8; anon., 'To-day's Debate on Woman Franchise', *The Times*, 28 Mar. 1912, p. 7. Wright's letter was reprinted (though certainly not endorsed) by *Freewoman*, 1/20 (4 Apr. 1912), 392–4, and in Wright's *The Unexpurgated Case Against Woman Suffrage* (London: Constable, 1913), 77–87.
21. L. Duffin, 'Prisoners of Progress: Women and Evolution', in S. Delamont

and L. Duffin (eds.), *The Nineteenth-Century Woman* (London: Croom Helm, 1978), 57–91, at 73.

22. M. Sinclair, *Feminism* (London: Women Writers' Suffrage League, 1912), dated 'March 31st 1912' on p. 46; anon., 'Our Little Brother', *Common Cause*, 3/156 (4 Apr. 1912), 880–1; anon., 'Prehistoric—or From Mars?', *Vote*, 5/128 (6 Apr. 1912), 281; E. M. N. Williams [review of Wright's *Unexpurgated Case*], *Common Cause*, 5/236 (17 Oct. 1913), 480; G. B. Shaw, 'Sir Almroth Wright's Polemic', *New Statesman*, 2/28 (18 Oct. 1913), 45–7; M. Sinclair, 'Sir Almroth Wright's Unexpurgated Case Against Woman Suffrage', *Jus Suffragii*, 8/3 (1 Nov. 1913), 30–1.

23. P. Fussell, *The Great War and Modern Memory* (New York: Oxford University Press, 1975), 270–309. See also Ch. 5, above.

24. e.g. B. A. Schlack, 'A Freudian Look at Mrs Dalloway', *Literature and Psychology*, 23 (1973), 151–63.

25. S. Freud, Introduction to S. Ferenczi et al., *Psycho-Analysis and the War Neuroses* (London: International Psycho-Analytical Press, 1921).

26. N. Ward Jouve, 'Woolf and Psychoanalysis', in S. Roe and S. Sellers (eds.), *The Cambridge Companion to Virginia Woolf* (Cambridge: Cambridge University Press, 2000), 245–72.

27. Woolf, *'The Hours': The British Museum Manuscript of Mrs. Dalloway*, transcribed and ed. H. M. Wussow (New York: Pace University Press, 1996), 156.

28. 'Insanity', *Encyclopedia Britannica*, 11th edn. (Cambridge: Cambridge University Press, 1910–11), xiv. 597–618.

29. 'Shell Shock' [leading article], *The Times*, 10 Aug. 1922, p. 13, and 'Courage and Character' [leading article], *The Times*, 2 Sept. 1922, p. 13.

30. 'Influenza', *Encyclopedia Britannica*, 11th edn. (1910–11), xiv. 552–6, at 555.

31. Woolf, 'An Introduction to *Mrs Dalloway*' (1928), in *EVW* iv. 549.

32. 'Insanity', 597.

33. Showalter, *Female Malady*, 179, quoting E. C. Southard, *Shell-Shock and other Neuro-Psychiatric Problems* (1919).

34. Lee, *Virginia Woolf*, 334.

35. For other approaches, see S. M. Squier, 'Invisible Assistants or Lab Partners? Female Modernism and the Culture(s) of Modern Science', in L. Rado (ed.), *Rereading Modernism: New Directions in Feminist Criticism* (New York: Garland, 1994), 299–319; and C. Webb, 'The Room as Laboratory: The Gender of Science and Literature in Modernist Polemics', in Rado (ed.), *Modernism, Gender, and Culture: A Cultural Studies Approach* (New York: Garland, 1997), 337–52.

36. G. J. Romanes, 'Mental Differences between Men and Women', *Nineteenth Century*, 21 (1887), 654–72, at 654–5.

37. Ibid. 655 n. 1.

38. Woolf, *Women & Fiction: The Manuscript Versions of A Room of One's Own*, ed. S. P. Rosenbaum (Oxford: Shakespeare Head/Blackwell, 1992), 3.

39. This section draws upon M. H. Whitworth, *Einstein's Wake: Relativity, Metaphor, and Modernist Literature* (Oxford: Oxford University Press, 2001), 166–9.

40. Unidentified, quoted by J. Needham, 'Biology and Modern Physics', *New Adelphi*, 2 (Mar.–May 1929), 286–8, at 288.

41. Woolf, 'Modern Novels', in *EVW* iii. 30–7; she also spoke of 'materialists' in the revised form of the essay, 'Modern Fiction' (*EVW* iv. 157–65), and in 'Character in Fiction' (*EVW* iii. 420–38).

42. R. J. Strutt, 'A Popular Book on Radio-Activity' [review of *The New Knowledge* by R. K. Duncan], *Speaker*, 13/320 (18 Nov. 1905), 162–3. Woolf first contributed to the *Speaker* in Jan. 1906.

43. J. Killen, 'Virginia Woolf in the Light of Modern Physics' (unpublished PhD thesis, University of Louisville, Kentucky, 1984), 84–117.

44. W. B. Yeats, paraphrased by S. Spender, *World within World* (London: Hamish Hamilton, 1951), 164; the occasion was probably 25 Oct. 1934: see *Diary*, iv. 255; *Letters*, v. 342.

45. A. S. Eddington, *The Nature of the Physical World* (Cambridge: Cambridge University Press, 1928), 224.

46. Ibid. 211; J. H. Jeans, *The Mysterious Universe* (Cambridge: Cambridge University Press, 1930), 120–1.

47. Eddington, *The Nature of the Physical World*, 211, 214.

48. C. Flammarion, *Lumen* (1872), trans. A. A. M. and R. M. (London: William Heinemann, 1897), 89–92; E. Slosson, *Easy Lessons in Einstein* (London: George Routledge and Sons, 1920), 42–45; C. Nordmann, *Einstein and the Universe*, trans. J. McCabe (London: T. Fisher Unwin, 1922), 76.

49. H. Henry, *Virginia Woolf and the Discourse of Science* (Cambridge: Cambridge University Press, 2003), 54.

50. C. Flammarion, *Popular Astronomy: A General Description of the Heavens*, trans. J. Ellard Gore (London: Chatto and Windus, 1894), 617.

51. For a contemporary account, see J. W. N. Sullivan, 'Popular Science', *Athenaeum*, 4719 (1 Oct. 1920), 444–5.

52. Whitworth, *Einstein's Wake*, 37–8.

53. The drafts appear in Woolf, Notebook 29, Berg Collection, New York Public Library, as reproduced on *Virginia Woolf: Major Authors CD ROM*, ed. M. Hussey (Woodbridge, Conn.: Primary Source Media, 1997).

54. V. Sackville-West, *The Letters of Vita Sackville-West to Virginia Woolf*, ed. L. DeSalvo and M. A. Leaska (1985; San Francisco: Cleis Press, 2001), 72, 149; Woolf, *Diary*, iii. 337; v. 107. For a fuller account of Sackville-West's references, see I. Blyth, 'A Little "Einsteinian" Confusion', *Virginia Woolf Bulletin*, 9 (Jan. 2002), 29–33.

55. Whitworth, *Einstein's Wake*, 181–6.

56. A. S. Eddington, *Space, Time, and Gravitation* (Cambridge: Cambridge University Press, 1920), 161–2; V. Sackville-West, 'Books in General', *Listener*, 4 (19 Nov. 1930), 844.

57. J. W. Graham, 'Point of View in *The Waves*', *University of Toronto Quarterly*, 39 (1969–70), 193–211, at 196.
58. Flammarion, *Popular Astronomy*, 617.
59. Beer, *Wave, Atom, Dinosaur*, 8; Henry, *Virginia Woolf and the Discourse of Science*, 101.
60. Jeans, *Mysterious Universe*, 1.
61. Ibid. 2.
62. 'Telephone', *Encyclopedia Britannica*, 11th edn. (1910–11), xxvi. 554, 556.
63. J. H. Heaton, 'An Imperial Telegraph System', *Nineteenth Century*, 45/268 (1899), 906–14, at 910; J. H. Muirhead, 'What Imperialism Means', *Fortnightly Review*, NS 68 (Aug. 1900), 177–87.
64. J. Romains, *The Death of a Nobody*, trans. D. MacCarthy and S. Waterlow (London: Howard Latimer, 1914), 16.
65. J. H. Jeans, *The Universe around Us*, 2nd edn. (Cambridge: Cambridge University Press, 1929), 240.

CHAPTER 7. Recontextualizing and Reconstructing Woolf

1. M. Cunningham, *The Hours* (1998; London: Fourth Estate, 1999); S. Daldry (director), *The Hours* (2002).
2. R. Campbell, 'Home Thoughts in Bloomsbury' (1927), and *The Georgiad* (1931), in *Collected Works*, 4 vols. (Craighall: A. D. Donker, 1985–88), i. 173, 182–216; F. Swinnerton, *The Georgian Literary Scene* (London: Heinemann, 1935).
3. J. Adam Smith, 'The Limitations of Bloomsbury', *London Mercury*, 39/231 (Jan. 1939), 353–4; F. W. Bradbrook, 'Virginia Woolf: The Theory and Practice of Fiction', in B. Ford (ed.), *The Modern Age*, vol. vii of the Pelican Guide to English Literature (1961; Harmondsworth: Penguin, 1964), 257–69, at 261.
4. F. R. Leavis, *The Common Pursuit* (London: Chatto and Windus, 1952), 257; N. Annan, 'Bloomsbury and the Leavises', in J. Marcus (ed.), *Virginia Woolf and Bloomsbury* (Basingstoke: Macmillan, 1987), 23–38.
5. A. Wilson, 'Diversity and Depth', *TLS*, 18 Aug. 1958, p. viii.
6. Bradbrook, 'Virginia Woolf', 257.
7. W. Lewis, *Men Without Art* (1934), ed. S. Cooney (Santa Rosa: Black Sparrow, 1987), 139.
8. e.g. B. Blackstone, *Virginia Woolf* (London: Hogarth, 1949), 9–10.
9. M. Holroyd, *Lytton Strachey: A Critical Biography*, 2 vols. (London: Chatto and Windus, 1968), i. 399, 402.
10. Albee's play was first performed on Broadway in 1962, and in London in 1964; the film was released in 1966. See B. R. Silver, *Virginia Woolf Icon* (Chicago and London: University of Chicago Press, 1999), 102–16.
11. The core acts were the Abortion Reform Bill (1967), the Sexual Offences Act (1967), the National Health Service (Family Planning) Act (1967), and the Divorce Reform Act (1969). For a sample of conservative

criticism, see P. Hitchens, 'Is Britain Civilized?', in *The Abolition of Britain* (London: Quartet, 1999), 285–96.

12. 'The Fears of Virginia Woolf', *TLS* (27 Oct. 1972), 1278 [unsigned, written by Joan Bennett].

13. E. Hawkes Rogat, 'The Virgin in the Bell Biography', *Twentieth-Century Literature*, 20 (1974), 96–113; Silver, *Virginia Woolf Icon*, 117–27.

14. e.g. S. Trombley, *All that Summer She was Mad* (London: Junction, 1981), and L. DeSalvo, *Virginia Woolf: The Impact of Childhood Sexual Abuse on her Life and Work* (Boston: Beacon, 1989).

15. Something noted by S. Raitt, *Vita and Virginia: The Work and Friendship of V. Sackville-West and Virginia Woolf* (Oxford: Oxford University Press, 1993), p. viii, and K. Lawrence, 'Orlando's Voyage Out', *Modern Fiction Studies*, 38 (1992), 253–77, at 256 n. 5.

16. Q. Bell and A. Olivier Bell (1982), quoted by J. Marcus, 'Introduction', in Marcus (ed.), *Virginia Woolf and Bloomsbury*, 2.

17. Silver, *Virginia Woolf Icon*, 35–40.

18. For the *Orlando* plays, see nn. 46 and 49 below. Marjorie J. Lightfoot's adaptation of *The Waves*, directed by Alan Kreizenbeck, was staged at the Tenth Annual Conference on Virginia Woolf at University of Maryland, Baltimore County, 9 June 2000.

19. G. M. Moore, 'In Praise of Infidelity', in Moore (ed.), *Conrad on Film* (Cambridge: Cambridge University Press, 1997), 2.

20. V. Payne, ' "I felt so at home" ', *Radio Times*, 238/3097 (19–25 Mar. 1983), 4–5.

21. My sources include: S. Lambert, *Channel Four: Television with a Difference?* (London: BFI, 1982); M. Poole, 'Films or Plays?', *Listener*, 108/2786 (11 Nov. 1982), 33; D. Cannadine, 'Brideshead Revered', *London Review of Books*, 5/5 (17–31 Mar. 1983), 12–13; P. Wright, *On Living in an Old Country* (London: Verso, 1985); J. Isaacs, *Storm Over 4* (London: Weidenfeld & Nicolson, 1989); T. Wollen, 'Over Our Shoulders: Nostalgic Screen Fictions for the 1980s', in J. Corner and S. Harvey (eds.), *Enterprise and Heritage* (London: Routledge, 1991); R. Samuel, 'Heritage-Baiting', in *Theatres of Memory* (London: Verso, 1994), 259–73; C. Brunsdon, 'Problems with Quality', *Screen*, 31/1 (1990), 67–90; I. Shubik, *Play for Today* (1975; 2nd edn., Manchester: Manchester University Press, 2000); J. Caughie, *Television Drama* (Oxford: Oxford University Press, 2000); A. Higson, *English Heritage, English Cinema* (Oxford: Oxford University Press, 2003).

22. Poole, 'Films or Plays?', 33.

23. Shubik, *Play for Today*, 69.

24. Cannadine, 'Brideshead Revered', 12; see also Samuel's more circumspect analysis, 'Heritage-Baiting', 264–5.

25. Wollen, 'Over Our Shoulders', 181, and Caughie, *Television Drama*, 211, respectively.

26. Samuel, 'Heritage-Baiting', 265.

27. [M. Poole], 'Co-produced Lawrence', *Listener*, 109/2797 (3 Feb. 1983),

33. Initialled 'M.P'. For a more detailed analysis, see Higson, *English Heritage, English Cinema*, 119–23.

28. P. Hardy, *Listener*, 109/2803 (17 Mar. 1983), 28; D. Hackett, *The Times*, 24 Mar. 1983, 8; J. Barnes, *Observer*, 27 Mar. 1983, 40; P. Purser, *Sunday Telegraph*, 27 Mar. 1983, 15; A. Mars-Jones, *Sunday Times*, 27 Mar. 1983, 56; P. Kemp, *TLS*, 1 Apr. 1983, 427.

29. C. Gregg, *To the Lighthouse*, 41.55.

30. Ibid. 68.38.

31. Ibid. 31.40.

32. The paintings in Gregg's adaptation were by Mali Morris. See also S. Bellamy, ' "Painting the Words": A Version of Lily's Briscoe's Paintings from *To the Lighthouse*', and I. Tucker Epes, 'The Liberation of Lily Briscoe', in A. Ardis and B. Kime Scott (eds.), *Virginia Woolf: Turning the Centuries* (New York: Pace University Press, 2000), 244–51, 252–6.

33. Gregg, *To the Lighthouse*, 35.45–41.55.

34. Ibid. 40.20.

35. Samuel, *Theatres of Memory*, 382, writing about *The Elephant Man*, dir. D. Lynch (1980).

36. C. Gregg, *To the Lighthouse*, 30.10; 24.15.

37. Ibid. 5.30.

38. Ibid. 12.45.

39. V. Sackville-West, *All Passion Spent* (London: Hogarth, 1931). Woolf's speculation about Shakespeare's sister has also inspired a historical novel, D. Gwaltney's *Shakespeare's Sister* (Charlottesville, Va.: Hampton Roads, for the Cypress Creek Press, 1995).

40. First performed at the Hampstead Theatre, London, 8 May 1989 (see R. Say, *Plays and Players* (July 1989), 35); later performed at Lamb's Theatre, New York, Mar. 1991 (see Silver, *Virginia Woolf Icon*, 215–22, 324 n. 18).

41. R. Dinnage, 'Creative Collaboration', *TLS* (16 June 1989), 666.

42. J. Marcus, 'A Tale of Two Cultures', *Women's Review of Books*, 11/4 (Jan. 1994), 11–13.

43. Silver, *Virginia Woolf Icon*, 217–20.

44. Ibid. 218.

45. Ibid. 219.

46. A. Chang Williams, 'Orlando', *Plays from Far and Near*, 3 vols. (London: University of London Press, 1959–60), iii. 29–50.

47. A. Carter, '*Orlando*' (1980), in *The Curious Room: Plays, Film Scripts, and an Opera* (London: Chatto and Windus, 1996).

48. Therese Grisham's account of *Freak Orlando* (1981), quoted in Silver, *Virginia Woolf Icon*, 223.

49. The first play is D. Pinckney and R. Wilson, 'Virginia Woolf's Orlando', first performed in German in Berlin, 1989; then in French in Paris, 1993; and in English in Edinburgh, Aug. 1996. The English text was reproduced in *TheatreForum*, 6 (Winter–Spring 1995), 77–87; the Edinburgh production was reviewed by J. Peter, *Sunday Times* (18 Aug. 1996), section

10 (Culture), 14–15. The other play, Robin Brooks's *Orlando* (premiered 1992), is summarized by B. R. Silver, *Virginia Woolf Icon*, 223. The ballet *Orlando*, presented by the Compagnie Buissonnière, São Paulo, 'mid-2002', is described by J. Thompson, *Virginia Woolf Bulletin*, 12 (Jan. 2003), 61–2.

50. J. Harpman, *Orlanda*, trans. R. Schwartz (London: Harvill Press, 1999) (first published in French, 1996).

51. E. J. Dickson, 'Time Switch', *Sunday Times Magazine*, 28 Feb. 1993, pp. 42–5.

52. L. Francke, 'Orlando', *Sight and Sound*, 3/3 (Mar. 1993), 48.

53. S. Potter, 'Immortal Longing' [interview with Walter Donohue], *Sight and Sound*, 3/3 (Mar. 1993), 10–12.

54. S. Potter, Introduction, *Orlando* (screenplay) (London: Faber, 1994), p. xiii.

55. Marcus, 'Tale of Two Cultures', 11.

56. Potter, *Orlando* (screenplay), 3.

57. Ibid. 16, 20.

58. Potter, 'Immortal Longing', 12.

59. Contrary to Marcus's claims, the inclusion of Crisp, Somerville, and Sherrin suggests that the film-makers were well aware of the novel's cult status in lesbian and gay culture; though sexuality has figured less prominently in Sherrin's career than in Crisp's or Somerville's, in 1993 he wrote the foreword to K. Howes, *Broadcasting It: An Encyclopaedia of Homosexuality on Film, Radio and TV in the UK, 1923–1993* (1993). However, while including gay men, the film has been criticized for underplaying the novel's lesbian aspect: see L. K. Hankins and E. Barrett in *Re: Reading, Re: Writing, Re: Teaching Virginia Woolf*, ed. E. Barrett and P. Cramer (New York: Pace University Press), 168–84, 197–9.

60. Higson, *English Heritage, English Cinema*, 39–41, presents a more complex version of this argument.

61. Potter, *Orlando* (screenplay), 5.

62. e.g. *Elizabeth R* (BBC TV, 1971), or *Elizabeth*, dir. S. Kapur (1998).

63. J. Pidduck, 'Travels with Sally Potter's *Orlando*: Gender, Narrative, Movement', *Screen*, 38/2 (1997), 172–89, at p. 176.

64. Van Os and Roelfs, quoted in V. Glaessner, 'Fire and Ice', *Sight and Sound*, 2/4 (Apr. 1992), 14.

65. Francke, 'Orlando', 48.

66. J. Pidduck ('Travels with Sally Potter's *Orlando*', 177) suggests this and further points of comparison.

67. Ibid. 179.

68. Potter, *Orlando* (film), 40.30; *Orlando* (screenplay), 32.

69. Potter, *Orlando* (film), 46.42; *Orlando* (screenplay), 36.

70. Potter, *Orlando* (film), 54.14; *Orlando* (screenplay), 40.

71. Potter, *Orlando* (film), 51.30; *Orlando* (screenplay), 38.

72. Potter, quoted in Glaessner, 'Fire and Ice', 14.

73. Potter, *Orlando* (screenplay), 3.

74. Ibid. 61.
75. 'Adapting Mrs Dalloway: A Talk with Eileen Atkins', *Scenario*, 5/1 (1999). Online at www.scenariomag.com, 3 Apr. 2003.
76. Gorris, *Mrs Dalloway*, 23.15; 26.15.
77. Ibid. 15.02.
78. Ibid. 10.44.
79. Ibid. 12.18.
80. Ibid. 15.02.
81. M. Cunningham, *The Hours* (1998); R. Lippincott, *Mr Dalloway: A Novella* (Louisville, Ky.: Sarabande, 1999).
82. Cunningham, *The Hours*, 30–1.
83. One of Cunningham's acknowledged sources, DeSalvo's *Virginia Woolf*, 177–8, draws attention to Woolf's association of the Duckworths with pigs.
84. Cunningham, *The Hours*, 116.
85. Ibid. 154.
86. Ibid. 211.
87. Lee, *Virginia Woolf*, 163–4.
88. Cunningham, *The Hours*, 211.
89. Ibid. 41.
90. Ibid. 207.
91. J. Urquhart, *Financial Times* (23–4 Jan. 1999), Weekend, p. 6.
92. M. Bostridge, *Independent on Sunday* (17 Jan. 1999), Culture, p. 11.
93. Lippincott, *Mr Dalloway*, 3, 16–17.
94. Most conspicuously, 'sidewalk' (ibid. 23); also 'blocks' (p. 29), 'gotten over' (p. 54), and 'Track Four' (p. 142).
95. Ibid. 153.

FURTHER READING

BIOGRAPHY

Bell, Quentin, *Virginia Woolf*, 2 vols. (London: Hogarth, 1972).

DeSalvo, Louise, *Virginia Woolf: The Impact of Childhood Sexual Abuse on her Life and Work* (Boston: Beacon, 1989).

Lee, Hermione, *Virginia Woolf* (London: Chatto and Windus, 1996).

Mepham, John, *Virginia Woolf: A Literary Life* (London: Macmillan, 1991).

Trombley, Stephen, *All that Summer She was Mad: Virginia Woolf and her Doctors* (London: Junction Books, 1981).

CONTEXTUAL MATERIAL

Art and Aesthetics

Robins, Anna Gruetzner, *Modern Art in Britain 1910–1914* (London: Merrell Holberton, 1997).

Shone, Richard, *The Art of Bloomsbury: Roger Fry, Vanessa Bell, and Duncan Grant* (London: Tate Gallery, 1999).

Education

Dyhouse, Carol, *No Distinction of Sex? Women in British Universities, 1870–1939* (London: UCL Press, 1995).

Mangan, J. A., *The Games Ethic and Imperialism* (1986; London: Frank Cass, 1998).

Gender and Suffrage

Eustance, Claire, Ryan, Joan, and Ugolini, Laura (eds.), *A Suffrage Reader: Charting Directions in British Suffrage History* (New York: Leicester University Press, 2000).

Kent, Susan Kingsley, *Making Peace: The Reconstruction of Gender in Interwar Britain* (Princeton: Princeton University Press, 1993)

Lewis, Jane, *Women in England 1870–1950: Sexual Divisions and Social Change* (Brighton: Wheatsheaf, 1984).

Strachey, Ray, *The Cause* (1928; London: Virago, 1978).

The Literary Scene

Carey, John, *The Intellectuals and the Masses: Pride and Prejudice among the Literary Intelligentsia, 1880–1939* (London: Faber, 1992).

Keating, Peter, *The Haunted Study: A Social History of the English Novel 1875–1914* (London: Secker and Warburg, 1989).

Miller, Jane Eldridge, *Rebel Women: Feminism, Modernism and the Edwardian Novel* (London: Virago, 1994).

Willison, Ian, Gould, Warwick, and Chernaik, Warren (eds.), *Modernist Writers and the Marketplace* (Basingstoke: Macmillan, 1996).

Philosophy and Science

Bradshaw, David (ed.), *A Concise Companion to Modernism* (Oxford: Blackwell, 2003) (includes chapters on the life sciences, eugenics, Bergsonism, technology, and physics).

Childs, D. J., *Modernism and Eugenics: Woolf, Eliot, Yeats, and the Culture of Degeneration* (Cambridge: Cambridge University Press, 2001).

Gillies, Mary Ann, *Henri Bergson and British Modernism* (Montreal and Kingston: McGill-Queens University Press, 1996).

Kolakowski, Leszek, *Bergson* (Oxford: Oxford University Press, 1985).

Levy, Paul, *Moore: G. E. Moore and the Cambridge Apostles* (London: Weidenfeld and Nicolson, 1979).

Showalter, Elaine, *The Female Malady: Women, Madness and English Culture, 1830–1980* (1985; London: Virago, 1987).

Whitworth, Michael H., *Einstein's Wake: Relativity, Metaphor, and Modernist Literature* (Oxford: Oxford University Press, 2001).

Political History

Bentley, Michael, *The Liberal Mind 1914–1927* (Cambridge: Cambridge University Press, 1977).

Davis, John, *A History of Britain, 1885–1939* (Basingstoke: Macmillan, 1999).

Searle, G. R., *The Quest for National Efficiency* (Oxford: Blackwell, 1971).

Taylor, A. J. P., *English History, 1914–1945* (Oxford: Clarendon, 1965).

Social History

Harris, Jose, 'Between Civic Virtue and Social Darwinism: The Concept of the Residuum', in David Englander and Rosemary O'Day (eds.), *Retrieved Riches: Social Investigation in Britain 1840–1914* (Aldershot: Scolar Press, 1995), 67–87.

—— *Private Lives, Public Spirit: Britain 1870–1914* (1993; London: Penguin, 1994).

McKibbin, Ross, *Classes and Cultures: England 1918–1951* (Oxford: Oxford University Press, 1998).

Pennybacker, Susan D., *A Vision for London, 1889–1914: Labour, Everyday Life, and the LCC Experiment* (London: Routledge, 1995).

Saint, Andrew (ed.), *Politics and the People of London: The London County Council, 1889–1965* (London: Hambledon, 1989).

Schneer, Jonathan, *London 1900: Imperial Metropolis* (New Haven and London: Yale University Press, 1999).

Stevenson, John, *British Society 1914–1945* (1984; London: Penguin, 1990).

War

Fussell, Paul, *The Great War and Modern Memory* (New York: Oxford University Press, 1975).

CRITICISM ON WOOLF

Articles or Chapters

Abbott, Reginald, 'What Miss Kilman's Petticoat Means: Virginia Woolf, Shopping, and Spectacle', *Modern Fiction Studies*, 38 (1992), 193–216.

Ayers, David, 'Aesthetics and History in the Novels of Virginia Woolf', *English Literature of the 1920s* (Edinburgh: Edinburgh University Press, 1999), 66–98.

Bishop, Edward L., 'The Subject in *Jacob's Room*', *Modern Fiction Studies*, 38 (1992), 147–75.

Esty, Joshua D., 'Amnesia in the Fields: Late Modernism, Late Imperialism, and the English Pageant-Play', *ELH* 69 (2002), 245–76.

Flint, Kate, 'Virginia Woolf and the General Strike', *Essays in Criticism*, 36 (1986), 319–34.

Hartman, Geoffrey, 'Virginia's Web', *Beyond Formalism* (New Haven: Yale UP, 1970), 71–84.

Horner, Avril, 'Virginia Woolf, History, and the Metaphors of *Orlando*', *Essays and Studies*, 44 (1991), 70–87.

Lanser, Susan Sniader, 'Fictions of Absence: Feminism, Modernism, Virginia Woolf', *Fictions of Authority* (Ithaca: Cornell UP, 1992), 102–19.

Little, Judy, '*Jacob's Room* as Comedy: Woolf's Parodic *Bildungsroman*', in Jane Marcus (ed.), *New Feminist Essays on Virginia Woolf* (London: Macmillan, 1981), 105–24.

McLaurin, Allen, 'Virginia Woolf and Unanimism', *Journal of Modern Literature*, 9/1 (1981–2), 115–22.

Marcus, Jane, 'Britannia Rules *The Waves*', in Karen R. Lawrence (ed.), *Decolonizing Tradition* (Urbana: University of Illinois Press, 1992), 136–62.

Rosenbaum, S. P., 'The Philosophical Realism of Virginia Woolf', in Rosenbaum (ed.), *English Literature and British Philosophy* (Chicago:

University of Chicago Press, 1971), 316–56; repr. in Rosenbaum, *Aspects of Bloomsbury: Studies in Modern English Literary and Intellectual History* (Basingstoke: Macmillan, 1998), 1–36.

Schröder, Leena Kore, '*Mrs Dalloway* and the Female Vagrant', *Essays in Criticism*, 45 (1995), 324–46.

Stevenson, Randall, and Goldman, Jane, 'Modernist Reading and the Death of Mrs Ramsay', *Yearbook of English Studies*, 26 (1996), 173–86.

Tate, Trudi, '*Mrs Dalloway* and the Armenian Question', *Textual Practice*, 8/3 (1994), 467–86.

Books

Banfield, Ann, *The Phantom Table: Woolf, Fry, Russell and the Epistemology of Modernism* (Cambridge: Cambridge University Press, 2000).

Beer, Gillian, *Virginia Woolf: The Common Ground* (Edinburgh: Edinburgh University Press, 1996).

Bowlby, Rachel, *Feminist Destinations and Further Essays on Virginia Woolf* (Edinburgh: Edinburgh University Press, 1997).

—— (ed.), *Virginia Woolf* (London: Longman, 1992).

Clements, Patricia, and Grundy, Isobel (eds.), *Virginia Woolf: New Critical Essays* (London: Vision Press, 1983).

Cuddy-Keane, Melba, *Virginia Woolf, the Intellectual, and the Public Sphere* (Cambridge: Cambridge University Press, 2003).

Hussey, Mark (ed.), *Virginia Woolf A to Z: A Comprehensive Reference for Students, Teachers, and Common Readers to her Life, Work, and Critical Reception* (New York: Facts on File, 1995).

Marcus, Jane, *Virginia Woolf and the Languages of Patriarchy* (Bloomington, Ind.: Indiana University Press, 1987).

—— (ed.), *Virginia Woolf: A Feminist Slant* (Lincoln, Nebr.: University of Nebraska Press, 1983).

Naremore, James, *The World Without a Self: Virginia Woolf and the Novel* (New Haven: Yale University Press, 1973).

Peach, Linden, *Virginia Woolf* (Basingstoke: Macmillan, 2000).

Roe, Sue, and Sellers, Susan (eds.), *The Cambridge Companion to Virginia Woolf* (Cambridge: Cambridge University Press, 2000).

Snaith, Anna, *Virginia Woolf: Public and Private Negotiations* (Basingstoke: Macmillan, 2000).

Warner, Eric (ed.), *Virginia Woolf: A Centenary Perspective* (London and Basingstoke: Macmillan, 1984).

Zwerdling, Alex, *Virginia Woolf and the Real World* (Berkeley and Los Angeles: University of California Press, 1986).

RECEPTION AND RECONTEXTUALIZATION

Brunsdon, Charlotte, 'Problems with Quality', *Screen*, 31/1 (1990), 67–90.

Caughie, John, *Television Drama* (Oxford: Oxford University Press, 2000).

Caws, Mary Ann, and Luckhurst, Nicola (eds.), *The Reception of Virginia Woolf in Europe* (London: Continuum, 2002).

Higson, Andrew, *English Heritage, English Cinema: Costume Drama since 1980* (Oxford: Oxford University Press, 2003).

Majumdar, Robin, and McLaurin, Allen (eds.), *Virginia Woolf: The Critical Heritage* (London: Routledge Kegan Paul, 1975).

Samuel, Raphael, 'Heritage-Baiting', *Theatres of Memory* (London: Verso, 1994), 259–73.

Silver, Brenda, *Virginia Woolf Icon* (Chicago and London: University of Chicago Press, 1999).

Wollen, Tana, 'Over Our Shoulders: Nostalgic Screen Fictions for the 1980s', in John Corner and Sylvia Harvey (eds.), *Enterprise and Heritage: Crosscurrents of National Culture* (London: Routledge, 1991), 178–93.

WEBSITES

http://www.utoronto.ca/IVWS/ International Virginia Woolf Society: contains many links to other websites.

http://www.pace.edu/press Pace University Press: contains many links, particularly to archival and research resources.

http://www.virginiawoolfsociety.co.uk Virginia Woolf Society of Great Britain.

http://www.tate.org.uk/ The Tate Gallery: the online collections section reproduces sixteen works by Roger Fry and twenty-five by Duncan Grant.

http://www.charleston.org.uk/ Website for the trust which owns Charleston, 'the country home of the Bloomsbury Group'.

FILM AND TELEVISION ADAPTATIONS OF WOOLF'S NOVELS

Mrs Dalloway (USA, UK, and Netherlands; director Marleen Gorris, screenplay by Eileen Atkins, 1997; starring Vanessa Redgrave)

Orlando (UK, Russia, France, Italy, and Netherlands; director Sally Potter, screenplay by Sally Potter, 1992; starring Tilda Swinton)

To the Lighthouse (BBC TV; director Colin Gregg, screenplay by Hugh Stoddart, 1983; starring Rosemary Harris, Michael Gough, and Suzanne Bertish)

INDEX

American Literature

British and Irish Literature

Children's Literature

Classics and Ancient Literature

Colonial Literature

Eastern Literature

European Literature

History

Medieval Literature

Oxford English Drama

Poetry

Philosophy

Politics

Religion

The Oxford Shakespeare

A complete list of Oxford Paperbacks, including Oxford World's Classics, Oxford Shakespeare, Oxford Drama, and Oxford Paperback Reference, is available in the UK from the Academic Division Publicity Department, Oxford University Press, Great Clarendon Street, Oxford OX2 6DP.

In the USA, complete lists are available from the Paperbacks Marketing Manager, Oxford University Press, 198 Madison Avenue, New York, NY 10016.

Oxford Paperbacks are available from all good bookshops. In case of difficulty, customers in the UK can order direct from Oxford University Press Bookshop, Freepost, 116 High Street, Oxford OX1 4BR, enclosing full payment. Please add 10 per cent of published price for postage and packing.